T0270526

LAND RICH, CASH POOR

MY FAMILY'S HOPE
AND THE UNTOLD HISTORY
OF THE DISAPPEARING
AMERICAN FARMER

BRIAN REISINGER

Skyhorse Publishing

Skyhorse Publishing books may be purchased in bulk at special discounts for sales promotion, corporate gifts, fund-raising, or educational purposes. Special editions can also be created to specifications. For details, contact the Special Sales Department, Skyhorse Publishing, 307 West 36th Street, 11th Floor, New York, NY 10018 or info@skyhorsepublishing.com.

Skyhorse® and Skyhorse Publishing® are registered trademarks of Skyhorse Publishing, Inc.®, a Delaware corporation.

Visit our website at www.skyhorsepublishing.com.

Please follow our publisher Tony Lyons on Instagram @tonylyonsisuncertain.

10 9 8 7 6 5 4 3 2

Library of Congress Cataloging-in-Publication Data on file.

Cover design by Kai Texel
Cover artwork by Getty Images

Print ISBN: 978-1-5107-7998-3
Ebook ISBN: 978-1-5107-8040-8

Printed in the United States of America

To my dad, as good and true a farmer as there's ever been.

TABLE OF CONTENTS

INTRODUCTION

SPRING WATER

They came from miles around, a few as far as Illinois, to see the old farmhouse before it was gone. The farm that sprang forth from it had been in existence for well over one hundred years. It was the Driftless region of southern Wisconsin, called such because the glaciers stopped short of this place thousands of years ago, leaving its soaring hills and plunging valleys intact. Sitting in one such valley, at the end of a steep, bending road where the township pavement ended and gave way to dirt, the old homestead and surrounding buildings were cordoned off—like a secret, holy place—from the rest of the world. The house was small, but tall in their minds with the memories it bore—of origins and hardships and shots at the middle class.

Their numbers had multiplied when they heard Helene was coming. She was nearly ninety years old then and the last of the generation who could tell stories of growing up in that house during the Great Depression; her only remaining sister was not able to travel, and the rest of the original fourteen brothers and sisters were dead. The summer sun bathed the farmyard and the valley of rolling green hills beyond as Helene stepped out of her daughter's car to look upon the place where she'd been born. A quiet fell. It was her first time seeing the home farm in sixty-eight years.

Helene smiled and nodded and began to talk, picking her steps and her stories with care, remembering those olden days. Helene's father and mother, Alois and Teresia, had started it all on that little farm. She told of survival—of Teresia giving birth to thirteen children in that house, until she bled so badly during her final labor that they feared for her life and went to the hospital. She told of hard work—as a young woman carrying eighty-pound pails of milk from the barn to the tank in the milk house. She told of a natural spring the family harnessed to draw water out of the surrounding hills. These were the stories, they knew, that made their lives possible. Without this place, there was nothing else.

But times had changed. The natural spring was buried back in the woods behind the house and offered no more water to the slumping buildings. The angular old farmhouse was crooked now, warped with age, and nobody lived in it anymore. It smelled of mold and wild animals. The squat, wooden milk house was weathered gray. All of it, the farmyard and memories, sat in what had been the orbit of the old barn—before it became so brittle that one day it simply collapsed.

Although the surrounding land was still part of a working farm, one now operated from another farmhouse up the hill, the faded farmyard here on the original homestead seemed to preserve in place what was happening to so many other farms—a steady but somehow sudden disappearance. At one time, nearly every family Helene had grown up knowing in that area was a farm family, and most of her fourteen siblings either farmed for a living at one time or worked on someone else's farm. Now nearly all of the extended family had jobs off the farm, save for her nephew Jim, who owned the property. He was still farming crops and raising heifers for other dairy herds and steers for meat, up the hill on the nearby farm.

Jim's grandfather and father—Helene's father and eldest brother—bought the land to expand upon the original homestead, back in the days when family farming was the future and not the past. But now

2

even Jim had to sell his herd of milk cows and alter his business model to keep the farm going, hoping as they all gathered that day that he'd done the right thing. There was only one other working farm left between Jim's and the highway.

The story of the disappearing American farmer is at once a sweeping economic history of the most urgent, unexplained socioeconomic crisis in our country today and a brutally personal hardship for the families living it. Small family farms like the one Helene grew up on once not only dominated the landscape of places like the rural Midwest but also defined much of the economy and culture in the United States.

In 1920, following the rise in American farming before years of economic depression hit, there were nearly 6.5 million farms in the United States. That came out to about sixteen people for every farm in the country[1]—the exact size of Helene's family. The number of farms had been on the upswing for decades, with families getting started in the Midwest and other agricultural enclaves across the country. In places like Wisconsin, America's Dairyland, such family farming took root just in time to face the devastation of the Depression.

The farms that survived the Depression emerged to power the rural economy with enough dynamism to deliver, within just one generation, middle-class status for countless families that began by digging their living out of the dirt. Along the way, America's identity became intertwined with the family farm—a connection that began with the ideal of the yeoman farmer Thomas Jefferson wrote about as the foundation of a young nation,[2] and stands to this day with a wide range of public-opinion polling consistently showing trust in farm families at well over 70 percent.[3]

And yet, just two generations after the Depression, American family farming had taken a hard fall. By 2020, one century after Helene's family typified the American experience, there were just 2 million farms in the United States, a nearly 70 percent drop. That meant there were approximately 162 people in the United States for every farm, compared to the sixteen people per farm from one hundred years earlier.[4] Economic devastation and changing times, from the Great Depression to the Farm Crisis of the 1980s to the recessions and other crises of the twenty-first century, all took their toll. By the 2010s, the loss of family farms had long been occurring not only during economic downturns but during boomtimes as well, while the rest of the United States economy was soaring.[5] The American economy had officially left the American farmer behind.

To be clear, some level of disappearance was inevitable, even natural. From the time America's westward expansion ended, there was going to be consolidation among all industries depending upon limited land—from farming to ranching to logging and beyond—as one competitor performed better than another. Given that there would also be some level of consolidation occurring in other parts of our food system and the rest of the American economy, there were always going to be farms growing through consolidation to keep up. Many farms also grew to support more than one generation at a time, a worthy reason to combine farms.[6] The problem is, that's not all that happened in America. We've experienced a much deeper shift—one that didn't need to be and that we must address.

The cost of this shift—from family farms clearing a path toward the middle class through the Great Depression to barely making ends meet in modern America—is impacting every American dinner table by putting our very food supply at risk, and fueling a broader economic and cultural crisis involving many of our country's deepest problems and divisions. For decades, America's food system increased production to provide as much food as possible,[7] as affordably as possible, a fact that some consider a modern wonder of the world while others fear it has degraded our nutrition and environment. In any case, that system succeeded in the goal of affordable food up to a point, but faltering supply chains and skyrocketing food costs[8] in the wake of the COVID-19 global pandemic have shown its limits. The disappearance of family farms has fueled this problem through the loss of economic diversity.

Rather than a mix of large, mid-sized, and small farms all playing a competitive role in the market, America's small farms and mid-sized farms—and even some of its larger farms—have faced economic ruin and fallen to bankruptcy or sales of necessity. Meanwhile, America is continuing to see ever-larger farms buying up smaller farms to keep up with a food industry dominated by far bigger companies. Those bigger companies, in turn, are trying to keep up with larger growing companies in other parts of our economy, and domestic and global demand. Such loss in the number of farms is part of a food supply chain that is less durable against disaster, less sustainable, and less secure because our farms are disappearing. It's the compromise of our most fundamental form of economic security: food security for every American. While it is a problem rooted in rural America, evidence of its effect is spreading from coast to coast, carrying a myriad of other economic and cultural problems in its wake.

In farm country, the pummeling pace of farms vanishing has not been limited by geography or industry.[9] It's a devastating hollowing out of rural America reverberating across the country, at various time periods and in often brutal ways, as family farms and ranches disappear, nostalgia the only monument left in their honor. Dairy farms in Wisconsin. Almonds in California. Cattle in Texas. Soybeans in Nebraska. Corn and pigs in Iowa. Oranges in Florida. All have faced some form of this decline. Sometimes the land ends up in the hands of other farms, or it becomes home to other industry or development. Other times, it lies fallow. Even when the land finds some new and valuable use, some parts of past economic life are extinguished—families going bankrupt or left with no choice but to sell the land that had been their stake in the American economy for generations.

The fate of these family farms reaches far past rural America—to the tables of millions of Americans who have never set foot in a barn. As more and more members of our agricultural industry slip away, our broader food system shifts ever onward toward consolidation, automation, uniformity, and the kind of mass production that increasingly has people questioning what's for dinner. Our country needs an economically diverse agriculture industry, with as many kinds of farms as possible operating in a competitive market in as many parts of the country as possible, to have a food system that is both affordable and resilient. Instead, we have fewer farms than ever carrying an increasingly perilous burden, and a food system with a stunted capacity for local options, even as consumers crave more farm-to-table choices than ever at stores, restaurants, and farmers' markets in every corner of the country.

Other dangers are emerging from this loss of economic diversity. Over half of Americans believe additives that are now a standard of our food industry pose a "serious health risk" as people crave more local, fresh food.[10] Meanwhile, the ecological decay that has accompanied this decline in family farms is not merely the source of an environmental debate, but also an existential issue for everyone to solve—entire societies have risen and fallen based on the availability of water and how they've treated the soil that sustains them.[11] Fewer farms—in place of a diverse industry of farms of many sizes competing—leave our food supply more vulnerable when disease or other systemic disasters, like contamination or invasive pests, strike. Even our control of the land on which we grow our food has fallen into peril. With consolidated farmland in fewer hands, foreign adversaries like the Chinese have the ability to sweep in and buy an increasingly larger piece of our country's food supply like a cheap hand in a global casino. As of 2022, 43.4 million acres of American farmland was owned by foreign investors, a total that remains small but is growing rapidly.[12]

Along the way, America as a whole has begun to lose something even more elemental as the control of our food supply has become suspect. Jobs have vanished, communities have declined, and powerlessness has replaced prosperity, crushing our country's economic mobility. The lack of hope has given our urban drug problem a rampant rural sibling. These farmers, so trusted by the American public in part because they represent America's vision for itself, are succumbing to depression, even killing themselves at troubling rates to end the pain of facing the families they fear they're failing.[13]

It doesn't end there. The resentment of being left behind is widening America's rural-urban divide, contributing to political parties that demonize rather than disagree, communities that don't trust each other, and people who don't understand each other well enough to solve problems together. A country that doesn't recognize itself. Each of these issues is a complex problem in its own right, often also driven by other forces. But each also ties back, in its own way, to the disappearance of the American farmer. We are losing not only the family farms that feed us but also a part of ourselves.

This book will uncover the crushing forces that have created this problem. Brutally quick, yet decades in the making, family farming's shift from economic powerhouse to past due in modern America leaves a confounding question: How did we let this happen? There are many fragments of an answer—spanning economic downturns, policies from Roosevelt to Reagan and beyond, a shifting American and global economy, and more. But there has never been an answer that traced this transformative timeframe from the Depression to the tumultuous 2000s and offered a truth worthy of the toll this problem has taken on our country's economy and culture. It happened not because our current food system isn't capable of modern miracles, which it is, but because we have made hidden decisions to have fewer farms in this country at almost every turn.

The full answer, then, lies in the untold history of the American farmer, a rare combination of revolutionary land ownership and ines-capable vulnerability to broader forces—walking so delicately that fault line between prosperity and failure as both landowner and work-ing class. So many of our farm families hold great wealth in the form of land that is increasingly becoming valuable only if they sell it, and harder and harder to make a living on if they don't. Unknowingly, decade after decade, our country sowed the seeds of decline of these farm families, until one day we'd left too many of them in the age-old but increasingly urgent dilemma of being land rich, cash poor.

This is a history that will shock those who haven't lived it and in some ways even surprise some of those who have. And it has the capacity to bring us all together around solutions to save America's family farms—and our food supply with it—if we are prepared to face hard truths. Family farms are part business, part labor of love. Since farms have always been bound by economics like any other business, as well as their love of the land, that means what will work economi-cally and practically for the remaining farms must guide our path forward—just as any long-term solutions would also need to make economic sense for consumers, companies, and others participating in our food economy. To have any chance in solving this problem, all Americans who care where their food comes from must find ways to bridge divides between rural and urban, right and left, defender and critic, and farms and consumers of all kinds. Despite the discomfort of hard truths along the way. Instead of taking the easy way out of demonizing one side or another.

In this book we will explore the roots, ruins, and road to revival of the disappearing American farmer on two parallel paths: an analysis beneath the surface of each of the key eras of economic history driving the disappearance, and a raw personal portrait of a family living out each of those eras, right there on that farm where Helene grew up in southern Wisconsin. We'll talk with some of modern agriculture's biggest champions and critics and see how life in rural America is more at risk than ever. Along the way, we will find lessons to redeem our future buried in our past. I'm here to share with you this unique look in part because I spent nearly a decade covering economic hardship as a journalist, the years after that trying in vain to address these issues in the public policy arena, then the years since as a columnist writing about the past and future of rural America. But most of all, I'm here to share this with you because I will forever be a farmer's son. And that family walking the old homestead—there in that sacred valley, where the pavement ends and the dirt road through rich farmland begins—is my family.

***

Inside the house that day we shuffled around on the dusty floor, listening to Helene and to the floorboards that piped up now and then with complaints of age from beneath the worn linoleum. Many of the family members huddled inside the house were offspring of one of the original fourteen children of Alois and Teresia Reisinger. My grandpa Albert was the eldest of that generation, and his eldest son, Jim, is my dad, still proudly carrying on the fight for our way of life. It was my dad's many cousins returning to the farm, to see where each of their parents were born, as I followed along to hear the memories aloud.

We saw the backroom, tucked behind a narrow doorway, where Teresia was so often in labor. We saw too where the fourteen children slept, up a steep, narrow staircase to spare bedrooms, most of which lacked heat in the winter. Back downstairs, we learned with surprise that the family later owned a piano that once sat in "the parlor," a small room just off the living room not big enough to fit more than six of us as we huddled to imagine the sight. Asked how poor the family was on its journey through the Depression to the middle class, Helene offered a youthful smile and an answer only a farm family could: "We always had something to eat."

Such are the stories that make this book about not only the great economic forces at play, but also the resilience of the rural working-class families of the heartland. I'll tell the stories of the kind of family farm that is owned and operated by the people who live on it—found in all corners of the country, but especially common in the "flyover country" of the Midwest and Great Plains. Throughout the book, we'll learn about forces affecting all farms, but there will be no claim that the experience of family farms like the one I grew up on was universal.

There are other types of farms with stories worth telling: farms with long legacies of migrant labor, tenant farms and sharecroppers of the South and elsewhere, and countless other individual circumstances. Some other farms are tangled in thorny issues, or have mainly become vehicles for wealth and mechanisms for exploiting government programs. But I don't think that's most farms, and it's not the kind of farms I know. There are parts of our way of life that fulfill some of America's deepest dreams about itself, and others that highlight our country's many disagreements. I will try to tell our story honestly and tie it to those larger forces affecting so many types of farms, because it's a true story worth heeding—for the sake of our food supply, and our humanity.

You'll join us in carving our living out of the ground. You'll see moments of joy as our family progresses and moments too of tragedy, from financial hardship to fickle weather to farm accidents that maimed and killed and still echo through the generations. You'll see our family's four-generation fight on up through today, as my sister runs the farm with my dad—and I struggle to help preserve our way of life, after walking away from it for a time. But you'll also see universal forces that have shaped not just my family but also every part of our country from coast to coast: immigration, economic upheaval, war, women's rights, addiction, and survival in a global pandemic. You'll see, I hope, that it is a truly American way of life vanishing— one we can only hope remains within our grasp to save.

***

In the final moments, before we took our picture and scattered back to our own lives, the family wandered about the backyard. Some wondered aloud what my dad should do with the old house. The barn outside had been gone more than thirty years now, and the nearby machine shed served as storage for our working farm up the road. Maybe the only thing to be done with the house was to bulldoze it—or burn it.

My dad and some relatives decided to crawl back into the woods to see if we could find the old spring that once supplied the farm with water for the better part of a century. I followed them back through the underbrush and the fallen branches. And then, through arching trees, we saw it: the spring's old one-room stone shelter, built into the hillside, one gray stone stacked on top of another by hand, so tight against the steep bank that the small square room seemed like a natural part of the earth that might have risen right out of the ground. Moss and brush had grown around it, and it took a few minutes of heaving to wrench the broken, old, wooden door open.

The open doorway was endlessly black, the darkness burrowing deep into the hillside. It might have looked like a tomb. But somehow there was a sense of life to it. Perhaps it was the green of the moss and the forest floor encircling the doorway, brightening it some. Or the sun, shining on it through the trees. And then, as we peered in closer and listened, we realized it was the water—pooling still in the bottom of the shelter, bubbling up out of the doorway and into the light.

CHAPTER 1

THIS LAND

America's Modern-Day Dilemma
After a Century of Disappearing Farms

There are more tears on this land than we want to admit.

My dad and I were on sacred ground, back at the small cabin I own on a forty-acre parcel behind the farmhouse where we both grew up. This is land upon which my grandpa turned out milk cows to graze years ago, and my dad journeyed to bring them into the warm barn each morning, and where I had escaped, for a few moments, the work I did on the farm since I was old enough to walk. His hands were big and calloused from decades of hard labor, his back still strong, but not as straight as it once was. We sat there on the porch in the sun, and the trees seemed to whisper of those things we'd lost. My father quietly broke into tears—like rain that starts suddenly while the sun is still shining, the Earth feeling more than one thing at once. So, too, for our family, with all that had been taken from us and all we had yet to save.

There are not many times a man will see his father truly broken. Especially not on the farm, where resilience is a crop grown no matter the season and children are raised to work onward when others can't—to be a stubborn people, for better and for worse. But there are such moments, and the broken times are all the more stark on the farm because of what it takes for our people to halt for even a moment: when my grandfather, Albert, saw his father, Alois, holding the bloody body of a boy injured in the fields; when my father, Jim, saw Albert lying in bed with a broken back; and now as I stood in this sacred place, with my own father mourning the loss of our milk cows after a century of our family dairy farming on this land. I wondered if there were answers in these times, if we felt able to look at them.

My dad hung his head. I put my hand on his shoulder, much sturdier than my own, and he leaned in and sobbed. He sold the cows the day before. Friends and family helped us load them onto the clanging trailers that would take them down the road to another farm that could afford to keep them. We still had our land and a plan to operate our farm on new terms; a plan our family worked on together that we hoped would keep it going. But we knew the unspoken stakes: those that come when you're not just fighting for your job but for your heritage. Our heritage on this land, where my great-grandpa first came to make a living four generations ago, then passed the farm on to his son, who passed it on to his in an ongoing family gamble. Losing the farm now—as my sixty-nine-year-old father was trying to pass it on like our ancestors did before him—would mean losing our home and our community and a proud line of farmland tradition. We had sold one part of that heritage, our beloved milk cows, in a bid to save the rest of it. And we did not yet know the outcome of our wager. I looked at my dad leaning against me and said words I could only hope he'd believe were true.

"You did so good, Dad," I said. "You held on for so long, and now because of you, we have a chance to keep the farm going."

There was more at stake than the farm, prowling beneath the surface of our loss. A danger that was not only unspoken but also thought of only in that deep, quiet place in the mind that is too honest for us most times to face—where secrets and fears and conscience reside. I had heard the stories for years of farmers taking their own lives over the loss of their cows. Some lost more than us: their land, their savings, or more. Some may have faced better or worse chances than us of making it with what they had left. There was no way to know, but the fear of losing our dwindling way of life allowed me to imagine how those farmers must have felt before they left this world by their own hand. Peering down at my dad, I let the thought surface for a moment, and then it was like a knife coming up through my stomach. I took hold of the thought and pushed it back down, then looked out over the sun streaming across the land before us and said a silent prayer.

The wind blew the wild grass, and I thought of my father's fields beyond and how hard we'd fought to keep them. For our family, the story of the disappearing American farmer—a threat not only to those living it but also to the life of our nation—began here, on this land. This plot turned our family from dirt poor to middle class in one generation during the depths of the Depression, carried two more generations forward, and gave way to the generation of me and my sister, and her kids. Until the rest of the world shifted and left us behind.

I thought of all of that and everything we'd survived since: not only the pandemic but also four recessions in my lifetime alone, the days of my sister milking cows through below-zero weather while pregnant, the days of my dad in the hospital when I was a boy trying to be a man, the farms of friends and family disappearing, people dying in tragic farm accidents around us. Surely, the resilience of the American farmer—paired with some new ideas and blessings from above or luck on the ground—could get us through.

And yet as I stood there with my dad, I feared the danger of him feeling that he'd failed us. And I knew that I had failed him.

There was a time, more than two decades ago, when I did my own crying on this same forty-acre parcel of land, hoping my dad wouldn't know. I looked into the woods and wondered again if there were answers back there in our past. Answers from a nervous twelve-year-old boy, struggling to follow his father's path, then as now. We had been hunting deer, my dad looming before me in a hard Wisconsin winter. I remembered seeing him there, in the sleet cutting sideways as we walked among the trees in the howling wind. Although we'd been hunting all morning, I felt alone somehow, like the snow blowing through the air was dividing us from each other and the rest of the world. Old trails, packed hard by cattle and wild game alike through generations of farming, twisted among the trees and underbrush beneath a thick and growing blanket of snow. I thought of those trails, and of the fields stretching across the hillsides beyond these woods, for even in the face of this harsh Wisconsin winter, we were always aware of the earth beneath us and the life that sprouts forth each spring, for us and our animals and the world beyond. Yet, on this day, the land was cold and spare, its trees black against the stark white of winter.

I knew by the time of my first deer hunt that things were changing, but I had no idea just how much. On that morning, I was doing as I had always done: following my father as he followed his, and his father followed his. The path was not yet broken, and I hoped, against the doubts I felt even then, that I could still find my way upon it. The cold stung against our sweat as we walked. Ice clung to my dad's dark moustache, visible in flashes as he looked back at me through the snow. He was tall, with an angling stride defying the limp of a broken leg he'd had years ago. I was small for my age, and rushing to keep up. Even though I was aware on some level I didn't fit this place, he was my dad, and I couldn't fall behind, or all I valued as a boy looking up to his father would be lost. The lever-action .30-30 I carried weighed heavy and foreign in my hands. The excitement in my chest rose and fell with the shifting currents of the howling wind. Its only rival was the quiet fear, lingering among the snow accumulating and drifting across the forest floor. I didn't know what I was more afraid of: not seeing anything or confronting whatever showed itself.

We reached the edge of a rock ledge extending out into the woods beyond, and my dad stopped. He peered over the edge, then motioned to me and put a finger to his mouth. There was a deer below, sheltering from the wind.

***

The memory could be a dream—that winter landscape that holds so much of the past, present, and future within its bounds—except for the ways in which it is all too real. It is, in fact, a rare genuine moment where I had an opportunity to please my dad, at a time when everything was about to change—for me and my dad, and our way of life. I come from a place where sons do as their fathers did, and I learned over the years to search for these times. Moments like these—annual November deer hunts that are a rite of passage in our world, or evenings when we would drive across our family's farm just to look at it—offered a chance to connect with my dad through the land, even as we grew apart.

I'd search for these times as I learned, whether I wanted to face it or not, that I would be the first of four generations of Reisinger men who would not take over our farm. I'd search for them as I left to find my own way. And I'd search for them when I returned years later to find that farms like ours had gone from the economic building block of a free people to a heart-rending relic of another time—slipping away at a rate of as many as three per day in Wisconsin.[14] I search for these times still, over two decades out from boyhood, as our family fights this rural devastation. My dad and sister first and foremost, working the farm together, but also my mom and me in our own ways, searching for how to help to save our way of life. This life that once rose with prosperity, like crops in the spring, but now for so many has fallen quick as corn cut down in a hailstorm.

I knew growing up that our way of life was special, in part because it was becoming rarer. Teachers talked about it, and I'd seen how many kids stepped onto the school bus each morning from dormant farms and how many more lived in town. Still, none of us could have known the depth of the devastation to come. A deep winter had set in on the American family farm as well as on the journey my dad and I were on together, as farms like ours went through a great, and perhaps terrifyingly final, shift.

From the 1970s—when my parents bought our farm from my grandparents—to 2017, America would lose a staggering 85 percent of its dairy farms.[15] The decline was driven not by any one American figure or force, and certainly not by a lack of farmland work ethic, but by a perfect storm of economic, governmental, and technological forces, stronger than any winter wind or snow we'd endured. And yet, there were also decades of bad decisions; seeds of decline so many had sewn, waiting beneath the ground and leaving the family farm too vulnerable to withstand the weather. It would all culminate in the years my dad's generation prepared to pass America's farms on to my own, making America's Dairyland the epicenter of an ever-closer slip toward extinction for family farms of all kinds across the country. From the Farm Crisis of the 1980s to the repeated recessions in the first two decades of the 2000s, the American economy would fundamentally change, adding to the uncertainty of a growing global marketplace. Family farms across the country, regardless of agricultural sector, had been seeing ups and downs and an overall trend toward vanishing—some through farm failures, some through industry consolidation—for nearly a century by then.[16] The forty-year fall in dairy, which was at one time one of America's more durable sources of family farming, would force a new level of urgency upon a nationwide shift that was reaching a troubling tipping point.

The decline would not simply be a matter of larger farms replacing smaller farms—an economic reality that has existed as long as one farmer discovered he could do a bit better by buying his neighbor—but also of a new level of economic devastation. In these decades, Wisconsin would go from number one in milk production[17] to number one in farm bankruptcies.[18] Still more farms would fall to voluntary sales with few good choices, where families still lost their land, livelihood, and way of life with it. And that decline in dairy would join the broader nationwide trend of disappearing farms, again marked by bankruptcies or devastating sales of necessity.

This decline, and the decades of economic upheaval that drove it, would change the face of land ownership in America. In the 1980s, mid-sized farms operated nearly 60 percent of our country's cropland. Within twenty-five years, as dairy and other forms of family farming fell, it would be just 36 percent.[19] Those still holding onto their land would either grow bigger to survive or find themselves less and less able to make ends meet. Over time, more of them became land rich and cash poor. This status was not outright poverty, as the agriculture writer Sarah Mock correctly notes.[20] But it was a paradox of grinding hardship: Keep your land and struggle to make a living, or sell your land and lose so much else.

Along the way, America itself would fall into a perilous trap as our food supply came under threat. A food industry capable of more than ever—larger amounts of food, in more places, at a cheaper cost—would somehow translate into a system that is less durable, less sustainable, and less secure. By the time of the COVID pandemic and its economic fallout, the problem would be clear, yet unbelievable: a supply chain struggling to provide the food Americans needed in the spring of 2020 and long afterward, while at the same time American farmers searched desperately for a place to sell their products with processing plants, restaurants, and other parts of our food system shut down.[21] Two presidential administrations in a row—from opposite political parties, agreeing on very little—said America was in a national emergency, as families struggled, for one reason or another, to put food on the table.[22] Ultimately the cost of food to consumers would spike by more than 10 percent in 2022, far faster than the inflation that was leading to increased prices across the rest of the economy.[23] And yet nobody seemed to understand all the ways our broader food system's failures tied back to challenges farmers had been facing for decades.

Every national trend meant hardship on the ground for farms like ours. In the same time period that American agriculture made its fateful shift, the farm our ancestors started a century earlier reached its highest point, then began to decline—imperceptibly at first, like the noon sun giving way eventually to cold black night. Those who came before us were men whose living rose not out of the latest job market but directly out of the land, and women whose strength and independence might have been celebrated by the feminist movement decades later, had they paused in their work long enough to tell their stories.

My great-grandfather, Alois Reisinger, had left pre–World War I Europe and lost himself in the rolling hillsides of southern Wisconsin, settling in 1912 on our farm in a deep valley filled with rich brown dirt. He and my great-grandmother, Teresia, built a future together as the Depression gripped the country. Out of their fourteen children came the eldest, my grandfather Albert Reisinger, who married my grandmother, Anna. Their generation helped expand our family's dairy farm up out of the valley to the hills above. And then his eldest, my own father Jim Reisinger, took over, feeling—like his father before him—that he had no choice with what he was supposed to do with his life. So he and my mom, Jean, rose each morning to milk the cows, bounced countless hours on the seat of a tractor, shoveled, carried, and heaved until they expanded the farm further still, buying a third farm once run by my dad's aunt and uncle and bringing the Reisinger family acreage to a height of six hundred acres.

My dad found, despite feeling he had no choice, that farming was his calling. Each day it sank deeper down into his blood and then his bones until it was a part of him. To me, he seemed to share the instincts of his animals and sense the changing weather bearing down on his crops. For forty-five years, morning and night every day of the year, he milked fifty cows in our old but sturdy red barn—sometimes rotating in more cows in shifts, when he could manage it, to make a little more money—and harvested enough crops each year to feed his herd and maybe sell a little extra on the side. He and my mom built our family a farm worth more than any point in its one-hundred-year history and gave my sister and I choices my dad never had. For me to find my own way, whatever it may be, and for my younger sister to decide to take over the farm in what had long been a man's world. And each year more people shrugged and told us little family farms like ours, so much work for so small a milk check, just couldn't make it anymore.

***

I nodded my head to my dad and stepped past him, slipping through the trees, aware now of every sound even in the sharp winter wind. My rifle weighed heavy in front of me. And I knew, as I walked out onto the rock ledge under the big black branches arching overhead to take a shot at my first deer, that something wasn't right. Perhaps it was the nerves of the hunt that brought it on, or the years of failing so many other tests from my father, or a fear of the unknown beyond that hard winter. But whatever the reason, I felt—from the tightness in my chest down to the emptiness in my stomach—that I was about to fall short. I had begun to understand not only that our way of life was becoming rarer but also that my father was a rare man, and becoming rarer still, and that there was a special weight to this. His devotion was something I had felt for years, ever since I was old enough to sit with him in the tractor as he worked our fields, but had been unable to name. Without fail, he was out in the damp spring and the hot green summer and the bright fall that gave way to hard winter. And I knew now, out there on that rock ledge, that what I was feeling was how truly rare he was—and how I might never measure up.

I reached the edge of the rock ledge and peered over. The deer, a big mother doe, was curled up under the ledge, braced against the snow blowing past. We had sat all morning and walked much of the day through the bitter cold to find her, and now I was unsure. She was no more than fifteen yards away, down over that ledge, but it was an awkward angle, and I was young and uneasy with my rifle. The wind took on even greater force, as if to test me further still. I struggled at first to find her in the scope fogging beneath my breath, trees and ground and snow passing before me. Finally, I caught my focus and aimed where I'd been taught to, right behind her front shoulders. In that final moment, the fatal shot felt elusive—the wind and my heaving lungs and the very pulse of the blood in my veins urging the crosshairs off course. I saw her there and thought she must feel tired and cold like me. I fired.

The rifle cracked, and I blinked against the kick as the scope went black. When I looked again, the doe was scrambling out from under the rock ledge and then bounding down the hill and through the trees to disappear behind the white curtain of falling snow. There was no time for another shot. I looked down, the bitter tang of the gunpowder lingering in my nose and mouth. I was old enough to know that what I was supposed to feel in a moment like this was shame. We strode through the snow toward home, and I waited to see whether my dad would tell me what he used to when I was a little boy and would miss squirrels in these woods years ago. *Holy shit, were you close.* But we said less to each other by then. Instead, we walked in silence, and I squinted against the tears rising in my eyes, hoping that my father would not hear me cry if I was sure to do it softly. The solitude offered by the wind and snow felt now like a small gift, despite the distance it placed between us.

I would get more chances to please my dad, on that first day of hunting and others, but the weight of failure would remain. Such moments, when he had the scarce and precious time to teach me something and I had the ability and interest to learn it, would prove elusive on the other side of this hard winter. So many other times over the years, one of those things would seem to be missing, leaving our attempts to relate to each other to slip and tumble down the distance that was growing between us.

And there would be more worries: how many families we knew that would lose everything; what such losses nationwide would do to the food supply of every American, as well as our country's broader economy and culture; how much territory rural prosperity would cede to hopelessness, addiction, and resentment. Increasingly rare farmers like my dad would help set records for new milk production despite these challenges,[24] while others like him would end their troubles with suicide—choosing death over facing the choice between failing to provide for their families by holding on, or losing their way of life by selling out.

We would face these worries, as a father and son trying to connect and a farm family struggling to make sense of a changing world, as the years passed. And it would take more years still to understand what I must do to live up to him—finding my own way and then looking back, deep into a precious way of life and four generations of family secrets. I would learn more than two decades later, as I saw my dad shed tears just as I had on this sacred land, that we must unearth our hidden history—that of my family and that of our country—if we are to save it. Buried times that would reveal who we are and what happened and *what is happening* to us, and what it would take to preserve our way of life so crucial to America's future.

Until then, as a boy still unaware of what was to come, there was nothing to do but trudge onward behind my dad. I followed his footsteps in the snow, looking up to make sure I hadn't lost him. The silhouette of our barn and silos marked the skyline before us, the snow getting lighter now. I wiped the tears from my wind-stung cheeks and hurried along again to keep up. There was work to be done. And truths on this land—from the past, and years still to come—we had yet to face.

CHAPTER 2

"DOWN IN THAT HOLE"

Surviving in the Early 1900s

The blood and memories run deep in the valley where our family first put our plow to the ground. Most of all, the blood. Flowing through our veins over the generations, but also spilling all too often out onto the land that offered a stage to the dreams and sorrows of a people who came to America hoping for better. My great-grandparents thought crossing the ocean would mean avoiding bloodshed—like their families seemed sure to face in the Old Country as Europe prepared for what would become the First World War—but it was a dream short-lived, and it disappeared one day in the summer of 1919, there in that rolling green valley in southern Wisconsin that held so much promise. For that was the day when they faced a tragedy that would echo for the better part of the next century. Our family would feel the tragedy reverberate, through happy times and other tragedies, and in quiet rooms where weary men and women grew old and thought of what they'd done, to themselves and to each other.

My great-grandfather, Alois Reisinger, came to the United States in 1909, and Teresia Roth came in 1911. They had grown up just three miles from each other in a pair of small farming villages in Bavaria, Germany, but never met. It would take the threat of continental war, a 4,500-mile journey over land and sea, and a chance meeting in the New World to bring them together. Alois was raw-boned with sharp features and ears that loped out from his head. In later years his features would sharpen further yet, and he would at times wear a dark moustache. But when he first arrived in the United States at the age of twenty-five, his face was smooth, albeit marked even then by a mouth set with stubborn determination. Teresia was kinder and softer faced, and would remain so through the years, but was no less tough, even if her strength showed itself in other ways. She was twenty-three when she came to America. They both hailed from a part of the world known for its industriousness but destined for global conflict.

Alois saw what would become World War I coming and wanted something different for his life. Ancestors in Bavaria, which had a legacy of resistance to German unification, remembered Alois as a lost brother who had served in the German military but left for America before the war broke out. Arriving with few friendly faces outside of those who sponsored him coming over, Alois worked on local farms amid the rolling hills of southern Wisconsin until he could find a way to buy his own farm.

Teresia's journey was less divorced from the support of family. Her father had once traveled to America and encouraged his children to go there in search of a better life. So Teresia made a trek that many in her family ultimately made. Where Alois found rich dirt that would allow the strength of his hand to go toward plowing up a prosperous and independent life—instead of clutching a rifle in the muddy trenches of Europe—Teresia found a place where perhaps she could build upon the promise her family was already finding in America.

But they were destined, despite the thousands of miles between Wisconsin farm country and the coming crisis in Europe, to wage another war—against the dirt poverty and physical hardship of what our family calls "the olden days" and what America counts as its pivotal shift from subsistence farming to industrial agriculture. It would be a furious fight for survival, one that would hold lessons for the modern-day fight for America's food supply generations later. And it would not be bloodless.

***

Alois and Teresia's arrival was a time of flux, flush with the hope and hardship that often accompanies such change, and one that established a simple fact: For the American family farm to reach its unique place in our country's economic system, it would first need to make it through this early era of survival from the late 1800s to the early 1900s. Farm families multiplied quickly in this era, but their chances of survival varied widely by region and class, in Wisconsin and all across the country. In 1910, one year after Alois arrived, there were more than 177,000 farms in Wisconsin, and nearly 6.4 million nationwide, numbers that represented a massive expansion from the time of Wisconsin's statehood some sixty years earlier, and that would grow more still before toppling in the decades to come. The amount of land going toward farming in Wisconsin in 1910 was more than 21 million acres, seven times what it was in 1850. America's farm acreage nationwide, meanwhile, multiplied by about three times in that same time period. In other words, midwestern states like Wisconsin were becoming booming economic engines, representing an outsized share of a large-scale expansion in American agriculture underway in the first part of the twentieth century. In fact, farms in Wisconsin held a total value of $1.2 billion by then, up from $30 million in 1850.[25]

But you wouldn't have known it by the conditions on the ground for farmers just starting out. The economic dynamism belied a farmland fight on the edge of poverty for some. Many farmers in the early 1900s, in many corners of America's growing agriculture industry, were still struggling to afford basic necessities like clothing, proper heat, and sufficient medical care for their families, even as they worked in a dynamic economic sector that was on the cusp of greatness. The future was bright and bountiful, but still just out of reach—perhaps down that next field row or over that next hill.

There are many roots of American agriculture, stretching back further in our country's history. But those roots from this period of upheaval in the Midwest are among the strongest, and they remain intertwined with the modern-day crisis of the disappearing American farmer—and the solutions to saving our food supply. In those early days, part of the reason such promise and poverty went hand in hand is because there was a revolution underway in the Midwest over exactly what kind of farming to do.

Wheat dominated many of America's newer agricultural hotbeds for much of the 1800s. Soon after, each state began to find its own unique niche in feeding the country. Wheat, for all its virtues, is hard on soil and required more and more acreage to be competitive on price and quantity as more farmland opened up in America. Wisconsin, featuring some flatlands but also more rolling hills, soaring bluffs, and plunging valleys than states to the south and west, lacked that wide-open acreage. Therefore, farmers, as well as the industry advocates and researchers trying to build an economy, had to find alternatives to make the production of each acre of land more potent and therefore profitable.[26] For a time, this meant mixed agriculture, with farmers experimenting with a range of cash crops (where crops are sold on the market) and various forms of livestock farming (where at least some crops go toward feeding animals that in turn yield another product, like meat or dairy). As a result, by the 1890s in Wisconsin, dairy farming—milking cows, then by hand, for milk, cream, butter, cheese, and other dairy products—emerged to overtake wheat.[27]

Farms surviving the transition from one crop or product to another face unique challenges. Like any business, a farm has to have one or more products it can produce to generate the income needed to make it another year. Unlike many other businesses, family farms—in Alois's day and today—are subject to fickle weather and all kinds of other uncontrollable perils in a way much of the American economy isn't. Expenses range from all the usual household expenses of any family, plus elevated fuel and energy costs, the cost of seed (genetically sophisticated in later years), fertilizer, ever-more-expensive farm equipment, supplies to care for animals and repair farm operations, labor, and so on.

The amount and kind of income can vary widely from one kind of farm to another, but farming is always a gamble rife with uncontrollable factors. A crop farm, raising say wheat or corn or vegetables, will generally plant in the spring and harvest at various times between then and fall, wagering that their yield will be strong enough to cover the expenses for the year. Planting and harvesting can take weeks or even months, depending upon the crop and weather conditions allowing farmers to get into the fields. That's true even with the modern conveniences of tractors and sophisticated equipment. Some goods, like alfalfa to make hay for cows, might have as many as five crops per year, each crop mowed and raked and then baled or chopped. All on the hottest and driest days, only to be done again a few weeks later, from late spring to early fall. In Alois's day, a good deal of fieldwork was done by hand, making it even more brutal and time consuming.

If the farm makes its money on livestock, meanwhile—such as milking cows to help produce dairy products—it may have more steady income, like a monthly milk check from a cheese factory or other milk processor. Periodic sales of livestock for meat, from beef to pork to chicken, are also forms of supplemental income. Such farms often also plant and harvest crops, betting that they'll yield enough to feed their animals and possibly sell some on the side. Farms that milk cows must do so at least twice per day, morning and night—by hand in the early 1900s, today by machine.

Then there's the other work in between: preparing ground for an upcoming crop; caring for animals, from birthing and feeding to dealing with sickness; repairing broken equipment; making or fixing fence; cleaning out barns or other facilities; and on and on each day. Such responsibilities make twelve-hour days often standard, and the sky is the limit in terms of hours worked during planting or harvesting season if the weather is good.

Whether a family's annual gamble will pay off is a matter of not only hard work, efficiency, and resourcefulness but also an extraordinary level of good fortune. A hard freeze at the wrong time, a hailstorm, a sudden drought, or overly wet conditions can all doom a crop that might make up the bulk of a farm's income for the year. An invasive insect can do the same. Some crops, like soybeans that soared in importance throughout the twentieth century, are so sensitive that reaching harvest at a time of slightly high or low moisture levels, even in an otherwise good year, can make a crop worthless. Sickness spreading through a herd of dairy cows, beef cows, pigs, or chickens—whether a preventable mishap or a freak accident—can wipe out the bulk of a farm's income for that year, and years to come if enough animals are affected. A farm accident that kills or lays up a family member can cripple a farm's operations or require hired labor the farm can't afford. What's more, all this is possible at any moment, even before accounting for commodity prices that can turn south on a dime, while input costs (like seed, fertilizer, fuel, and more) continue to rise. That makes many farms at risk of losing money any time, no matter how efficient they are.

Cruel ironies exist along the way: a good growing season means farmers have more to sell, but lower prices as supply increases; a bad growing season might drive prices up because of scarce supply, but farmers are unable to capitalize because their production is down. This creates a trap for farmers that often has them defying economics.

They're often left striving to produce more in good years and bad alike, even if what they should be doing is reducing their supply to help correct prices. Even if they wanted to restrict their supply, it's not a simple matter of holding back inventory like a store or factory might. Farms have to destroy crops or livestock to quickly reduce their supply, and often can't increase supply again until a year later or more, such as the next growing season or the day when a young animal is finally mature enough to generate income.

Many businesses face some of these perils, but fewer face them all at once, let alone face them as a small family operation. Most farms don't have the big budgets or diversified revenue streams that allow large corporations to hedge against disaster in one part of the globe, with good fortune in another.

The need for a reliable food supply for the country through all of these perils—including in years where food has been needed at below the cost of production—would lead to major government intervention within just a few years of when Alois arrived. From there, endless debates would unfold for decades to come over where the government should end and the market should begin, in the quest to put food on every American dinner table.

However, many families in the early 1900s were simply searching among the various crops and animals they were raising for the products that would help them make enough money to survive. This period of mixed agriculture in the Midwest—which played out at various times on farmland all across the country—is where the popular image of the American farm truly came into its own.

Today, most crop farms specialize in a few main cash crops, and most livestock operations focus on one kind of animal and the crops needed for feed. In Wisconsin, for example, that's often dairy farms with a herd of milk cows and fields of corn and hay for animal feed. Any given farm may feature a side crop or novelty animal here and there. Yet, in the early 1900s, farmland brimmed with any crop you might take to market and every kind of animal you could imagine milling, waddling, and pecking about the farmyard. The mix of crops was myriad, on farms of all sizes in Wisconsin: hay, oats, corn, barley, rye, potatoes, dry peas, tobacco, the whole spectrum of garden vegetables, apples, cherries, plums, pears, strawberries, raspberries, blackberries, and more.[28] Livestock ran the gamut too: dairy cows, horses and mules for the fieldwork, pigs, sheep, chickens, geese, ducks, turkeys, and so on.[29] All these crops and animals represented the fight for survival on two levels: the search for products that could make a profitable farm and the raising of food that these farm families could live on. That's money in the pocket and food on the table—or stored away on shelves and in cellars, in anticipation of a brutal winter.

This is a history that is repeating itself, over a century later, in ways we do not see. Modern conveniences like heat and running water, miracles of medicine, and easy travel to grocery stores mask the fact that today, American agriculture—and with it our country's food supply—is again going through a period defined by devastating economic circumstances. Many of the forces driving our agricultural crisis today, from economic upheaval to technological change, mirror the challenges of these early days. The loss of farms is destroying our capacity to feed ourselves in a durable way and provide the stable food supply our country needs, as well as the kinds of choices consumers want. All of this makes the American farm family's fight for survival in the early twentieth century the best place to start in determining the path forward in the twenty-first century.

Alois's fight for survival met him in his first moments in America. He arrived by boat on March 31, 1909, with a secret from his days in the German military. Its shadows ranged across the wood-planked docks of Ellis Island, then followed him over hills and valleys of midwestern farm country. Reaching southern Wisconsin in a year when winter lingered all the way into May,[30] he worked first on the farm of a family that had sponsored him coming to America, a common practice to facilitate immigration in those days, then on another farm nearby. Despite the work from fellow immigrant families and the growth of Plain, a German Catholic village made prosperous by local farmers, Alois seemed to keep to himself in those first two years.

For a time, according to family histories, he considered returning to Bavaria—even as he avoided contacting family for fear of the secret from his military days being found out. But he was encouraged to stay by a man whose sister was coming over soon, a young woman excited to see America. They met at a funeral adorned with the spare crucifixes and other symbols of the Catholic heritage they'd shared just three miles apart from each other in Bavaria. Her name was Teresia.

That winter of 1911–12 was the hardest on record.[31] The Great Blue Norther cold snap swept the northern United States, plunging the Midwest into a spate of extreme weather: dangerously cold temperatures, deep snow, howling wind, and even winter tornados springing forth from the sudden shift in conditions.[32] And yet, in that hardest of Wisconsin winters—with the Old Country and the Atlantic Ocean and another thousand miles across land already behind him—Alois traveled further. Up, into the surrounding hills, in search of a farm to buy with the woman he planned to marry. He'd come to America with $25 in life savings in his pocket, a decent amount equaling about $800 today, but only a fraction of what it would take to buy a farm. Since then, he'd saved wages for more than two years and was preparing to risk it all on land he hoped would turn enough profit to pay off the debt it would take to buy it.

The 180-acre plot he found was even more isolated than most family farms in those days. It had begun as three separate land grants from US President James Buchanan, one of them granted to a US military veteran.[33] The land changed hands a few times over the decades until local farm families consolidated the properties into one farm. It was several miles from the nearest town, up and over a series of hills from the nearest main road, tucked in a valley down a road so steep it would imperil many a horse-drawn wagon, as well as cars, trucks, and tractors for generations to come.

Standing at the bottom of that road in his customary overalls and a heavy coat, Alois looked at the secluded farmyard and valley beyond, covered in snow. He knew the dirt beneath that brutal winter landscape was brown clay loam—frozen and bound to be tough and muddy after the spring thaw, but fertile, nonetheless. Good for growing hay, corn, apples, and everything in between, this soil could provide everything that a family needed to survive, if Alois was willing to work it hard enough and could traverse the hills and dodge the fickle weather well enough.

Stretching out southwest from the rough-sawn log farmhouse, the farm's fields sprawled across rolling hillsides on either side of the valley before eventually giving way to dueling forests further up each hillside, reaching into the sky. The farm's acreage extended nearly half a mile down the valley, then reached a fork. One path continued straight ahead to fields belonging to another farm. The other curved northwest to complete the property Alois was eyeing, around a bend in the wood line that gave way to more fields, again sloping up hillsides that led to woods. He had found this place to start a new life just as Wisconsin's dairy industry was preparing to come into its own.

Over a century later, his grandson, my father, Jim, would wonder aloud why Alois was so eager to settle "down in that hole," instead of on easier ground nearby. The young immigrant farm laborer could have turned away from that valley and looked to the rolling hills nearby offering less treacherous slopes, to flatter land out by the main road where he had first worked, or to softer soil in other parts of the county. Perhaps he did. But whatever his reasons—cost, availability, the way the fields struck his eye beneath that deep blanket of snow— there was still one reason raising the stakes of survival, in a way no other reason could.

Alois was, in fact, only supposed to be in America on borrowed time before returning to the bloody business of war in Europe. It was the secret that had burdened him across land and sea. Before leaving, as a condition of going to America, he had signed an official-looking government document stating that he would return to service if war broke out in Europe. Some members of our family have a hard time believing he came to that valley for fear of being found out and taken back to war. There were many good, and less shocking, reasons to buy a farm. Others feel it is the only reason that truly made sense. It was why he'd kept to himself in America and avoided contacting family in Bavaria, resulting in his years of loneliness. Whatever the case, Alois took out a mortgage on the farm—down in that valley so far from anyone who could inquire about his foreign military obligations— buried his secret there in the snow of that hard Wisconsin winter, and married Teresia just a few short weeks later in January of 1912. He didn't speak of it to his family for four decades.

The promise was immense, if unreachable by a people any less determined, as Alois and Teresia awoke those first mornings in that valley in 1912. Knee-deep snow buried not only Alois's secrets, but much of the work in the farmyard in those days. Each morning the plumes of their breath rose—first, in the colder corners of the house far from the wood-fired stove, and then in the frigid farmyard air as they ventured out into the early-morning darkness for chores. It was below freezing almost always, and below zero often. A hard wind howled down the valley, but it was softer there in the farmyard, nes- tled against the hillsides guarding it. And come spring, there in those fields, spreading down the valley and around the bend, they could find prosperity against the elements, if they worked hard enough and the Lord smiled upon their toil.

Alois and Teresia's bet was that, with enough rain to nourish their fields and enough dry periods in between—and no disastrous weather—they could raise enough crops to feed their animals and hopefully find the products that would make them a living to survive. Across the yard from the house, a hulking red barn with a stone foundation provided shelter where Alois could keep cows. The land offered space close at hand where their family could not only pasture the cows but also ultimately keep pigs, chickens, and geese; where small sheds could store machinery; where a stone root cellar built into the hillside could store food.

Out back of the barn, up past the apple orchard, Alois would keep a still to make hard liquor. Perhaps there would be money to buy beer on occasion to give the threshing crews—area farmers who would band together to share the machinery and labor needed to complete the fall harvest, then drink the hours away when the work was finally done.

The farmhouse sat tucked against the hillsides. When the sun rose in the east from behind, it shined in earnest first across the valley before working its way back toward the farmyard. Finally, the sunlight would conquer the towering hillsides and shine directly upon the house, passing through the spare rooms. Out back of the house there was a natural spring that they could harness to supply cold water to the family inside the farmhouse, to the animals in the barn and sheds, and to the garden Teresia would tend. She came to love gardening, her hair tied back in a knot as she leaned over the brown soil in her heavy work dress and grew every food the earth would welcome. Down the valley from the house and barn, grape vines and berries tangled their way about the woodland surrounding the fields. They canned all they could and kept sauerkraut in crocks in the basement. Occasionally, they'd butcher meat when they could spare it—to eat and preserve for later.

By then, milk was their best chance at survival. They couldn't compete in the wheat market alone, flooded as it was by flatter states with bigger fields. They couldn't buy enough beef cattle to make it selling meat alone, the kind of thing only established cattlemen could afford in those days.[34] But Alois had seen the farmers nearer town making real money selling milk and cream, and there was a growing local cheese industry. Farmers were using the acreage limited by the hills and valleys to grow feed for dairy cows, from reddish Guernseys to black-and-white spotted Holsteins. Over the years, as young couples like Alois and Teresia fought for their stake, Wisconsin would prove to be fertile ground also for some specialty crops, like potatoes, cranberries, and ginseng. But none would direct the state's economic future, nor exemplify the plight of every American farmer, like Wisconsin's dairy industry. Milk was becoming Wisconsin's currency in the growing but tumultuous world of American agriculture.

The move toward niches in Wisconsin and other states would begin as a source of innovation, but ultimately shift so far that many farms would lose their diversified farming in favor of specialized farming. This would become a problem so pronounced that a century later, we would learn we never should have lost these roots of mixed agriculture—and that returning to them would offer a path forward toward more innovation again. But for the time being, Alois and Teresia found, like so many Wisconsin farmers as the midwestern farm states carved their place in the nation's growing economy, that they were destined for dairy farming.

They would also find, all too brutally, that when you go from almost nothing to something, you have more to lose.

***

In January of 1913, Teresia gave birth to their first son, my grandfather, Albert. And the kids kept coming, with Sophie born in October of 1914, and Herman in December of 1916. There was no electricity, heat only in those rooms close to the wood-fired stove, and no money for medical care. Herman would be the youngest for the first few years, but the family's struggle to survive would be something all the children, whatever their age, would come to know. Helene, the second youngest of the fourteen, born in the early days of the Great Depression, recalls her father selling mainly milk and cream, but also eggs, pigs, and young bull calves. The family kept the rest of the food they grew to survive, serving it on the long wooden dinner table in the cramped kitchen.

"They grew everything," she said. "Money was always tight."

The work and determination of Alois and Teresia to support their family bound them. Alois stayed there, down in that valley with his wife and children, as global war broke out in 1914. While Alois found certainty about leaving his old life behind, Teresia gave up thoughts of another life as well. Years later, her daughters learned she had not wanted to be married at first because she wanted to explore America. Instead, together in that valley, with a place to raise their animals and crops and a family, Alois and Teresia waged a decades-long labor to pay off the farm and prepare it for the next generation. Their farmland fight would never completely subside, even as brighter days came to the American family farm. The enduring challenges of everyday farm life and being the little guy in a growing world infused in them an eternal sense of fighting against the odds. They would learn, like all farm families, that their first job was as simple and serious as it comes: Survive. Persist, each day, each season, each year, so that perhaps there is something for those who come next.

Maybe that's why Alois whipped those horses onward with such drive as he made hay on that fateful day in 1919, so weighted still with blood and memory. The hard winter and soggy spring of Wisconsin farm country had given way to warmer summer days by then, for the hay was tall enough to be in need of cutting. It was tall enough, too, that there were things in the fields a man could not see.

At thirty-four years old, Alois was doing what animated him most—working, harder each moment, to grow a living out of the ground for his family. His legal status would have been difficult to classify in today's terms. On one hand, he'd arrived legally. On the other, he was not yet a citizen and had by then stayed in America years past the outbreak of World War I, when German authorities claimed he must return to fight on opposite sides from the country he now called home. His children saw him ceaselessly working—plowing and planting and milking and heaving and pounding—never letting loose of that which he'd found in that valley in place of war in Europe. Teresia was given to small kindnesses, offering a bit of jam on a piece of bread, or quiet words of comfort in hard times. But she was a taskmaster in her own way, urging her children to tend to their chores in the house and farmyard and fields.

"*Schaffen, schaffen,*" she said. The children knew what it meant—*work, work*—but the translation is something more precise. *Create.*

So Alois drove the horses hard. Cutting hay meant steering a horse-drawn mower across the rolling green fields that stretched southwest down the valley and around the bend. Once the hay was cut, Alois would have to let it dry in the sun, then load it by hand with a pitchfork onto the back of a wagon. As acre after acre of hay dried and went from field to wagon to barn, it kicked up dust and chaff to mix with Alois's sweat and coat his hands, neck, and face. Over and over until his fields were cleared. There was never any time to waste if he wanted to get his acreage mowed and dried and harvested under the hot sun before the rain bore down on his valley.

Then, strangely, the horses stopped in the middle of the field, not wanting to go further. Stepping clear of them, Alois walked through the hay, thick and green with multicolored clover, to see what might be halting his progress. He looked around and around through the tall hay but saw nothing. Turning back, he got behind the horses again, and whipped them onward. We'll never know what he heard or saw next—whether it was the screams of his young child that came first, or the horses jostling against the obstruction. But in seconds that would hold the weight of decades, Alois broke from the horses and found his two-year-old son Herman beneath them. His boy's leg was shattered, red blood staining the field. Young Herman, moments earlier lying peacefully in the swaying shoots of hay mere steps from his father, was now screaming and bloody, no different than a soldier on a battlefield.

Picking the little body up, Alois held Herman in his arms and struck for the house. Perhaps he questioned, suffering in solitude with his bleeding little boy as he strode across his fields in that valley toward home, whether he should have whipped the horses onward like he did. Or perhaps it made him feel all the more why he pushed so hard each day—even if he would have taken that fateful moment back—seeing yet again that they must strive forward, for fear of a tragic accident or other catastrophe that could at any moment knock them back. The dangers surrounded them in all directions: failure to beat the weather, failure to provide for their children, failure to keep the farm going. And now, failure to avoid bloodshed. They were so close to making it. The war in the Old Country had ended a few months earlier.

Finally, Alois reached the pasture, then the farmyard, then the stoop of the farmhouse. When he burst into the kitchen, his face was stark with panic. Family recalled that as he stood there and Teresia finally saw him—holding Herman bloody and pale there in his arms—their little boy's leg was hanging on his body by a thread.

CHAPTER 3

THE FORGOTTEN DEPRESSION

Economic Devastation of the 1920s and 30s

The fire started, they believed, with kerosene. That first bit of oil slipped from the glass lantern, flame following fast and close behind like the devil chasing a straying soul. In an instant, the blaze had caught and the flames danced across the room, orange and yellow and nimble and angry. Little Albert was the only one there to see it. He was barely big enough to carry his baby sister then, let alone know all the dangers that could befall them on the farm. But he could see there, blazingly clear, that fire was one of them. As the flames grew taller and louder, seeking and swallowing everything in their path, Albert turned to Sophie, picked her up, and began to run across the room for the door, the fiery glow casting flickering shadows upon the walls and searing across the floor. Albert was small and afraid, but he knew the way out. Through the door, onto the porch, then out into the farmyard where his parents worked as their house went up in flames.

There weren't enough prayers or hands or water to be had as Alois and Teresia scrambled toward the house. These were days when there was no telephone to call the fire department, no hose to spray water— only the speed and courage of the family to fight the fire themselves. If Albert was older, they maybe could have sent him to town by horse to fetch the fire department. But he was still too young, and they could spare neither the manpower nor the time for the six-mile journey across soaring hills and through winding backways to the main road and into town. And so, they fought. Yelling and shuffling from one spot to the next to head off the fire, Alois and Teresia threw buckets of water to knock it down. They couldn't pump water fast enough, so they even cast buckets of milk on the fire. That smooth white fruit of their labor, the raw equivalent of money, splashed against the rough sawn wood of the house that contained so many hopes and dreams, the inferno dodging and roaring and hissing. Until finally, they put it out. Woodsmoke and fear filled the air long after the flames were gone, rising into the sky above the valley so big, as the family sorted through all they had left.

And still, there were more fires to come.

***

No more than four years old then, my grandpa, Albert Reisinger, would come of age during unimaginable disaster. He and his family were destined to each take their turns, over and over, on our land fighting not only the Great Depression but also a series of hidden calamities that would befall family farms and bring our country's food supply to its knees. It was a time of apocalyptic proportions, during which the American family farm would face its greatest economic, environmental, and existential challenges. For farm families to not only survive but also emerge poised to enter the middle class demonstrates just how deeply their resilience ran, and just how much economic opportunity lay in the ground at that time. Their emergence against such unimaginable odds also reveals the potential to overcome the systemic vulnerabilities to our own food supply today due to economic upheaval and entrenched debates over our environmental future, so long as we find new ways to harness the heartland, rather than abandon it.

If some of America's deepest farming roots grew during the early 1900s shift to industrial agriculture, then the earliest flames of today's farmland failure first showed themselves in the apocalyptic era of the 1920s and '30s. However, this account is not the typical narrative of the Great Depression that swept the globe, hitting farmers as well as everyone else; it's one of a forgotten farm depression that began nearly a decade earlier and in some ways never left. For the American farmer, the fire of economic devastation started in a rural financial crisis in 1920[35] and persisted in a series of disasters that struck while so few outside of farm country were watching. And, like the loss in any fire, the cost of the crisis was noticed at first in those things lying among the ashes, but not fully realized until forgotten things are remembered years later. From 1920 to 1925—for the first time in recorded history—America would shift from a growing number of farms to a shrinking number of farms, from more acreage being used for farmland to less acreage being used for farmland, and from farms gaining value to farms losing value. That loss in cash value, more than 25 percent in five years, would be surpassed in history only by the loss that would come a few short years later in the Great Depression.[36] However, the impact, even with devastation of this magnitude, could not have been fully realized until later: The disappearance of the American farmer had begun, and would persist even during boomtimes that offered invitations to the middle class for some.

Such a treacherous fall requires reaching a great height. In 1919 the American family farm was flying high, by the standards of the day. While many farmers in the heartland had only just a few years earlier moved from subsistence farming into a stable business, and much of the prosperity of the 1910s came also in the midst of World War I from 1914 to 1918, the demand for food grown all across the heartland had skyrocketed.[37] In fact, there was a common belief that a victorious America would have to feed a smoldering Europe. That growing demand came at a time when many agricultural states had found their footing in the nation's food supply and coincided with what economists and farmers widely remember as the "golden age" for all of American agriculture from 1910 to 1914. The seemingly endless need for food, and the growing ability of the American family farm to deliver it, were in a moment of harmony.

Unfortunately, it was never built to last. Like the sun still shining as the first rumble of a dark and angry thunderstorm rolls in, it was a temporary sight that would soon enough seem too far off to have ever been real. The price farmers got for their goods hit a high point before taking a furious fall—down a third from the previous year by November of 1920 and down 85 percent by the summer of 1921.[38] Europe's recovery, and ability to feed itself, came sooner than expected.[39] Meanwhile, farmers had taken out debt—be it from the private sector or government loan programs established in this era to encourage more lending to farmers—to meet the previous demand for food. By 1920, farms nationwide had more than doubled their mortgage debt from a decade before, the total tearing upward more than 130 percent, to just north of $4 billion. Every single region of the country showed an increase, especially in the Midwest and other major agriculture states.[40] There were more farms, more farmers taking out mortgages, and more debt per farm.

And now they were in trouble. The drop in the price of farm goods, for farmers deep in debt, kicked off a rural financial crisis, with prosperity that once seemed endless snapping back with an equally unbelievable amount of economic pain. Banks that once doled out ample loans now had customers unable to make payments on their debts.

Soon enough the banks themselves were in trouble, piling up losses on loans farmers couldn't repay. From 1921 to 1927, more than 4,600 banks failed.[41] Consequentially, money became even less available to local farmers, spreading financial pain to neighboring banks all across the heartland.

Rodney Ramcharan, a former economist at the Federal Reserve who now serves as a professor at the University of Southern California, and Raghuram Rajan, a former economist with the International Monetary Fund, have painstakingly exhumed the records of these thousands of individual banks from this time period. Their finding: the rural financial crisis of the 1920s reveals why bank failures then, and still today, spread like a fire from one room to the next. With so many farmers and bankers struggling so deeply, the land they were all depending upon—the land that the farmers worked to make their living, and that banks could claim and sell when loans went bad—fell in value. There was already the lower price an individual farmer or banker might have to sell land for if they were in trouble, but the drop in the value of land went far beyond that. The repeated fire sales of land hurt the value of land owned by other farmers and bankers who weren't in trouble too, Ramcharan said. That loss of "fundamental value" in farmland meant that soon thereafter those financially healthy farms and banks were also struggling. Loans became harder to pay off for farmers and riskier to keep on their books for bankers, further exacerbating an ongoing spiral of economic devastation.

"It reduces the value of those loans, and gets those farmers into trouble," Ramcharan told me. "You get this kind of cascade, or contagion, that takes place."

The result was an economic depression that swept farms and rural communities a decade before the Great Depression. However, the devastation in farm country also started earlier for reasons that went well beyond this forgotten agricultural depression. Farmers in broad swaths of the heartland—specifically the Upper Midwest—faced their own ecological crisis that began before the better-known Dust Bowl of the 1930s. All the way back in the late 1800s, farmers in the Midwest were facing catastrophic erosion. Like the Dust Bowl of the Great Plains to come later, this erosion was the result of farmers doing their level best to make as much money as they could by plowing up their small slice of God's creation before modern soil conservation efforts were developed. The problem accelerated throughout the 1900s and was out of control by World War I, years before the Dust Bowl hit the nation's breadbasket, said Stanley Trimble, a professor and researcher who has written extensively about the time period.

"They started into these virgin soils," he said. "And they thought that would last forever."

But unlike the Dust Bowl, it wasn't just dry weather that did them in. Farmers moving in from other regions who had not experienced the heavy rainstorms of the Midwest found they had plowed too much ground and were suddenly deeply vulnerable to rushing gulleys of rainfall washing over their hillsides and sweeping their virgin topsoil away, Trimble said. This threat was not immediately apparent, but one that set in over decades. Soil that might have been rich for many years over time began to lose its organic material, structural soundness, and other crucial characteristics—suddenly becoming less fertile and more vulnerable to erosion when the heavy rains came.[42] Farmers who worked those rich virgin soils for years without trouble now trudged across high ground sapped of nutrients and low ground transformed into a flooded and muddy wasteland.

All of this came before the stock market crash of 1929. After years of agricultural depression, compounded in some parts by the catastrophic erosion of midwestern farmland, many farms and farmland lenders went under—and those still standing were battered and barely getting by. Although some economic recovery occurred in the years that followed, it was well-known that many crops and products were often selling for less than the cost of materials needed for production, regardless of a farm operation's efficiency.

When the stock market crashed on Black Thursday, October 24, 1929, it sent shockwaves through the national financial sector and signaled what we now know was the global descent into the Great Depression. In farm country, it was yet another wave of economic devastation searing across the land. Then came the first dry periods of the Dust Bowl on the Great Plains, foretelling another ecological disaster ahead. By the early 1930s a nationwide drought was killing crops and feeding a compounding crisis—topsoil blown away on the Great Plains and further damaged in the Midwest after years of already being weakened by gulley erosion. All of this beat down on farmers knocked flat by years of economic depression.

The depths of the devastation—from the forgotten economic and ecological crises of the 1920s, to the Great Depression and Dust Bowl of the 1930s—unleashed a level of unrest in farm country that continued despite temporary economic rebounds, and even turned violent. In 1933 the federal government moved off the gold standard, which in basic terms meant it could print more or less money to put into the financial system without needing to have each American dollar backed up by a certain amount of gold. That allowed the government to pump more money into the economy, which decreased the value of the dollar in world markets and helped drive up commodity prices, including prices paid to farmers for crops and food products.[43]

Researchers say the increase in prices of farm goods contributed to the beginning of a recovery from the Depression, but it wasn't enough—economic decline returned off and on for nearly a decade, through the 1930s.

Aside from that, a great deal of economic damage had already been done in farm country, so many didn't feel the effect of any brief recovery. Foreclosures hammered farms nationwide. Farm bankruptcies were rampant for the better part of two decades. In total, nearly ninety thousand American farms filed for bankruptcy from 1920 through 1939—just under fifty-two thousand during the agricultural depression of the 1920s, and thirty-eight thousand during the nation-wide Great Depression of the 1930s.[44]

In the Great Plains and American Southwest, farmers with depleted soil struggled to grow what they needed to survive, for their table or their pocketbook. In midwestern agricultural enclaves like Wisconsin, milk prices hit a point that was two-thirds lower than it was at the end of World War I.[45] Dairy farmers went on strike in 1933, dumping their milk and blocking the production of cream and cheese. A chain of escalation among authorities, farmers, and inter-loping vandals led to violence—including the bombing of cheese fac-tories and a striker shot to death.[46]

For those families that kept their farms, the economic pain took many forms. Each new child—a regular occurrence for the big families of the era—brought the hope of more hands to help with the work, and the fear of another mouth to feed each day. In our family, all fourteen of Alois and Teresia's children would come of age during, or be born into, economic depression. The eldest, Albert, would find his life shaped by the traumatic conditions in ways that would echo for decades.

***

The sky above them was so big and so dark you could lose yourself in it if you stared upward long enough. On overcast nights it was pitch black, and everything—the farmhouse, the outbuildings, the fields, the valley beyond, and the little dirt road running through it all—disappeared under a shroud of darkness, so heavy a hand in front of your face was barely visible. Other nights stars appeared like so many promises from the heavens above. The deep dark sky took on a nebu-lous purple hue then, the countless stars letting pinpricks of light shine through to help color it.

Alois, Teresia, and the children rose before daylight, moving from the house to the barn and working in both by lantern light. Draft horses nickered and blew in the dark. The cows mooed low as they journeyed in from pasture. Albert and the other children would milk the cows by hand and do their other morning chores while Teresia fired the stoves, began to prepare what food they had, and tended to those children who could not yet take care of themselves. The sunrise in the east came slowly. It was as if the light from above tended to the rest of mankind before seeing fit to find the growing brood of farmers in this valley so deep, working in their way. Morning's earliest hints peaked from behind the house, up over the hill.

They could only pray that by the time the Lord saw fit to give the valley light, nobody had been hurt in the dangerous work at hand and that the good fortune would last throughout the day. There was little money for a doctor or other needs. Family after family lost farm after farm around them—just up the hill, between there and town, and in the hills and ridges beyond. One costly tragedy or another could bring the same to their valley.

By the time of the Great Depression, Albert was sixteen. He had first cried and toddled as his parents weathered World War I and climbed out of subsistence farming in that valley. Sophie, Herman, and Mathilda (known as "Tillie" for much of her life) were born not long after him. Next was Bill—within just two years of when Herman was trampled and left with a wooden leg by their father's team of horses—and then through the rest of the 1920s came Marie, Catherine, the twins Ann and Clara, then Alois Jr., and Edward. As the eldest of the children, Albert worked alongside his father first and for the longest, as a boy during the agricultural depression of the 1920s, then as a young man in the Great Depression. Milking cows and shocking grain and carrying heavier loads and graduating—when he could—on to other tasks as his siblings grew old enough to work. Joseph and Helene would arrive in the early 1930s. It would not be until 1936 that John, the family's last child, would come—as would the greatest danger of all, after two decades filled with it.

The economic and physical peril could not extinguish the joy of a family living close to the land. Though the children huddled together in the winter, sharing when they could the only room with a heat register from the wooden stove below, in warmer weather they slipped out onto the porch roof from their second-story window. And despite the fact that there was work to be done every day of the year—and most hours of each day, except for Sundays—they took what little time they could to play baseball in the farmyard. During the week, the children walked across hills and fields to school after morning chores. Their parents spoke Bavarian German, and the children would answer back in English. Every now and again on Sundays, Alois and Teresia would hitch a ride to visit relatives and neighbors. The children would descend then on the old Ford car, the family's only automobile, and crank it alive to drive it around the yard, rumbling and jerking and honking about in the dust. Helene, the second-youngest child, remembers learning to drive that way. Afterward, the children swept the dirt yard with sturdy straw brooms to conceal their joyous tracks from their parents.

Work and play alike could turn to physical danger in an instant, though. And the family—financially strapped and injured often in the brutal conditions—owed so much money to the hospital they often couldn't get the medical care they needed. Of course there was Herman, who survived the horses running him over in the field at age two. He lived from then on with a wooden leg that he worked on over the years—reminding his family, each day, without a word, of the dangers they all faced. But that was only the beginning. Other siblings survived accidents with machinery and tools and dangerous falls off buildings and down chutes. There was more than one instance, over the years, of Alois looking up from the head of the long wooden dinner table to ask where one of the children was, only for he and

Teresia to learn of an accident the boys and girls lining the table on both sides were afraid to disclose.

Alois had become stern and hot-tempered over the years of work and disaster and physical danger. He worked from before the sun came up to whenever the tasks of the day were done and expected the same devotion of his children—and enforced strict discipline. Physical punishment was common in those days among families of all stations, and that was true of our family as Alois pushed his children to do what was needed on the farm. Some of the brothers and sisters would look back and feel it was just a sign of the times, knowing Alois loved them and the method was only a product of the harsh world he came up in, while others remembered wanting nothing more than to get away from it all.

When Alois was angry, his children recalled, it was mainly about keeping the farm going and his children on the straight and narrow. He hardly drank, unlike many of his fellow German immigrants, though he kept a bottle of brandy on the stairway to the basement, and he made sure the local men were fed and could drink their fill of beer when they helped him finish the harvest. Teresia had a sense of humor and heart for her children. Now and then she'd sneak a sip from Alois's idle bottle of brandy, replacing it with water. On the rare occasion when she was angry enough to threaten her children with punishment, they suspected that she had no intention of using the whip she would chase them with. More likely it was just for show to keep their father from scolding and supplying harsher penalty. It was often Teresia, or her eldest daughter Sophie, who would find the children hurt and help them.

As the eldest, Albert would not only live this world first but also remain in its grasp for years to come. Like so many large farm families of the day, as the two eldest, Albert and Sophie assumed second in command behind their parents. In the years since they had emerged from the flames of the burning house, they were both charged with growing responsibility. In addition to working alongside his father, Albert oversaw the farm work of his siblings as they came along, while Sophie cared for the children as a second mother with Teresia so often pregnant.

Catholic devotion wound throughout life, in all its forms—inspiring commitment to family and moral behavior, embedding guilt over sins real and imagined, and directing the course of dreams both realized and not. Albert was smart, but after years of working with his father he lorded being the eldest over his siblings and had an odd sense of humor. He could recite Catholic Mass in Latin and would do so in the barn, purporting to bless or condemn his brothers and sisters as they worked. Sophie was beloved—caring like her mother, but firm when she needed to be. She would sew her siblings' clothes, take them to the doctor when Alois could afford it, and care for them herself when he couldn't. One of younger sister Helene's earliest memories was as a toddler, when she cut her neck on some glass. It was Sophie who removed the glass and cleaned her wound, the blood filling two bowls before the little girl was safe and laid down to rest.

Albert struggled with how to break free of these days of depression and danger. As he grew through his teenage years and into his early twenties, he talked of leaving the hardship of the farm behind to enter the Catholic seminary. Over the years, there was disagreement between him and various family members on whether he could have. It was common in the Old Country for eldest sons to inherit their parents' land—a tradition that would fuse with the American practice of small land ownership to create farm families that were forever grooming their eldest sons to take over the farm. Albert would say for all of his life that he wished he could have become a priest, but he had to abandon his dream to work with his father, who expected him to help get the farm through the Depression and carry it forward into the next generation.

His mother told others in the family that if Albert had wanted to go, they would have let him. Many of his siblings saw him over the years in charge on the farm and believed it was what he really wanted. Whatever the case—whether the signals from Alois were orders or hopes and whether part of Albert wanted to stay or simply lacked the courage to leave—he did not go. Instead, Albert stayed and worked and grew into a young man who was at turns shy and arrogant and guilt-ridden. His eyes were quiet. His smile, on the occasions when he wore one, was halved, curling into a sly end when he had an idea, a joke, or a secret. He liked to fix things and took to repairing machinery and jerry-rigging solutions to problems, more than he did tending animals or shouldering heavy labor—of which there had been so much when it was only him and his stern father. At some point, he turned to drinking.

When it came time for someone to break free and leave, it was Sophie. Faithful even from a young age, she had wanted to go to the convent to become a nun since grade school but knew she must stay to care for her siblings. Finally in 1935, when she was twenty and Albert was twenty-two, Sophie saw her teenage sisters coming of age and old enough to help her parents, so she felt she could leave. Albert watched as the children cried, and their mother lamented the loss of her most steadfast companion. Alois spoke of it in the only terms he knew.

"Let her go," he told Teresia. "If she sticks around, she'll get married, and she'll be gone anyway."

***

The hardship would deepen and persist as Sophie climbed out of the valley toward the convent. And the farmland she left behind would be totally transformed before it was over.

For the rest of the 1930s the American family farm blew back and forth in a hot alternating wind of recovery and relapse. President Franklin Delano Roosevelt had come into office in 1933 on a wave of discontent, and one of the first actions of his promised New Deal was congressional passage of the Agricultural Adjustment Act. An entirely new level of government intervention in agriculture, it set up the federal government to pay farmers to produce less and to keep land idle—limiting production in an effort to reduce oversupply and increase prices for farmers, while fanning controversy over the destruction of food as many Americans starved.[47] FDR's intervention also kicked off a battle over the role of government that would shape the next half century, yielding a combination of public and private sector action that reshaped rural America.

At its worst, that battle revealed the early fault lines of political fights that still rage, in one form or another, to this day. Talks with a wide range of economists, historians, and advocates on all sides of the question reveal unresolved dilemmas from this era that run the gamut, the only real consensus being that the needs of World War II represented the single largest driver of recovery. At its best, the battle over the role of government reached a balance that helped farms move forward, with government providing infrastructure like roads and rural electrification, and the private sector driving innovations like tractors and other machinery that only America's entrepreneurial spirit could accomplish.

Farmers were not only affected by this battle, they exemplified it— while often defying the neat political boxes either side of the American political system might have liked. Farm groups, from those representing farmers broadly to narrower industry niches, at times cooperated but often found themselves at odds. Organizations like the American Farm Bureau Federation championed finding broader markets and cooperation within the industry, often aligned with business interests and at times opposing subsidies. Meanwhile, a wide variety of labor-oriented and progressive groups promoted more government action and attempted to organize farmers into their own labor movement.[48]

A broad reading of history and accounts of the times show individual farmers fell all across the political spectrum and were at times deeply divided among those who sided with industry and those who sided with labor. Often, they were many things at once: opposed to government interference in the market; outraged by prices set by large industry players; willing to strike to force changes in prices and policies; willing also to collaborate among industry, government, and academia; and more. This was borne out of farmers dealing with the consequences of real-world realities, not abstract political ideas, as they carved out an increasingly unique place as both landowner and laborer. On any given day, the American family farmer played the role of property owner, investor, manager, and worker—economic classes often separated into groups in other sectors of the economy.[49] While this position had its advantages, in debates over economic devastation, farmers were caught between owning small businesses trying to keep costs down and being workers seeing the world stacked against them by the powers that be.

Over time, innovative solutions emerged, like farm cooperatives. Once politically divisive groups, farm co-ops became professionalized organizations that operated within the market economy, banding farmers together to buy services and market their products on a larger scale. The moments when the public and private sectors struck a balance, combined with the resilience of the American farmer, got 6.1 million farms through the Depression to the full recovery that came with World War II.[50]

The advances of this time still tower over us. Government helped bring electricity to farm country through loans to local electric cooperatives.[51] Greater soil conservation practices through the US Department of Agriculture[52]—along with research by universities and action by private and public organizations locally—helped address the catastrophic erosion of farmland. Industry, meanwhile, produced new technology that would enable surviving family farms to emerge stronger. Although the Depression kept many from affording them at first, private sector innovations included better tractors and machinery replacing horses, sophisticated seeds increasing crop yields, and milking machines and other electrically powered farm equipment easing hard labor. Running water became possible in the farmyard and the home alike. The advancement wasn't uniform, and for farmers, modern conveniences didn't always mean greater comfort. As of 1938, dairy farmers in Wisconsin were twice as likely to have running water in their barn as in their home, seeing how it could improve their farm's economic prospects before moving on to household convenience.[53]

Back and forth farms went, receding and progressing in an era of prolonged turmoil. As the initial economic recovery of 1933 gained traction, farmers who had avoided foreclosure or forced sales would put a little more money away and occasionally invest in tractors or other machinery that helped them move forward. There was, in fact, a brief period in the Great Depression, after the initial drop in America's number of farms a decade earlier, when the number of farms increased. From 1930 to 1935, the number of farms nationally went from 6.3 million to 6.8 million, an increase of 8 percent.[54] Some historians attribute that to people returning to farm country for lack of jobs in the city.[55] But it didn't last. In 1937, the Depression again deepened, and the decline in the number of farms became worse than ever.

The great technological shifts of the era, combined with the economic hardship, drove the disappearance of farms, economists say, showing the flipside of changing times. For example, moving from horses to tractors meant farmers could take on more farmland with less labor and that it took fewer farms to produce the same amount of food. That gave farmers who could afford it even more reason to buy out struggling neighbors or pick up nearby land out of foreclosure.

After the brief increase in the number of farms in the early 1930s, the double dose of economic depression and technological change drove the decline in farms to a level never before seen in the recorded history of the American farmer—a 10 percent drop in farms from 1935 to 1940.[56] Despite waxing and waning from year to year, the trend of the disappearing American farmer that began in the 1920s was deeper than ever. And because of the structural changes underway in the economy and society, and more changes to come, it's a disappearance that's continued for the better part of a century.

Taken in total, the Depression era showed the American family farm the dangers of excess, a lesson that reverberates today as the crisis of the disappearing American farmer again endangers the food on every American dinner table. Excessive debt in farm country during the high-flying prices of World War I. Excessive spending, speculation, and large living in much of the rest of the country in the Roaring Twenties before the Great Depression. Excessive land plowed up in the Midwest and Great Plains, only to have gulley erosion, wind storms, and prolonged drought leave farmers struggling to grow the crops they needed to make it. Only after surviving the terrible scarcity that came with the years of depression did the American family farm fully benefit from the innovations of the era and restore the food supply that's again at risk today.

But for all these lessons, as our family would see, the human cost of hardship would remain for generations to come.

***

She shouldn't have been bleeding so much. Teresia had given birth to thirteen children within the walls of the farmhouse. The lack of money for medical care during the Depression and the remoteness of the valley made getting to the doctor rare. And so, she had given birth to her children on the farm—Albert first, and then all the others, year after year. She had labored in bed and wherever else she needed to, Alois with his rough work-calloused hands and blunt ways serving as her only help. She had even survived discovering in the middle of labor that one of her pregnancies was twins—when her labor was not over, Alois looked and told her to get back in bed because baby Ann was coming right after baby Clara.

So, when Teresia went into labor with her fourteenth child, Johnny, in 1936, the family had reason to think she would again be fine. But Teresia was forty-eight years old by then and had endured hard labor in the house, garden, farmyard, and fields that took a further toll. When she went into labor this time, it was different. She began to lose blood. The color drained from her warm, round face, and she was weak. Alois knew she must go to the hospital. They drove up out of the valley, through the same soaring hills and winding backroads that had kept them from outside help during the fire some twenty years earlier. When they hit the main road, they slammed the car into high gear, hurtling even further still. When they made it to the hospital, they found the trauma had left a mark that would last their lifetimes. Teresia would never again become pregnant. Alois, so stern and unsentimental in the face of life's challenges, would reveal his fears in a letter to Sophie. Much of the family did not know he wrote letters to her, secretly sharing news and hopes and doubts from the valley to his faithful daughter in the convent. The letters were confessions, of the brutal hardship he so rarely acknowledged as he tried to make a better life for his family.

"We almost lost the both of them."

CHAPTER 4

THE TORTURED PATH

The Vanishing Rural Workforce of the 1940s

The path to the middle class began in the valley, and it was a stiff climb. Up the steep and winding road, away from that spot where Alois first looked upon the farmyard and fields beyond. Albert and then his siblings for years afterward journeyed upward, finding as they came around the bend and leaned into the final hill that the sunrise was waiting for them, more visible with each step as they journeyed closer to the horizon. Further and further up the road, finally the sunrise peaked up over the edge of the earth and beamed its golden rays across the countryside, great shafts of light extending in every direction. And there was a choice, standing at the top of the hill in the golden-orange glow of the morning light—toward the endless possibility of town or deeper into the life from which they'd came.

Yet another hill to the north, gentler in slope, led to another farm. There was the bright red barn, a white farmhouse, and surrounding outbuildings, all of it sitting in a cup in the land, nestled among the hillsides rolling onward for miles. This was the first stop on our

family's path to the middle class: a second farm for the next generation. Here on the hill, the sun rose earlier than in the hidden valley
below, more eager it seemed to extend its light upon this corner of the
world than on their original homestead. The fields curved with the
shape of the earth more naturally, less treacherous than some of the
hillsides the brothers and sisters knew from down below. But not all
was gentler and richer. Sunnier mornings and easier hills, yes, but
tougher ground with rocks close to the surface in the clay soil. And
on the hill the wind roamed more freely. While the wind was good
for drying fields when the crops needed it, it also blew dust in work-
worn faces and ushered in great storms that filled the wide-open sky
above and split it with lighting and shook it with thunder. The world
on the hill moved in ways it didn't in the valley.

Albert lived in the white farmhouse facing the sun and the wind
and the rain. He was a bachelor, seeing if he could make it here while
his parents farmed in the valley. This neighboring farm on the hill
had been foreclosed upon once already, and Alois had taken out debt
to buy it after years of penny-pinching in 1935, then sold it to Albert
in 1940—lending his twenty-seven-year-old son a financial hand that
also came with the responsibility to make good and pay the farm off.

Albert's face still harbored the quiet eyes and sly smile, when he
smiled, and he was handsome in those years. His hair was dark
brown—although it began to thin and retreat up his forehead early in
life—and a long straight nose sat almost noble atop the filthy overalls.
He was not an especially tall man, but he was lean and work-hard-
ened in those early days, with big farmer's hands. The hardship had
marked him, in those and other ways. Inside, the house was spare.
There was a sink in the kitchen with a pump atop it in place of running water, and an old stove. There was no indoor bathroom. Wood
sat stacked in the woodbox and in the woodshed outside to heat the
stove and the house. The countertop in the kitchen bore bruises from
where Albert had fastened it—nailing it down with a hammer, instead

of gluing it like he ought to have done. Albert had seen too many families lose their farms in the Depression and wanted to pay his off before he was married. He boasted about the wife he would take one day, saying he wanted to make sure he "got the coop before I got the chicken."

However, Albert's family knew also that he was afraid of the world beyond, as he looked upon it from the porch just off the kitchen. He could see the sunrise start to the left in the east and knew that soon enough it would fill the sky and light the fields where his livelihood sat buried. Under the sink was generally a bottle of booze, the liquor hot and thick in his throat. He drank it any time of day, and he bought it by the case.

***

This was the American family farm as the 1930s turned to the 1940s: on the precipice of prosperity, with irreparable change underway that would introduce new risks to farm families through good and bad economic times alike. While the reasons for the continued trouble were many, most boiled down to an emerging threat that was uniquely difficult for farm country and would last for decades to come—the problem of vanishing labor. Many farms were still facing the lingering effects of the Depression into the 1940s. When the recovery fully took hold, it was tied to World War II, initiating a draft that sapped most of the American economy of the workforce it needed. In farm country, however, the challenge was even deeper. The sons and daughters of the American family farmer were leaving home in droves, not only because of the war but also because of job opportunities and the wide-open world the city offered a generation of children raised up in rural hardship.

In 1940 a majority of Americans—57 percent—still lived in the country, but rural America was destined for a transformational fall.[57]

Those in rural areas who didn't face the draft saw an increasingly diversified economy rife with opportunity. America was on its way to becoming the industrial giant needed for the war effort, and to fuel broad prosperity in the years afterward. This postwar economic expansion was capping a massive shift already happening, away from agriculture and toward manufacturing, the service industry, and government.[58] That kind of economic expansion moved people—away from rural areas and toward urban ones. Kenneth Johnson, a rural demographer at the University of New Hampshire, said in an interview that the overall rural population wouldn't fall in raw numbers until the twenty-first century, but the share of America's population tilted from rural to urban far earlier.

The proportion of the population that was rural compared to urban began to plummet in the 1940s, he said, as the number of people migrating from rural areas to urban areas soared. And it was largely young people—the kind parents needed to take over the farm—who were leaving. In the 1950s and for decades afterward, rural counties experiencing depopulation nationwide lost an average of 43 percent of residents between the ages of twenty and twenty-four years old.[59] Our family, and so many others in the hills and valleys beyond, would exemplify this shift. Years would pass before anyone would fully see what the move from family farm to urban factory would do to rural America.

There was great opportunity in this time, as well as grave risks that would further set the course of the disappearing American farmer. Prices for crops and farm products were on the rise in the 1940s: by 1947, the ratio of prices farmers were paid for their wares versus what they paid for materials they needed to produce—known as the *parity ratio*—reached its most favorable level since before the agricultural depression following World War I.[60] Those who had made it through the years of Depression may have increased their holdings at an affordable price, if they were able to acquire a neighboring farm from a family or bank that was forced to sell. Some may have done so in rare moments when they felt they could take a risk, as Alois did in helping Albert get his start, while others may have waited until recovery took hold. And since many families had more children than they did farms, there was the opportunity for two tracks of prosperity: those who took over the farm from their parents or bought another local farm themselves, and those who left the farm to work in burgeoning industries, from manufacturing to food processing and beyond.

The lingering effects of the Depression, though, kept times tight for many farmers until they could put away savings and build equity in their farms. Many of the technological advances and modern conveniences that completely remade urban life, like electricity and running water, came to rural areas much later. Some parts of the nation's farm states had electricity in the late 1930s as a result of rural electrification, whereas others didn't until the 1940s. Jerry Apps, a prolific Wisconsin historian who grew up in the Depression, remembers his family's farm not getting electricity until 1947. Electricity granted farmers electronic milking machines, refrigeration of milk at the flip of a switch, electrically powered elevators to move feed, and more, Apps said. At the same time, the types of tractors and machinery available expanded greatly, and more farms finally got running water in their homes. Apps's father doubled the size of his family's milk herd. Things were changing, however slow the pace.

"Farm people moved in that time from hopelessness to hope," Apps said.

Still, there was the problem of farming's vanishing workforce. The first, and most devastating, was the number of soldiers shipping off to war—primarily men, but also hundreds of thousands of women, while other women filled roles in industry left vacant by the war effort. American military personnel during World War II exceeded 12 million by 1945, many of them leaving behind jobs on the farm and in the city alike. More than four hundred thousand of them died.[61] The risks to the country of having America's farms deprived of crucial labor was well known, as evidenced by Congress passing legislation in 1942 instructing local draft boards to exempt agricultural workers from military service, if they could show their work on the farm was essential to the war effort.[62]

Beyond that, and as part of a much larger underlying trend, was America's shift from rural to urban. In some ways, that shift was less obvious, not only because it was separate from the trauma of the war but also because some farm families were so large that it was inevitable: A certain amount of children from farm country would need to find opportunity elsewhere. Johnson, the rural demographer, said it's important to remember that the picture isn't so simple as young people choosing to flee to the bright lights of the city. One trend driving long-term rural depopulation was the pull of opportunity in urban areas, he said, but the other was fewer jobs in rural areas as technology made farms more efficient with less labor.

Despite the need for some farm kids to find jobs in the city, the overpowering trend of sons and daughters leaving had long felt like a slow death to rural areas—a fear, it turns out, that was founded. Since at least the 1880s, young people leaving rural areas was a concern for many.[63] The trend picked up in the 1940s and beyond and would become a crisis that would last decades. The simple fact is there were more farmers finding fewer sons and daughters to help with the labor and one day take over. Johnson elaborated on the impact of losing such a key demographic: When a rural area loses people in their early twenties, it means not only fewer workers and fewer successors for work-weary farmers but also fewer young aspiring parents to give birth to more young people. As the average age of a county increased, it sapped vitality—more deaths and fewer births, Johnson said, until more people were dying than being born. The problem proved impossible for some communities to reverse.

"You would see decade after decade of substantial outflow of young adults out of these counties," Johnson said.

The vanishing population of this urban-to-rural shift would have impacts that would far outlast the war—a problem that would compound on top of the trauma farm families already carried from the years of economic depression.

***

In the early mornings, Albert's sister Catherine walked the pastures searching for the milk cows. She was the seventh eldest, working as a teenager for her bachelor brother while he ran his farm. He paid little, and the work was endless. But she knew also that life on his farm meant freedom from the watchful eyes of her parents. And so, each morning she journeyed over the green hills and into the whispering woods to listen for the lolling bells around the cows' necks. Urging the herd over the hills toward the barn for morning milking was only the beginning of the day's tasks. There was more to be done in the barn and house, in these in-between years as the Reisinger children followed their eldest brother—one by one—up the hill, to work on his farm, and find what else the world had to offer.

Over time, for one reason or another, all their eyes turned upon the horizon beyond.

Each of the siblings had worked first for their father and mother, just as Albert had done, and some tried to farm the homestead for Alois as he aged. But life in the valley would only last so long, for each of them. There were the brothers who helped on both farms for a time, then left for the military or to try to make a living in town, most often at factories over forty miles away in the capital city of Madison. Sisters like Catherine took turns working for Albert before they were married, as he ran the farm on his own with no wife at his side. Others left to get married sooner or to pursue their own work in the city, after leaving the home farm. Some of them, brother and sister alike, considered following Sophie, now Sister Mary Bede, into the Church, but didn't go through with it. And on it went, the Reisinger family trying its hand at finding greater prosperity both in the rural economy—with father and son now each owning their own farm—and in the urban economy.

There was splendor and squalor alike.

Near Albert's farmhouse stood an apple orchard, bathed so often in the ample sunlight that spread over the rolling fields stretching in every direction there on the hill. The family came to call Albert's farm "the upper place" and Alois and Teresia's farm "the lower place," a simple mark of geography that nonetheless suggested the progress that the climb up the hill could offer. The progress was both social and economic, although Albert paid as little as $1 per week for the work they were bound to by family duty. The brothers and sisters knew that on Albert's farm they could do as they pleased, so long as the work was done. They went out at night to dances in nearby Plain and Roxbury, without incurring Alois's wrath. Sometimes, Albert would drive them there and back; other times the girls might get a ride from a boy they'd met.

But life on the hill had hardships of its own. Albert's house stayed rough and dirty, despite the constant work of his sisters. Rats pored over the basement, gnawing in their dark refuge on the apples picked from the sun-bathed orchard. Mice scampered in the pantry and the rest of the house, sprinklings of mouse droppings often the only evidence of their passage. The dishes to feed Albert and the other men working the farm stacked so high and filthy that they stuck together, and his sisters had to soak them in a deep pool of hand-pumped water before they could come apart to be cleaned. The work of the upper farm was daunting: milking and feeding and plowing and planting and harvesting just like the lower place, and so much more to repair and to change and to build. Albert added a chicken house, machine sheds, and other improvements over the years. Just like on the home farm, the sisters did the housework on top of working in the barn and the fields like their brothers. They were continuing for a second generation the unsung paradox of social progress that farm country afforded—women doing the work of any man in a way the big shots in the city would have never imagined, yet left caring for their families and depending upon the men who held the money just the same. And though the brothers and sisters alike found that there was money now and then, for dances and drinks and cigarettes, times were still tight.

Albert remained stuck, meantime, between the old and the new. The talk of becoming a priest never truly left, simply waxing and waning with his mood and years. Soft-spoken and sensitive as he was, Albert had shed his father's sternness and anger, but never his worry over whether the farm would make it. Albert remembered always the Depression, bossing his siblings and pressing work upon them and penny-pinching. Alois and Teresia had given Albert a good start, selling him the farm on the hill for $1, provided he assumed the debt it had taken to buy it up. It was a common practice in those days, and a good turn from Alois—dispensation to the eldest son who had endured the longest years alone of work and strain and angst under his father. But Albert had a debt of $6,500, more than $140,000 by 2024 standards, to pay off as decades of economic depression gave way to world war—all while facing the uncertainties of weather and natural disaster and the market, and other forces that left farms always at risk. And so, he watched every penny that went out of his pocket. Albert felt it was foolish to pay more than he must for anything, whether it was bargaining for a piece of farm equipment or buying the cheapest item on the shelf or paying one of his siblings for the help they gave him. He kept a log, detailed but rough, noting in terse lines every item he had to buy to keep the farm going. Motor oil, fertilizer, tools, belts for the machinery, groceries. Drinks at the tavern while he was in town. Cases of booze for the farm.

Even in excess, he was thrifty—noting each beer he drank, buying his alcohol by the case to ensure he got it at a cheaper price. But then, there would have been no need for such attention to the amount if it had been taken in moderation. If Albert drank in the morning before chores, it was often a pull straight from the bottle. The times he felt able to sit and enjoy his drink, it might be a nice full glass of brandy or whiskey. *Schlucks*, he called the splashes of booze from the bottle, be they straight to the back of his throat or in the bottom of a glass, using an old German word for drink that harkened back to our family's Bavarian heritage.

And he loved nothing more than to offer a schluck to a visitor, be it a neighboring farmer, someone from town, or one of his many brothers and sisters. It was his own drinker's version of the old farm family tradition of making sure visitors were well fed, even if you had little else to offer. And, it was a way to ease out of his solitude. With a glass of brandy, he could not only extend a welcome to his guests but get them to sit and talk with him—there on his own farm, with his own liquor warming them, where he didn't need to feel shy. Sometimes he'd offer dandelion wine as well. He made it himself, in the granary just down from the house, and drank it sometimes even before it was ready. The alcohol filled the spaces between his moods and perhaps deadened those burdens that drove them.

"I think he probably drank just to be happy," my dad, Jim, said years later.

It was one of many ways Albert wrestled with life, as he strode from the poverty and harshness of his childhood to the middle-class status and independence of adulthood. Out from under the direction of his stern father and religious mother, Albert swung back and forth between sin and virtue. He had a colorful sense of humor, full of sayings about this or that, which became dirty after a few too many schlucks. And yet he talked often of right and wrong and good and evil, and now and then got around to talking of love—if it was with the right person, and he sat long enough and drank long enough to let the feelings come. There was God's love, which Albert believed in despite the hardships, and then earthly love, a more complicated thing. He wrestled with his feelings in the hallowed glow of St. John's Church in the nearby town of Spring Green, where a woman with the most beautiful voice sent "Ave Maria" soaring through the rafters. His sisters suspected he had an eye for her, but he never talked with her. Whenever that kind of love came up, Albert deflected.

"I want a woman willing to walk knee deep in cow shit," he said.

Some of that was bluster. They all knew he was bashful. And yet, his family saw he needed someone who was strong enough to withstand all the pressures that life with him meant: the work, risks, and dangers of the farm, and the drinking he did along the way.

Albert wrestled with that earthly love, too, when it came to his family. He watched the brothers and sisters who worked for him leave to do other things he envied. Other times, he relished chances to sit and have a drink with them—on his farm, or now and then even in their homes—to see how they'd gotten established. And he wrestled with earthly love as Alois appeared on the upper farm each day to inspect his son's operation, as though Albert could have forgotten about the pressures that came with making sure his farm would succeed. On one such day, Alois was checking on the pregnancy of one of the family's heifers, searching with his hand for the calf to see how soon the heifer might give birth and join the milk herd. The heifer was restless. Alois pressed on her abdomen in one spot, then another. In a blink she cocked her leg and kicked him in the stomach. The air shot out of Alois, and he fell to the ground, his children scrambling to get to him.

"He was blue by the time we got him to the hospital," his daughter Helene said.

***

Alois would survive, but it was a harsh reminder that he wouldn't be around forever. In that way, this reality underscored one of the great challenges of America's recovery from the Depression: finding successors to take over the farm, with so many sons and daughters finding opportunity elsewhere. While the concern about young people leaving the country for the city was not new, its true impact on the American family farm did not take root at first. Large families cycled through successors, starting with the oldest and working their way through the family as necessary, but finding someone to take over became harder as the workforce vanished. In our family, one child after another of the fourteen who grew up in the Depression found opportunity somewhere other than the home farm. Some of them wanted to farm and gave it a shot but couldn't work out the transition with Alois. Others didn't want to farm or found better economic opportunity in the city, with employers like food processor Oscar Mayer taking on more workers after moving its headquarters from Chicago to Madison in 1957.[64]

The world Alois found when he came to America in 1909, where less than half the US population lived in far-off cities like Madison,[65] was coming to an end. In fact, during the 1950s, Sauk County—where our farm sits and an especially rural place in the mid-1900s—lost more than 47 percent of its residents aged twenty to twenty-four. Although that would ease some over the years, the county would never stop experiencing a net loss in that key age group for the next six decades.[66] It was a problem that took deep root across the heartland for decades to come and would help ensure the disappearance of the American farmer would continue. Pam Jahnke of the *Mid-West Farm Report*, one of the most trusted broadcasters in agriculture, said a lack of young people to take over farms makes succession challenges among the biggest reasons today that farms don't make it. And the most personal.

"Nobody's getting any younger," she said. "I'm sure that it goes on in business board rooms, but this is around the kitchen table."

The decrease in successors in the 1940s has completely transformed rural America. Jerry Apps, the farm historian who grew up in the Depression, said the shift in rural population that dealt a blow to family farms also affected small towns and surrounding areas, denying them the local residents needed for economic vitality, to the point that some communities have simply disappeared. We've gone from a world where farmers brought their wares to town—selling and buying in local markets that ensured a deep bond between the American farmer and the American consumer—to one where rural and urban America are increasingly isolated from one another, Apps told me. That disconnect contributes toward the rural-urban divide that existed even in those days. A world that once had the opportunity to close that divide with greater ease of travel and communication—and perhaps did, for a time—is in some ways more divided by geography than ever. Our hyperpolarized political environment consistently breaks down along rural and urban lines as much as any other divide.[67]

That loss—of people moving from rural to urban and the divide it breeds—was not the only reason why the farmland prosperity after the Depression was destined to be temporary. But it may have been the first. Solving the problem of our urban-rural divide decades later, Apps said, is one of the most important tasks our country could undertake.

"The country as a whole cannot continue to prosper in any sense of the word, unless we have both strong agriculture, strong rural villages and cities, as well as vibrant urban centers," he said. "For a country to succeed we must all respect and learn to work together."

Our family would experience the turmoil of these changes, and the opportunities and challenges that came with it, for generations. We would experience it in ways that directed most of my own life—and a guilt I couldn't name—without me knowing it.

***

The man downstairs was quiet and seemed nice enough, but Ann Ruhland was skeptical. She was a tenant in the house, staying there while she worked for a local family in town, and she tended to keep to herself. Having grown up on a farm outside of Plain, she was used to work coming early and had already turned in for the evening, when the grinning boys from around town came piling up the steps and beckoned her to join them downstairs. They refused to tell her why. Ann was not one for nonsense, but she also believed in getting things over with, and so she got ready and came down. She was tall for a woman—long and slender, but strong—with sharp features and eyes dark like gun barrels. When she got downstairs, she discovered why the boys had interrupted her solitude. There was a table, a deck of cards, and a man who wanted to meet her. His name was Albert Reisinger. He didn't say much as she sat down and began to play cards with the rowdy group. Mainly he spoke with his eyes—shy glances, now and then, over the cards and glasses of booze. She wasn't exactly against the idea, but this also wasn't exactly how she'd envisioned it happening.

After that first night, he would come by regularly. Albert was older than Ann by more than eleven years, but she was in her mid-twenties already, and unsure of whether she'd find anyone else to care for her. She could see that he was determined. And he had a farm of his own.

"He was always there, before I ever got home," Ann said. "So, I thought, *Well, we'll have to see how it goes.*"

This was how my grandma decided to marry my grandpa, and it says as much about their time and place as it does about them, as the 1940s gave way to the 1950s. Marriage was often still an economic prospect, part of moving forward in those promising-but-cautious days that came after years of economic depression and war. Although delaying marriage and children was not uncommon as a result of the Depression, it was still a few years later than most when Albert finally got over his shyness enough to bring them together.

Born in 1924, Ann had come from a place as rough as he did. The farm she grew up on was also tucked in among the hillsides, several miles away from the Reisinger farm, over what they called "the ridge." "The ridge" was so tall and loping that it earned the distinction among the many hills and draws and valleys that it dwarfed for miles around. The family relied on horse and buggy for travel and draft horses for work, after some other farms had bought cars, trucks, and tractors. She grew up working in the fields, hauling manure by hand, and raising chickens in the basement. Her real name was Anna, which she preferred, but most people called her Ann or Annie—which she hated, but endured, as she did most things, without dwelling on it.

They married in 1950 and settled in on Albert's farm to build a life. Although, by then, the American economy was booming and it was a good time for many farmers, prosperity was not a given. But the farm was paid for, the milk price was mostly good, and they found they were able to afford newer machinery and put a little money away. Soon enough, they began a family: my dad, James, was born in 1951, and David in 1954. Albert was stubborn in the ways he wanted the farm run. Most often he was soft-spoken, and he didn't beat Ann like she'd seen happen to so many women. Still, Albert's drinking persisted.

Down the hill on the home farm, the struggle continued. Alois and Teresia had retired to town in 1948, but they kept the farm, with several of the children trying, one after another, to run it after Albert left to get his own start. Some even tried living in the house, which would have been a step toward taking the farm over, if it had worked out. Yet, one after another found Alois too set in his ways and angry at times about change to find a way to work it out—no matter how much they wanted to farm or how badly they felt. As his grandson Jim put it, he was a "strict old German" who struggled to let go after so many years of clinging to the farm through hardship. Finally, after years of struggle to keep the lower farm going, Albert stepped in. Alois and Teresia were contemplating a sale outside of the family, some of his siblings recalled, when Albert convinced them to sell it to him for less instead in 1955. Some of the lower place's operation would be folded into Albert's: the acreage to pasture more animals and raise more crops; the buildings to keep young heifers before they joined Albert's milk herd up on the hill; the house to rent out to hired hands or other tenants. The rest would be sold at auction. It was a way to keep the farm in the family and for Albert and Ann to start making a little more money for their children. However, it also meant one less local family farm, exemplifying the trend of disappearance that was taking hold. Albert, who already had a farm, would take over in place of another of his siblings getting their start there, or another family wanting to make a go of it.

Jim was still a little boy as he stood on the porch of his father's house, seeing his grandfather's things go down the road. Horses that had pulled the machinery in a bygone era. An old side rake, for use behind a horse or a tractor to turn the cut hay as it dried in the sun. A rickety wagon, then another. Though he was only three years old then, watching with his mother, he knew somehow it was an important day. What he was watching was both an end and a beginning, one that furthered his family's move into the middle class but that was also part of a broader trend none of us would have wished to go on forever. For, in that moment, our family exemplified the trend of disappearance that had been born in the agricultural depression of the 1920s and would accelerate now even in good times. We went from spreading our prosperity across two farms, with one son starting a new farm after buying it from his father, and another son or daughter perhaps taking over the homestead, to one farm swallowing up another.

It was a shift that would not stop, no matter how good the times became, and Albert's prosperity would remain at risk. The promise on the horizon could not save him from the danger on the hill.

***

One morning, in the winter of 1959–60, Albert strode out to the corncrib to try to set things right.

There was snow on the ground and the bitter cold of a Wisconsin winter clutching the morning air. Albert was nearly bald by then, his brown hair lingering on the sides and back, a few strands dancing across his head when he didn't wear a cap. The corn crib was thirty feet high, with doors near the bottom and the top to let the corn out when the family was ready to feed the cows. At the very top, perched at the apex of a slanted roof, was a hole that was supposed to be plugged with a cap. The cap had become dislodged somehow, perhaps blowing in the winter wind overnight. Albert reached the corn crib and set up a ladder against its towering frame. Looking up, he gripped the ladder and began to climb. The air got colder and wilder with each step further from the ground, but he didn't think much of it. He had done it before. And he had eluded, somehow for years, the first threat to every farm's workforce—those daily dangers that had maimed and threatened the lives of so many of his brothers and sisters, and sent his father to the hospital.

Still, the metal was cold, matching the frozen ground getting further away. Steel band after steel band marked the climb higher into the frigid air as he ascended, cobs of corn poking out in between. When he got to the top, he eased out onto the roof, crawling part way onto the metal surface, cold and slanted and smooth. He reached as far as he could. Straining there, in the cold air so far from the cold ground, to put the cap back in place. And then in an instant he slipped and was sliding. Down the pitched roof and off its edge, flailing and grasping, falling and falling and falling—thirty feet through the rushing winter air—until he hit the ground.

CHAPTER 5

BACK-BREAKING WORK

*1950s–60s: Becoming the Little Guy
in an Ever-Bigger World*

Only a dark set of curtains separated Jim from his father.

Jim was eight years old and had been sent away—to live in town with his aunt, after Albert fell off the corn crib and cracked his back on the frozen ground. They didn't tell Jim why or that anything was wrong, and he got to play with his cousins. However, it wasn't long before he asked to go home, where there were baby calves to play with and clean country air. When they wouldn't take him home, he wondered why. He asked again, over and over, for a time longer than a young child could measure. Finally, one day, they took him home to the white farmhouse on the hill to see the truth. He stood before his parents' bedroom, that set of brown curtains concealing what they'd hidden from him. Jim crept forward and pushed through.

What he saw on the other side was a world different from the one he'd left: his father, in bed, flat on his back. Jim stood there and stared. Then his mother grabbed him.

"Get outta there."

The curtains fell back into place, and Jim could no longer see his father. But the new world on the other side of that curtain remained—a world where his father's back was broken and where his family needed his help; where a little boy would work alongside the uncle and neighbor who came to help with the milking every morning and night, and alongside his fast and fearsome mother; where he'd haul hay bales and scoop corn and oats from a wheelbarrow to feed the cows, scrape the barn's driveway of manure, and struggle now with the rowdy calves he loved, to make them drink milk from a bucket; where the days were so long, Jim would miss too much school to pass out of third grade; where all the while his father laid in bed, shattered somewhere deep inside. It was a world where a boy would learn to do the work of his father, and not stop until he was grown himself, and then continue on. And nothing would be the way it was before.

***

When the war ended and ushered in a new era of prosperity—neither smothered by economic depression nor hobbled by bloody global conflict—the American family farm rose with it. Bolstered by years of high prices to feed the war effort, technology that was now fully available for civilian needs, and all the benefits and trappings of a mature industry, the American farmer was ready to grow. What should have been a time of optimism (and in many ways it was) was in fact deeply fractured. Something was broken about the way the economy would change that America failed to see, our country's eyes fastened as they were on the work at hand and the horizon beyond. During this time of seemingly endless possibility, the structure of the American economy would undergo a fateful transformation.

The new middle-class status of family farms would prove fragile—subject to the market power of larger players across many industries, and the whims of government under both political parties.

Consequently, family farms would be put on an irreparably different path: The American farmer became the little guy in a world of big business, big government, and increasingly bigger forces that would eventually set in on all sides. Farm families did not have the luxury of total ignorance others did, for even amid the prosperity they could feel the new pressures and the weight on their shoulders. But nobody—not farmers, consumers, or national leaders—saw it as clearly as we might wish, now that we know about the unexpected farm loss to come.

The money was good for those who were prepared to navigate the new era. Following the end of World War II, the emergence of the new humming economy—combined with the run-up to the briefer Korean War—created a rapid economic expansion in America, from the late 1940s to the early 1950s. The 1950s remained relatively strong, then gave way to the longest expansion in history during the 1960s.[68] Despite bumps along the way, farmers across the country often found good prices for their crops and products, and the value of farmers' holdings were skyrocketing. In 1950 the cash value of farms in America surpassed $75.5 billion, a 63 percent increase from five years earlier—the largest increase in thirty years, finally putting farm values above where they were before the agricultural depression of the 1920s.[69]

Wisconsin exemplified what had become America's ideal of the family farm, with farms there more likely to be owned by the families operating them and to remain midsized even as they became more prosperous.[70] Farmers' productivity was also on the rise, thanks to economic opportunity, technological advancement, and improving efficiency of farm operations. That productivity was destined for a decades-long surge that would define the American farmer, beginning in the late 1940s and stretching into the next century.[71]

This era should have been a thing of beauty. But the problems with America's surging prosperity—the result of those internal cracks beneath the surface—were coming fast.

Some seemed harmless, even inspiring. In 1948 Richard and Maurice McDonald, entrepreneur brothers who had struggled for years before finally running a successful hamburger stand in southern California, had an idea. They'd apply the principles of the manufacturing assembly line to making food in a kitchen.[72] Of course, we now know the ability of McDonald's to sell more of the food Americans wanted at a cheaper price launched the brothers' successful small business into the stratosphere. Another example of the American Dream unfolding didn't have to mean trouble to come—nor did opening up franchise opportunities that could offer ways for other small business owners to try their hand in every corner of America. An alternative universe exists where it could have simply meant more demand for locally grown food, in regional economies all across the country. Of course, McDonald's was just one of many fast-food chains changing the restaurant industry,[73] part of a much broader shift in the entire American food system—and broader American economy and culture—toward the lowest possible cost, highest possible convenience, and most plentiful possible quantity. The many food and agribusiness companies, from buyers and processors of fast-food ingredients to other foods all across our economy, would have to grow to keep up with the demands of a growing America.

Consolidation within mature industry, whether it was these growing agribusinesses or the farmers in turn trying to keep up with them, was in some ways inevitable. Such consolidation also had its benefits that wouldn't automatically mean economic trouble to come. There are two basic types of consolidation: *horizontal integration*, where one competitor buys another that does the same kind of business, and *vertical integration*, where a player in the industry gets control of additional parts of the supply chain. As companies in the food processing industry grew larger, the more economic scale they could achieve— buying supplies in bulk, having large systems that created efficiencies across their operations, and so on. By squeezing cost out of their production process, they could sell food more cheaply to the American consumer and keep up with the many other industries where consolidation was occurring. Additionally, America would have a more sophisticated supply chain to meet growing needs and contend with increasingly global markets.

However, there was a flipside to too much consolidation, the topic of historic debates in American society before and since: monopoly—and if not monopoly, something close to it. As America shifted toward its fully industrialized economy, it was more likely to have certain industries dominated by a few large players that could afford entering expensive and complicated markets.[74] In the case of a monopoly, or an oligopoly, there comes a point where the large controlling players lack real competition and can shift from squeezing costs out of their own operations to squeezing others: beginning to set prices across the entire industry rather than just their own, moving the market themselves, and preventing new competition.

As the economy soared, there were warning signs that the agriculture industry was becoming more and more subject to the risks of a less competitive market—and one less open to the American farmer who ranked as the little guy. In 1965 Harold Breimyer, a farm boy and celebrated agricultural economist who had worked under both Democrats and Republicans (Roosevelt's New Deal and Republican President Dwight Eisenhower's Council of Economic Advisers), issued such a warning. Noting the shift from flexible farm labor costs to off-farm costs like energy and fertilizer that farmers didn't control, and the growing market power of agribusiness companies that both sold to and bought from farmers, Breimyer wrote, "Only if markets are freely open to farm producers and essentially free of oppressive power can traditional institutions of a 'free' agriculture be maintained."[75] Still, the consolidation of the 1950s and beyond might not have been so significant if it weren't one part of a relentless chain reaction to come across much of the American economy. Decades later, it would become a surging controversy and surprisingly biparti-san concern.

There were other threats, more immediate. Agriculture was becom-ing a drastically smaller part of the American economy. As the size of the service industry and government grew and manufacturing recov-ered from the Depression, agriculture steadily declined in its share of national income.[76] Within that agriculture industry was greater pres-sure than ever to meet the demands of the era. The prices farmers were getting for their products versus what they were paying for the things they needed to produce—the parity ratio that hit its nearly two-decade height of 115 in 1947—would drop below 100 in 1953 and fall continuously, with few exceptions, into the 1970s.[77]

While technology made greater productivity possible, it also meant fewer farms were required to produce the same amount of food—and subsequently that some farmers would be able take on more land while others would face increasing pressure to get out. All this was happening as more sons and daughters continued to move from farms to the city. Meanwhile, expanding cities, residential developments, airports, and more all created great demand for open farmland and led many farms to sell. It was the flipside of greater economic oppor-tunity in the city and greater productivity on the farm.

America's amount of farmland, often one of the more stable num-bers over the years, would decline in the 1950s—shifting from rural to urban just like its people were—and fall for the rest of the centu-ry.[78] The farmers who sold had the chance to get out of debt and try something new, and in some cases could clear enough to become incredibly wealthy. Those who held on and didn't get bigger by buying up other farms began to struggle, exemplifying in modern terms what it meant to be land rich and cash poor.

Farmers' time in the sun, although clear and bright, was fading sooner than it would for the rest of the country they were feeding. The result of all these economic forces: The American family farm disappearing at record rates, even as nearly everyone else in the economy—including those farmers who were surviving the shift—launched further into greater prosperity. From 1954 to 1959, the number of farms in America would plummet 22 percent, the largest five-year drop in recorded history, outpacing even the worst of the Great Depression.[79] Those farmers who were surviving often had to do so by buying up other farmland, perhaps picked up from their neighbors, to become more profitable. Those who weren't making it were shifting, by choice or necessity, into more lucrative jobs in other industries like manufacturing, or falling into ruin. There was a certain amount of consolidation that was inevitable, as with any competitive marketplace, and some considered the farms that sold or went under to be too inefficient.[80] But to reach record levels of farm loss at a time of such American optimism goes beyond the natural selection of the marketplace. And coming far from the heartland were more reasons for that contradiction.

During this time, the family farm was barreling toward a future of unexpected hardship, just as it got the opportunity to step free of its perilous past.

***

There was a time, however brief, when hardship might not have come so soon for my dad too. Tender moments, soon lost.

As a little boy, Jim was often with his mother. Although the work was always there, she had known it all her life and wasn't as stern as she'd become. Standing there on the porch as Alois's auctioned horses and machinery made their way down the road, there was great opportunity before her family, even if it came amid the sad circumstance of the home farm struggling to find a successor as it had. Ann allowed herself little moments of joy in those early days. She laughed when Jim, as a toddler, took fresh eggs and dropped them one after another onto the kitchen floor. She enjoyed playing cards and sewing and baking and watching flowers bloom. She would love those things even as the moments to appreciate them became few.

Such tenderness was not to last. There was the farm work and the stress of children, like any farm family faced, but Ann's burdens set in more deeply. With her husband laid up in the bedroom, his back slowly healing as winter wore on, Ann took on a heavier load, a good deal of which she would not lay down again. There was helping with the milking morning and night, cleaning all the milking equipment, throwing down hay from the mow above the barn, hauling in bedding for the cows to lie on, feeding and butchering chickens and collecting eggs, carrying and stacking wood to heat the house, overseeing Jim's work, and endless tasks in the farmyard, from morning to night. Then there were her duties in the home—caring for her crippled husband, on top of cooking, cleaning, and raising two boys. Her only good fortune in these cold winter months of Albert's recovery was there would be no fieldwork until spring.

Albert's back finally healed, but some damage would not be undone. When he could stand again, Albert stepped into his overalls and laced up his brown leather work shoes and strode across the farmyard. He fixed tractors and other machinery and directed his family's work, watching closely again to ensure that his farm made it through this strange era of opportunity and peril. However, the lives of his wife and eldest son would ease little, if at all. Albert and Ann fell into a pattern of both cooperation and strife.

They came together in times when the work overtook all else—like hay season, when the family had to cut and rake and bale and haul hay back to the barn for days on end in the summer heat, on top of the morning and evening milkings and other chores. Ann would drive the rumbling Allis Chalmers WD tractor, eight-year-old Jim sitting alongside her on a toolbox mounted on the fender, while Albert worked on the wagon stacking bales under the beating sun as the hay chaff and dust flew. Other times, they were divided over the strain. Albert preferred to work on machinery in his shop alone, while Ann listed back and forth between doing the other work she saw languishing and prodding her husband onward as his drinking intensified.

Although he drank alone more and more as time went on, Albert was not alone in his affection for alcohol. Not in the rural midwestern alcohol haven of Wisconsin, with its proud history of breweries—and hearty people like the Germans, Polish, and others who worked hard and drank harder when they could. For Albert, however, the alcohol by now had become both a cause of trouble, and a remedy: sapping his drive in a way that taxed his family, deadening his senses when his wife would protest and set to yelling. Albert was stubborn and kept a tight hand on the money but was always gentle with his wife and children, and usually soft-spoken, outside of the times he had too much to drink and would holler and stomp off to the shop. And Ann had found by now that tenderness, for her husband or her son, was too vulnerable a thing to allow in herself if she wanted the work to get done.

If she was to have loving times with her eldest son Jim, it would be only through their work. She and Albert would prepare him—each in their own way—for what it would take for the farm to survive.

***

America's prosperity would conceal so much. Not only would the economic injuries of this mysterious era remain, but the prosperity on the surface would also cloud the reality needed to have a true debate about government's role in farming, from President Franklin Delano Roosevelt to President Ronald Reagan and beyond. This failure to address the deeper issues that solidified in the 1950s would affect the American family farm in unforeseen ways for decades. The debate born in the Depression—of whether to have more government or less—would continue, with a certain level of bipartisan acceptance of some of Roosevelt's New Deal programs emerging, and the desire for more food for less driving the debate. That debate may have correctly started with whether to have more or less government, but it needed to dive at least two layers deeper to address the dilemmas shaping the future: how to best structure whatever role America agreed the government should have, and how to ensure real competition for every American farmer to get a fair shot.

Instead, the debate over agriculture would settle into a rut filled with unintended consequences. It's a rut that persists today but that our country dug in the 1950s—during the shift toward bigger government and bigger business that began to define the American economy in a more lasting way as the emergencies of the Depression and World War II faded. We can't solve the crisis of our disappearing farmer without facing these fateful places where America started getting bogged down, and checking the preconceived notions on both sides of our political debate that have set in since. Jumping into such muddy fields—and engaging with smart people from all sides of the debate—reveals unexpected challenges to long-held assumptions and lessons for new steps forward.

On the government front, World War II ended, and the programs that some believed were emergency measures in the Depression largely continued. Rather than have the full debate about which programs should continue and which shouldn't, America fell into a pattern of both political parties adjusting the programs at the margins, adding more measures as needed, and only rarely approaching real reform when things weren't working. Farm programs have run a wide gamut ever since: government-supported lending, price supports through the government buying excess supply and other means, various kinds of direct payments to farmers to incentivize or limit certain kinds of farm production, regulations setting the terms of the market, barriers to imports from other countries, government-backed insurance, and more.[81]

Many economists, historians, and farm advocates contend that if not for government intervention—including price supports and paying farmers to produce less—far more farmers would have been wiped out in the Depression and afterward. Wisconsin historian Jerry Apps, who grew up on a farm in the Depression, argued programs like the Civilian Conservation Corps were also crucial, providing jobs and building infrastructure. Ultimately, it was government that drove rural electrification.

"I make no bones about supporting FDR's idea that we cannot wallow in our misery," Apps told me. David Danbom, a rural historian and former professor at North Dakota State University, said there's an argument the New Deal should have spent more money to spur recovery when compared to today's standards of government stimulus during the Great Recession and COVID lockdown.

Some advocates say what worked in the 1930s and 1940s should be replicated today, instead of the shift toward other programs over time. Sarah Vogel, an attorney who represented farmers during the Farm Crisis of the 1980s, said America consistently asks farmers to produce food below cost, and taxpayer support is the only way that's possible without wiping out more farms. She said farmers deserve government action to ensure parity—addressing that problem in which farmers receive insufficient prices for their goods, compared to the cost of materials needed to produce in the first place. And, she said, any critic of government involvement in agriculture should remember a strong food supply is crucial to America's national security. (Without robust domestic food sources, the argument goes, America would be beholden to other countries in times of crisis.) Oftentimes the parity argument, one made by many farmers for decades, focuses on achieving prices similar to the "golden era" of farming before World War I, from 1910 to 1914, or a similar level of balance between the prices farmers receive and the prices they pay.

The counterargument, from conservative economists as well as free-market advocates, portrays a nonsensical system—a "Rube Goldberg machine" of complicated mechanisms to accomplish what should be a simpler and more efficient task, as Dennis Jansen, director of the Private Enterprise Research Center at Texas A&M University, put it. These conservative economists say government spending to boost prices incentivizes farmers to produce more of something (say, wheat) to capitalize on said better prices. That's at the same time the government pays farmers to produce less, as it so happened during the Depression and at other times.

Alexander Salter, an associate professor of economics at Texas Tech University, said these government programs cause farmers to produce goods to satisfy the demands of one contradictory incentive after another, rather than what makes sense both for their pocketbooks and for consumers. Those kinds of perverse incentives prevent innovation, these economists argued, while wasting taxpayer dollars and inflating food prices. Then there's the constant challenge of certain kinds of operators benefitting most from government programs—those farms already able to turn the highest profit, or businesses and investment vehicles that aren't even farms. Jansen, who as a kid would visit his grandfather's family farm, said it's fair to ask who is really benefiting in a world where the largest organizations have the money to influence policymakers and pay accountants and lawyers to navigate the programs.

"I don't think it's my grandfather on a small farm in southern Illinois," he said.

Here's the irony: although some of the debate tying back to this 1950s shift and persisting today falls on philosophical lines, farm policy challenges the belief system of anyone, past or present, who cares about family farms. There are certainly farms that would not have made it, in the Depression or the decades since, without price supports and other programs. It's a truthful refrain that generally farmers of all sizes are "price takers, not price makers." Selling goods on the commodities market, increasingly the case since America's 1940s and '50s shift toward an urban economy, means farms have less hand in setting their own prices, while also having to buy their inputs (animal feed, seed, fuel, and more) at whatever price they're given as well. Decades of data from the United States Census Bureau and other entities show the prices farmers get are often insufficient compared to the cost of production materials.

On the other hand, it's a fact that government programs favor some over others, such as the largest 10 percent of farms receiving more than two-thirds of all government-backed crop insurance payments.[82] Danbom, the historian who noted Depression-era spending was small by today's standards, also said the same New Deal programs that saved certain farms displaced others and favored the largest players from the start. Endless examples of subsidies have run amok in the decades since—including people who aren't farmers benefiting from farm subsidies.[83]

With so many cross-cutting facts, our political parties fell into a mushy middle ground in the 1950s and beyond—when such ideology-defying problems could have instead led to innovative ideas from both sides. The same happened to another unaddressed dilemma from this era: where the line falls between bigger being good and bigger being bad. When do larger companies in the agriculture and food sectors, or any part of our economy, provide cheaper and better service? And when are they so large they're limiting choices—or worse yet, dictating artificially high prices, colluding with their few so-called competitors, or pursuing other anticompetitive practices? Although our government maintained a clear antitrust position in the 1950s, *big* began to define the American economy in ways it never had—from the fast-food chains that emerged from the carhop days to major industrial brands—and regulations governing the size of companies waned over time.

Both political parties have seen their arguments upended since this issue set in. The political left criticized corporate power for decades but struggled to gain traction as bigger companies delivered low prices to consumers. The political right championed the market and won a bipartisan shift away from antitrust enforcement as more goods became affordable,[84] only to find years later that many conservatives would be just as angry at big companies as at big government.

As it would turn out, the move toward "big" in our economy, from the 1950s into the twenty-first century, has made antitrust one of the rowdier debates in American government today. There's now a shift underway on the competition-minded political right, as well as the equality-minded political left, about the market power of giants in all kinds of industries. This includes the administrations of both President Donald Trump and President Joe Biden moving forward a range of cases against Big Tech.[85] In Congress, conservatives like Senator J. D. Vance and liberals like Senator Elizabeth Warren are targeting the financial industry.[86] Agriculture has received increased attention too. Watchdog efforts led by Republicans and Democrats alike allege that pesticide companies like foreign-owned Syngenta have loyalty programs designed to limit competition from generic products—and lock farmers into higher-priced pesticides—by paying off distributors to block competitors from the market.[87] The companies argued there was no violation of laws protecting competition, in part because there was no specific requirement that farmers purchase from any particular manufacturer.[88]

Antitrust issues can be battled out in Congress, where the rules get written, or in the courts—where opposing parties argue incredibly complex cases over pricing, intellectual property, and business practices that show how difficult it has been to find the right balance over the decades. In theory, a large company becoming calcified and noncompetitive should be open to disruption by a smaller entity. However, critics argue disruption is not possible if a company is so large it can shut out meaningful competition or has won government favor.

The shift toward a "bigger" American economy that took off in the 1950s—and led to a shift away from antitrust enforcement by the 1980s—has reverberated through the decades and remains a dilemma affecting family farms. Antitrust crusader Matt Stoller, the director of research at the American Economic Liberties Project, said the more recent bipartisan support for antitrust action is a "revolution in antitrust and antimonopoly thinking" that still isn't enough. A consensus in Congress remains far off. Litigation can take years. And antitrust is only the beginning, Stoller said, with laws around trade, fraud, and more needing enforcement. Meanwhile, he said, not only are consumers, farmers and others paying higher prices or getting less choices in the absence of competition, but the American food supply is also at risk. Say a food supplier withholds its products from the market to increase prices, or the United States becomes a net food importer as its farms disappear. That could be catastrophic, Stoller said, if another pandemic shuts down food processors again—similar to the consequences of COVID—or halts imports. Another disaster scenario would be agribusiness companies limiting the genetic traits of seeds to only a few strains that suddenly become vulnerable to a new kind of pest, he said.

"If we don't fix this," Stoller said, "we will eventually starve."

While the left reprises its antitrust bearings, the debate about what to do within the American right is raging. Many in conservative circles share a concern over government favoring big companies or are trying to speak for working-class voters who feel trampled on by the elite. The economic policy is more complicated, though, with plenty of skepticism that government action is the answer. Jansen, of the Private Enterprise Research Center—as well as numerous other economists focused on the study of free markets—said antitrust laws have a limited role to prevent things like collusion. Outside of that, they said, such laws tend to stop companies from reaching their full potential, which hampers innovation and increases prices.

"I think efficiency matters," Jansen said. "I don't think by itself big is bad, period." Salter of Texas Tech generally agreed, saying he needs more proof of big players improperly increasing prices over the years. At the same time, he's open to the idea that government should act to preserve competition against too much market power. He argued there are other reasons for everyone, including economic conservatives, to be concerned about "giganticness" dominating the economy. A large number of small businesses ensures greater competition in a market, naturally incentivizes more decisions to be made locally, and gives citizens faith in both a market economy and American democracy, he said.

The lessons from these debates of the post–World War II period forward—what has worked and what hasn't, and what's changing in American politics—offer a chance for innovative solutions we've missed in the past. For the moment, the failure to solve these dilemmas so far has raised the stakes for family farms, ever since America's troubled rise from the economic ashes.

***

The challenges of this era, as the American family farm became the little guy in an increasingly big world, made the middle-class status of millions of families shockingly fragile in the 1950s and '60s. While the generation that grew up in the Depression eventually got to ride the economic dynamism that came with World War II and lasted for years afterward, the future for the next generation of farmers would be more fraught than anyone would have predicted.

There was little room for error. That's why the most important thing about Jim's childhood—and to our farm's future—was that he didn't like the taste of liquor.

For years Albert drank more and more, be it alone or with visiting friends and family. By the time Jim was old enough to walk, Albert was drinking each morning, taking a schluck before chores, maybe another after breakfast. It was brandy by then, stowed under the sink. One day he took a pull from the bottle, considered that thing which gave him such joy, and handed it to his son. Jim tried it but found none of his father's happiness in it. He hated the smell, that deceiving sweetness that stung up through his nose and eyes. The burning taste. The way it made him dizzy, then sleepy, and sick. Most times after that, he didn't drink it—not the searing booze in the morning, the big bottles of beer on the hot days, nor the whiskey and sodas on the table in the evenings. Jim's temperance meant a different path for the farm.

Over the years, as Jim got older, a powerful-but-informal delineation of duties, more subtle than the family's more formal decision-making, began to emerge. Even though Albert milked and did every task on his father's farm or his own at one time or another, he eased back from some duties whenever he had the help over the years and as the drinking took deeper hold. Albert still milked cows in the morning while Ann readied the family for school. But in the evening, it was often Ann and Jim who milked, while Albert worked in his shop or lingered on a trip to town. Milking was heavy labor in those days: bringing the cows in from pasture and corralling them into their stanchions in the barn; cleaning their udders; placing straps over each cow's back to hold the hulking milking machines in place and heaving them from one cow to the next, feeling them become heavier still—some forty pounds—as the metal pails attached filled with milk; lugging the milk out of the barn. The process repeated over and over, dozens of times, from cow to cow, one end of the barn to the next. For a grown man, particularly one with a few drinks in him, this was hard work. It was even harder work for a woman and boy of ten. Around age twelve, Jim began driving tractor in the fields, and by his teenage years and afterward, there was hardly a job on the farm he didn't do. Slowly but clearly, the father left more and more to the son.

However, Jim liked the work and the time with his mother. Stern by then—and willing to threaten punishment with the razor strap when Jim didn't behave—Ann was quieter when they worked together. She moved quickly, from one task to the next, and Jim followed, each learning the ways of the other in silence. In time, they came to work independently of one another but toward the same goal, anticipating what the other would do: from one cow to another in the barn, one load to another in the farmyard, one row to another in the field, one day and week and month to another as they moved the farm forward over the years. They fell into a rhythm common among farm families but special to mother and son in the precious harmony it brought, so different from the strain that had set in on the family.

On occasion, the whole family fell into work together, but the harmony was not nearly so sweet. Albert still worked harder, as he had in the olden days with his father, during the summer hay season that came periodically and during the harvest of corn in the fall. He would mow the hay, sitting atop a bright red Super H tractor, pulling a mechanical sickle that clattered and cut as it went. Ann would follow on the WD tractor with a hay crusher, another piece of machinery that would pick up the hay between two steel rollers to squeeze out the moisture and lay it back down on the field. A day or so later, Albert would come through again with the tractor pulling the side rake, yet another piece of machinery with rows of tines that shuffled like a deck of cards as it rolled, picking up the hay and turning it over to dry further.

When the hay was ready, it was no longer a two-person job for Ann and Albert, but for the whole family. It was still Ann driving another red tractor, the popping and jaunty Super M that pulled the baler. Only now it was Jim doing the hot work on the wagon—striking at each bale with the hand-held hay hook, pulling it out of the baler, and stacking row by row. When they had a load of bales, Albert would drive an empty wagon out to them and swap, then haul the full wagon into the haymow above the barn. There, he ran the great hay fork that swung down from the wooden barn rafters and closed around the hay bales, hoisting them through the dark and dusty air and piling them in the mow. It was hot in the haymow, with little air, and Albert drank all the while—most often quart bottles of beer to cool off. It was hot in the field too. The harmony of the family's work would break when Albert, cloudy from the beer, would forget to bring water out to his wife and son, Ann yelling from the tractor in disbelief.

The machine shop where Albert retreated from his troubles was an old Quonset hut, long and cylindrical and low to the ground. It was made of galvanized steel, better to withstand the wind and the rain, and to hold the secrets of his thoughts and feelings. The darkened windows sat like sleepy eyes upon the farmyard, concealing what went on behind them. Inside, it was warm. A little potbelly stove burned wood behind its iron door, the dirt floor upon which it sat offering up direct commune with the earth. Next to it was a steel workbench where Albert pounded and fiddled until the pieces of machinery he was working on fit together, in a way they hadn't outside in the farmyard. Along the front wall was a long row of wooden drawers, holding tools and machine parts and supplies he used to set the world right.

Albert was proud of his shop, and sometimes he let his son into his refuge. Jim would sit on an overturned pail and watch his father fire in the stove, piling wood inside, embers flying. They liked to peer deep into the pit of the stove together, to see how red it got as it warmed them. Albert drank less in the shop, if at all. There, he was a man about his work, fixing a tractor in the back or tinkering with parts on the workbench. He was happy then and would smile and laugh and talk to his son about the farm: crops, cows, how a good farmer organizes tools. It was here, in the warm solitude of the shop, that father and son built their closeness. It was a closeness that would fuse with farmland tradition, and acknowledgment of the work ethic Jim showed over the years, until one day Albert said it to his son directly:

"Someday this is gonna be yours."

The expectation of the eldest son, which Albert always said Alois had of him, passed now from the second generation to the third—like the sun soaring ever higher over the farmyard on a hot day, strong and glorious, but also heavy and punishing. During these changing times, Alois and Teresia died, both in 1967. Alois had become difficult to care for and spent his last days in a nursing home, asking to go home. And Jim knew, as the weight of tradition passed from his grandparents to his parents to him, that everything he and his parents did now would shape the future of the farm.

One day, he came home from high school to see the yard lined with cars and trucks, and men working at the far end of the big red barn. Albert was adding on, to expand the barn beyond the thirty to forty cows it had held all of Jim's life. There was a chance to make more money and a need to keep up, by getting a little bigger in the rapidly growing economy that was giving more and taking more from the American farmer. Jim wandered among the construction at the back of the barn that was to be his someday: the walls of heavy brick and wood framing, the big beams overhead, the sand floor awaiting cement. He looked out the window—still free of glass so the cement trucks could ease their spouts inside the barn to pour the floor—and gazed upon the farmyard with excitement. Albert was proud but worried the addition wouldn't be enough for his son to weather the days to come.

"We should've added another forty feet," he said.

Sometimes as a young man, Jim wandered out past the back of the barn, toward the woods where the sun set each evening with its oranges and reds and purples. It was his own retreat, just as his father had his machine shop, to clear his mind. Jim would go often to an apple orchard that sat on the hill behind the barn and walk among the fruit-bearing trees. When he reached the hill, he'd peer back upon the expanded barn, then upon the yard and house and fields beyond. Past the land that he could see, over the hills and down in the valley, was the original farmland his grandfather Alois first bought, then sold to his father.

All of it, he thought, would be his someday.

Other times, especially on Sundays, Jim would leave earlier and wander further, carrying a .22 rifle past the apple orchard and still more fields, and along a great ravine, until he reached quiet woods where he loved to hunt rabbit and squirrel. The sun would shine brightly upon the forest floor. Stopping upon a knoll, Jim would peer down through the trees, staring at the place where his father's property—one day his—found its end.

CHAPTER 6

DEADLY WEATHER

The 1980s Farm Crisis and Its Lasting Cost Today

The winter storm blew in from the northwest and was a subzero disaster by the time it hit southern Wisconsin. Snow first, then rain turning to shards of ice, shot through the sky on a howling wind—hitting the fields and the roads at night and clinging to the power lines strung tight in the darkness. Jim awoke in the pitch black, daylight still far away, and journeyed down the stairs to the first floor of the farmhouse. It was 1976. The power had gone out, and the farmyard outside the windows was darker than it had been for decades. No barn light was shining in the night, no moon, no stars offering a glow from the sky above. His fiancé Jean was on the couch in the living room, the only place his parents would allow when she came out on the weekends between now and when they were set to be married later that year. Snow was piled outside, but it did not blow in the wind because the ice had capped it all in frozen stillness. They were due to start morning milking in the barn, so it didn't make any difference if the electricity was out or the weather was harsh. The cows had to be milked or they could become sore and sick. The large red barn loomed obscure and distant in the darkness outside, no light nor machine to aid them in their plight.

All four of them—Jim, Jean, Albert, and Ann—shrugged into bundles of work clothes and stepped out into the vicious dark. Albert tried to get a generator running for temporary power. His tools clicked in the cold, but the generator would not run. The ice was so thick and slick that Jim and Jean had to ease to the ground, and slide down the hill on their backsides, descending slowly under the black sky until they reached the barn. The warmth of the cows' body heat as they stepped inside was the only comfort they would have that morning.

The milking machines that were among the technological revolutions to farming some forty years before would be of no use to them now. They required electricity to run and sat lifeless in the darkened milkhouse. Instead, Jim and Jean would have to milk by hand. It was a task from another time: when farmers in Wisconsin usually milked far fewer cows because of the labor involved, and when each cow yielded less milk. Crouching there alone—with more than forty cows that could each give thirty pounds in a good milking—Jim and Jean warmed their hands in careful consideration of the cows, reached down to the animals' shivering udders, and began. Short tight streams of milk sounded against the bottom of the pail as they tugged. They closed their eyes, leaned their heads against the cows, and fell into a workmanlike trance in the streaming darkness until each cow was done and they could move on to the next.

Finally, the faithful milker pump blared, and the long yellow overhead lights came back on, bathing the barn again in modernity. The cows, in two rows down the length of the barn, swished their tails, peered about, and adjusted their hooves in the soft golden light. They hadn't milked all the cows by hand, but they'd done enough of them to make their hands throb. Jean—a "city girl" from outside Madison who had only just begun farming in the months since she'd met

Jim—felt the pain coursing from her hands up her arms and into her shoulders.

"I'm not sure I can lift my arm," she said.

The rest of them—her kindly but drink-prone future father-in-law, his leather-tough wife, and their dedicated son—had little to say. There was work yet to be done. As it would turn out, the family would have to dump the milk before it spoiled, with the milk truck unable to make it up the ice-laden hill. Later, in the house, Jean curled up in the fetal position, clutching her aching hands beneath her aching arms, and cried.

Though it was the last time they would perform that trying task, it was only the beginning of farm families of the era getting knocked back into an earlier time by an unholy blend of forces descending upon them. And those forces would usher in a level of economic devastation we're still wrestling with today.

***

The Farm Crisis of the 1980s is commonly referred to as a perfect storm of economic, geopolitical, and governmental forces. In reality, the storm was not a temporary mix of bad weather, but the confluence of those booming forces and a completely unknown technological threat all battering the American family farm far longer than history remembers. It was a singular disaster in America's story not only for the severe financial ruin farmers faced—although that was reason enough—but also for the cruelty of how preventable it was. American prosperity followed by financial crash, the movements of hostile nations, policies under both political parties, and more all provoked an epic era of failing farms, banks, and rural communities. And that tempest of forces, timed so precisely as technological change and one American institution after another failed us, would impact family farms in secret ways we still don't understand.

The first winds were just beginning to blow as my parents battled the ice storm that foretold further disaster to come. Once again, it was a time of prosperity mixed with warning signs. Commodity prices, especially grain, were rising, a reflection of strong worldwide demand[89] and a growing economy stretching into the 1970s. President Richard Nixon's administration negotiated for America to sell grain to the Soviet Union,[90] opening up international markets that were among the many reasons for farmers' optimism. Government officials encouraged greater food production than ever before, highlighting the increased opportunity while also pressing farms to get bigger and more productive.[91] Farmers responded not only by forcing greater efficiency on their farms—a virtue good farmers had embraced for decades and bad ones missed at their peril—but also by taking out debt to buy more land, expand operations, or upgrade capabilities. Farm-operator debt hit $33.7 billion in 1974.[92] This usually happened in times of opportunity—it had in the midst of World War I before the crash that caused the farmland depression of the 1920s, and it had to some degree in the World War II era, but with memories of economic depression tempering the appetite for debt.[93] By the time of the Farm Crisis, our country boasted supposed safeguards, both via private-sector lending practices and public policy, but some of it was false hope. America's institutions would fail farm families, and by the 1980s too many had forgotten the Depression-era lessons that could have saved them as they did after World War II.

Meanwhile, the positive economic winds of the moment carried a political crosscurrent. Selling to the Soviet Union was a new market and gave the United States government Cold War leverage against the Communists because America had something they needed. Nixon's agriculture secretary, Earl Butz, revealed the truth of the time with four fateful words: "Food is a weapon."[94] By supplying Russia with grain, farmers were giving American government officials what they believed was a diplomatic asset they could also withhold to influence their Soviet rivals, a weapon that both political parties—Republicans under Nixon and President Gerald Ford, then Democrats under President Jimmy Carter—would hold in their arsenal. It was a rare area of agreement in American politics that would slip from being a widely accepted solution to bipartisan problem.

Too few people saw that at the time, however. With so much opportunity on the horizon, land was getting more expensive. Farmers saw a need to get in on the action while they could, said Pamela Riney-Kehrberg, a distinguished professor of rural and agricultural history at Iowa State University.

"God isn't going to make anymore," Riney-Kehrberg said of the mindset at the time. "I need to get this land now or I'm not going to be able to afford it later."

Unbelievably, those forces of the Farm Crisis to come weren't the only problems. Nor even the deepest. Another wind bearing down on family farming was technological change, and it would blow longer and carry undetected danger partially because it also drove so much economic opportunity. The rush of technology that had brought constantly improving tractors, electricity, sophisticated seed and fertilizer, and other modern miracles to the family farm after the Depression turned now toward machinery covering more field rows than ever and science that allowed farmers to raise more animals than ever.

Jim MacDonald is an economist who has studied farm consolidation for decades, as a professor at the University of Maryland and for the United States Department of Agriculture. His research reveals how technology would become the one overarching force of this era leaving fewer farms on our country's landscape—in ways America didn't see until far too late. For decades, MacDonald said, economists and farm-technology researchers were trying to address the difference between high factory wages and low farm wages that were pulling people off the farm and driving the heartland's workforce shortage. Part of the answer was technology that could give farms greater economic scale with even less need for labor: massive planting, cultivating, and harvesting equipment that could cover more acres; expansive buildings and feedlots with equipment to tend to hundreds more animals. All that expansion, with fewer workers. This major technological advance—one that was often too expensive or impractical for small farms—increased pressure for farms to get larger and crowded out the kind of small-scale innovation that previously gave smaller farms a shot at keeping up.

Then, in the 1970s, the economics changed, MacDonald told me, with farm wages catching up with factory wages and thus lessening the need to cope with a declining labor pool. The problem was nobody seemed to notice. The technological shift promoting large farms over small farms rushed onward for the rest of the century. The research of MacDonald and his colleagues, distinct from most studies of the issue, shows that fifty-three out of fifty-five crops reviewed—from wheat to corn to fruits and vegetables—underwent almost constant consolidation in the next twenty-five years in the wake of the Farm Crisis. While the pace differed, exponential consolidation also occurred for five of the seven forms of livestock studied, from dairy cows to chickens and beyond.[95] The only force that was a constant across so many sectors, MacDonald said, with government policies changing and market forces varying, was technology less geared for small farms than before. And it's a force that still continues today.

None of this was apparent at the time. Inflation was setting in, but the transition from prosperity to rising prices and other economic woes was happening without much regard for the risks facing farmers. The farm consolidation going on at the time in the 1970s was far slower than the record-breaking 1950s, when family farming's emergence into the modern economy forced so many farms to the wayside.[96] The growing need for food, it seemed, was arriving at a time when family farms were ready to meet the challenge. For now, the perfect storm that would become a timeless tempest was gathering in the distance. Until it finally broke the sky, America's farmers and their families would stand on a pedestal, where everyone could see them rise higher than ever before—and the prospect of falling was all the more dangerous.

***

The summer of 1976 was so dry in southwest Wisconsin that the land broke into pieces. Like a cosmic counterpunch to the hard winter a few months earlier when Jim and Jean had milked by hand, the dry weather hit the farm and plunged it into drought. Rich brown dirt, usually soft and damp, grew so brittle that the ground cracked like the cobblestones of a lost civilization. Jim crouched in the field and found that he could place his forefinger three inches into the cracks between the fragments of earth. By late summer, it was so dry that there were hardly any crops to harvest. Jim couldn't have put his plow into the ground to prepare the soil for next spring's planting even if he'd wanted to. And he didn't want to, for the wind whipped so much dust across the fields that he knew if he plowed his ground up, all the topsoil would blow away.

Jim was about to be married, and it wasn't supposed to be like this. He had met Jean on a blind date the year before in 1975, and they'd been through so much already. At first, Jean had not been the kind of woman Jim would have pictured; she was from a prominent family just outside the capital city of Madison, working in a hospital. For her part, Jean would have never dated Jim—tall and handsome as he was, with a brown moustache and shy smile—if she'd known he was a farmer. Her father had grown up on a farm, and she was well aware of the back-breaking work of her relatives who still farmed. But there was something there, in their first conversation. Jim liked her cheerful personality, beaming from a soft face with kind eyes. Jean found that although Jim talked only about farming, he was still open-minded, and she was attracted to him knowing what he wanted: to farm. That was a virtue in the world she knew of aimless men with money, even if it wasn't what she'd have picked for her life.

The culture shock for the farm boy and the city girl had been on full display on the summer afternoon in 1975 when Jim had brought Jean to meet his parents. The introduction came after a local parade, when Jim returned home to do chores and milk before they could go back to the town festival that night. Ann stood there in a work dress, her hair tied up in a bandanna, her face twisted into disgust over standing around in the sun doing nothing. Jim's parents wanted a girl who was a devout Catholic, wasn't "damaged goods," and grew up on a farm. For Ann, Jean meeting the first two criteria did not entirely make up for her missing the last one. But Albert abandoned those notions in the first moments of meeting. He pranced over, happy again to have someone on his farm, where he could shed his shyness and welcome, of all things, a beautiful young woman from the city who was interested in his boy. He shook her hand and talked and talked, telling her about the farm—first there in the yard and then later in the barn—and making little noises like a squirrel barking in a tree to joke with her.

"I love my son Jim. He's gonna take over the farm," Albert said. "Everything here is bought and paid for."

Buoyed by Albert's kindness, Jean stuck it out despite the challenges—afraid at first of the cows when she walked down to the barn, upset when the dog covered in cow shit jumped up on her nice clothes, offended by Ann's standards for her, worried she'd made a bad impression. She wanted nothing more than for Jim to finish his work so they could get away together. It was only a few weeks after that when Jim proposed. He bought the ring with money he'd made picking wild ginseng, in the woods above the valley where his family had gotten its start two generations earlier.

Standing in the cracked fields now in August of 1976, a little over a year after Jean's first visit to the farm, Jim could not believe what they'd been through together. The woman who was once scared of cows had milked them by hand with him when the power went out the winter before, and did not waver now with drought setting in. But they could not have known how bad it would get.

As Jim and Jean had prepared over the summer to be married and officially buy the farm from Albert and Ann, only one decent hay crop rose up out of the ground in June. The cornfields choked in the heat, too, the stalks struggling to break up through the ground. Now Jim looked out over the brown and gasping fields that would soon be his. He could tell by the next hay crop—thin and spiny when it should have been lush under the summer sun—that they wouldn't get another. They'd have to use what corn they already had stored away from past years, and whatever they could afford to buy. Their wedding was a little over one month away. And Jim asked himself, before he and his wife-to-be could even get started, the question every farming generation asks at some point: *Are we going to make it?*

The fear lifted for a few short days, as Jim and Jean were married on September 25 of 1976 and they took Jim's only long weekend off at that point in his life to go fishing up north. They returned home to move into the farmhouse where Jim grew up, while Albert and Ann retired to town in Plain. The economic woes came crashing back in. Jim and Jean were rebuilding their herd after the sale of several cows, making the milk check small. The failed harvest would make the milk check smaller still; short on feed, the cows wouldn't produce. All this came as Jim adjusted to running the farm on his own: bills, taxes, and the new financial weight of buying the farm from his parents. Luckily, there was no debt left on the farm—Alois and Teresia, and then Albert and Ann, all worked so that the family could own all of the land free and clear, and no lender could claim it in tough times. But there was still a financial burden. The common practice by the time Jim came along was for the younger generation to buy the farm from the older generation under *land contract*. This was an arrangement by which Albert and Ann sold the farm to Jim and Jean and let them pay it off to them gradually. It avoided the younger generation taking out debt, as their grandparents and parents had, and still afforded the older generation income in a world where Social Security and savings were rarely enough to get by.

Left with dwindling money and few options as fall turned to winter, Jim and Jean lived a life more meager than they'd ever imagined. Jean closed off unused rooms in the farmhouse to save on the wood they needed to fire in the big woodstove for heat. Jim trapped rabbits and hunted squirrels so they wouldn't have to buy meat in town. They still had chickens, and so they collected eggs and butchered birds when they were fit. When a cow wasn't producing, they made the hard decision to sell it and save on costs, rather than try to get it milking better. Jean baked homemade bread in between the long work days and tried, when she talked with family, to hide the pain. She was not only worried but also alone. Her parents, siblings, roommates, and friends she'd had in the city were all an hour away, and a day off to go see them was rare with so little money and so much work to do. The job she'd had in the cardiac unit of a hospital, another social outlet and work she had been proud of, was gone now. Having all those things replaced with a struggling farm left her unsure of where to turn. Jim had never asked Jean to leave her job, and Jean never told Jim how alone she felt.

It was neighbors who saved them. A tall and cheerful neighbor who had farmed down the road long enough to be better established had let them gather loose hay off his barn floor for nothing. Another neighbor, a blunt old man named Leo Hetzel who was known to walk barefoot through the wetlands that merged with his pasture, had welcomed them to old hay in his barn too. His farm was down the road from the end of the valley where the Reisinger family got its start, and he and Albert had banded together to harvest each other's crops in the days when most farms lacked the machinery to do it themselves. Now, the partnership had crossed into the next generation. When Jim needed more hay, Leo had agreed to "go halves" on whatever new hay they could get off his fields—if Jim would do the fieldwork, he could have half the crop. However, the old man took less than his share, saying they could "settle up later." No matter how many times Jim walked into Leo's smoky living room to offer the old man money as he chain-smoked cigarettes, there was never any later. Finally, one day, Leo's famous grouchiness emerged to state it plain.

"You don't owe me nothin'." He gave Jim a candy bar and a glass bottle of Sundrop on his way out to let him know it was okay. "You just got married. Take it and go."

That hay from neighbors, gathered over the summer and early fall, got the farm through the winter. It kept Jim and Jean from taking more drastic measures, like buying feed, and maybe even borrowing money for an operating loan at a time when they'd have risked failing to pay it off. Staying clear of debt in the late 1970s would be the difference between life and death for many farms in the years to come.

***

Prices had been falling and times tightening when the first big wind of the Farm Crisis blew in from Washington, DC, in fall of 1979. The way it changed the economic atmosphere surrounding the American family farm was sudden and lasting—with a level of economic whiplash that shocked the heartland.

It was the moment Paul Volcker, chairman of the Federal Reserve, implemented a sharp increase in interest rates.[97] The Fed's ability and willingness to control the money supply—putting more money into the financial system with low interest rates, and less money into the system with high interest rates—had expanded since the Depression. The increase in interest rates, as with other times since, was meant to help curb inflation. Prices for nearly all goods were rising for American consumers, as economic growth became stagnant. By increasing interest rates and decreasing the amount of money in the system, Volcker aimed to slow inflation—a feat he is widely credited with achieving—in advance of another era of American prosperity that would eventually emerge in the 1980s and 1990s. However, for farmers, this meant a sudden reversal of fortune. The higher interest rates meant farmers had to pay more interest on loans they needed, and that banks were operating in a tighter financial environment. Many historians and economists blame this chain of events for kicking off what Iowa State professor Pamela Riney-Kehrberg called a "rolling crisis" of one economic catastrophe after another.

Farmers once flying high were now in deep trouble, not because their operations were falling behind, but because the financial environment had made debt more expensive to have and harder to get. Soon enough, lenders—both private sector banks and government programs like the Farmers Home Administration—began to stumble as farmers struggled to pay off their debt, Riney-Kehrberg said. Unlike the Great Depression, when most people experienced economic pain on some level, this crisis was specific to rural communities. Farmers felt it first and most painfully, but then it spread from farmers to rural banks to the communities surrounding them. Everyone in farm country found it harder to get a loan because of the sudden storm and suffered as economic activity slowed down.

"When family farms go awry, it ripples. . . ." said Sarah Vogel, the lawyer who represented farmers during the Farm Crisis and went on to author *The Farmer's Lawyer*, a book about her experiences in the depths of the crisis. "It ripples into small town Main Street, it ripples into implement dealers, it ripples into utilities. It ripples, it ripples, it ripples."

The wind kept blowing, bringing new storm clouds to bear even before the last ones passed. On January 4, 1980, the moment came when the United States government decided to put Earl Butz's "food is a weapon" theory into maximum practice. Seeing the Soviet Union invade Afghanistan against America's wishes, President Carter picked up the Nixon-era weapon and wielded it, announcing in an evening national address from the Oval Office a ban on the sale of many goods to the Soviet Union.[98] The grain embargo closed off a key market to sell crops, just as farmers were facing the credit crunch. Riney-Kehrberg said the embargo's impact was most of all psychological. Although the loss of the market to the Soviet Union may have initially slowed sales, she said, soon enough there was the ability to sell to other countries that were now selling more to the Russians and experiencing a shortfall of their own. But to see the United States government under Carter closing off a key market that the government under Nixon had encouraged—while farmers built up massive debt in between—showed farm families that if food is a weapon, they were the ones in danger. The upheaval of shifting markets, and proof they were expendable on a bipartisan basis, all came as the broader crisis worsened.

Farmers responded with outrage. Some of them might have initially agreed with parts of the 1970s sentiment of Butz, the Nixon agriculture secretary who grew up on an Indiana farm, that farms needed to modernize and continue their march toward greater productivity. Others may have also related to Carter—whose political image was famously tied to his background as a peanut farmer—and understood the need for a response to Russia. However, the chain reaction set in motion by various parts of the United States government, whether justified in each individual action or not—encouraging massive debt, then making it more expensive; opening the Russian market, then closing it—was too much. Meanwhile, groups like the American Agriculture Movement were growing, organizing farmers into protests reminiscent of the Great Depression.

In February of 1979, thousands of tractors from all over the United States rumbled into Washington, DC. After "tractorcades" all over the country organized by AAM, some ten thousand tractors, trucks, and other vehicles rolled toward Capitol Hill, hauling the plight of the American farmer on full display for a national audience. The episode snarled traffic, damaged the national mall, and led to clashes with police when farmers refused to let authorities corral them into a perimeter that would limit disruptions to the city.[99]

The demonstration also led to moments where the nation witnessed that blend of independence and willingness to help your neighbor that makes up America's farmland spirit. When a blizzard brought more than twenty inches of snow to DC over Presidents Day, weekend, farmers plowed much of the city out, drove doctors and nurses to hospitals, and came to the aid of stranded motorists.[100] As spring broke later, farmers planted fresh grass on the national mall before heading home.[101]

Despite farmers being heard nationally, the Farm Crisis got worse. In 1981 interest rates hit a historic high never reached in recorded history before or since.[102] Farm foreclosures climbed throughout the 1980s. This was fueled partially by the crisis already underway. But the need for credit also ran up against efforts to get the economy moving by President Reagan's administration. Reagan advisors argued there was a need to decrease government spending, part of a broader effort to unleash economic growth with tax cuts and deregulation during the ongoing fight against inflation.[103] Some farmers may have agreed with Reagan's goals, just as there were varying views of Nixon and Carter. But the government's actions to address the financial troubles of the Farmers Home Administration, a government program that was among the lenders now struggling as farmers struggled, led to further outrage. Generally speaking, when a borrower is struggling, a lender— be it a private sector bank or a government program—can deal with it in a number of ways. It can restructure the loan in various fashions, work out an alternative payment plan, and implement all kinds of intermediate steps before foreclosure. Vogel, the lawyer who represented farmers during the Farm Crisis, said the government made a drastic turn, sometimes giving farmers just fifteen or thirty days to pay off debt they previously had decades to repay. Vogel filed a class-action lawsuit for farmers to fight back.

Part of what was unfolding, in the middle of farmers facing foreclosure, were echoes of the unresolved debate over the role of government in agriculture. Vogel—as a champion of government providing the support needed for farmers to produce America's food below cost—said having a strong government loan program is crucial. The Farmers Home Administration, one of the main lending programs during the Farm Crisis, had what she called a crucial strategy: helping farmers starting out who couldn't get a loan, then working them toward a private lender. Officials with the Reagan administration, though, argued that the government was spending too much money to be sustainable and that federal loans—backed by government subsidies—had fueled risky loans farmers willingly took out. Members of Congress from farm states on both sides of the aisle took on the Reagan administration, countering that the government helped cause the crisis, leaving farmers with a sudden reversal in fortunes.[104] Alexander Salter, the Texas Tech professor, said that across most economic sectors time has proven that "Uncle Sam is actually a pretty bad allocator of credit" because the government lacks the right incentives and information to pick borrowers most likely to pay their loans back.

The debate from this era reaches far beyond lending and still rages today. Although the Farm Crisis dealt mainly with lending issues, debate over farm programs in the late 1980s and early 1990s drove America away from direct price supports and toward "risk management," like voluntary insurance both farmers and the government pay into for days that prices drop below a certain level. Vogel said New Deal–style programs that helped address parity—the issue of farmers left to sell at prices that are insufficient compared to the cost of the goods they need to produce—have been weakened over the decades and would provide greater stability that farmers deserve. Salter thinks government programs that alter prices like that are exactly the kind incentivizing farmers to rely on government subsidies, rather than make decisions based on what makes economic sense. He worries that programs layered upon programs, even if some of them make sense on their own, is a problem itself.

"The end result is a very complicated mashup of policies," Salter said. "Now what we have here is a fragile Jenga tower."

Jeff Lyon worked for United States Representative Steve Gunderson, a Republican from Wisconsin during the Farm Crisis, before going on to work for years as the general manager of Farm First Dairy Cooperative, where he had to help dairy farmers appeal to both sides of the aisle. Meaning, he's seen firsthand efforts to change the government's relationship with agriculture and the realities farmers face. He said the period showed some of America's capacity for reform that can enable innovation. For example, cheesemakers used to create large amounts of "government cheese," like cheddar, that the government would buy in bulk to help regulate the price. When that program went away, he said, it freed cheesemakers to start producing provolone and other varieties that have thrived. However, he laughs when asked about those who want the government out of agriculture altogether or think farmers can just produce less to increase prices.

By the 1980s most farmers were "price takers" selling their products on the commodities markets. A commodity is any product that has become so uniform it's no different from one producer to the next—a tank of milk or a bushel of corn—usually sold on an exchange where the prices are based on market-wide demand. So, one dairy farmer restricting his or her supply isn't going to affect the milk price. Furthermore, since cows have to be milked rain or shine, that same farmer would have to sell or slaughter milk cows to restrict supply. If the price goes up and it's time to expand, it could be months before that farmer's young livestock can rebuild the milk herd.

"That's been a never-ending discussion," he said of how to handle limiting supply in farming. "It's hard to take a sharp turn and reduce your production."

The dilemma over supply management—through government or private-sector means—is one of many still-unresolved issues that resurfaced with a vengeance during the 1980s Farm Crisis. Meanwhile, farmers on the ground were struggling to survive in a way they hadn't since the Great Depression.

***

Jim heard the talk about dumping milk to force higher prices. It was a throwback to the 1930s, when striking farmers had tried to decrease supply, to increase prices—and get enough attention to force change. Now, the debate was reignited between farmers who saw dumping milk as the best way to take action in the 1980s and farmers who saw it as foolishness. People argued at social gatherings in town, at community meetings where farmers gathered for updates, on the steps outside church after Mass. The debate even occurred in Jim and Jean's own home, when a persistent neighbor huddled around their kitchen table trying to convince Jim to join in. Jim was polite—the neighbor was another who kindly mentored him in those early years—but didn't commit.

"We'll have to think about it," he said. And when he did, he and Jean could never get around the fact that farmers who needed money more than ever were being asked to discard their main source of it. "They're losing money," he said to Jean. The organizers of the milk dumps said that kind of thinking was the problem—it would only work if everyone did it.

While not all farmers dumped their milk, most took action to survive in one way or another. The crisis was especially hard on crop farmers who had dramatically expanded during boomtimes around grain, wheat, and other crops, which meant those in the Corn Belt in Iowa and states like North Dakota, South Dakota, Nebraska, and others. But dairy farms also got hit, Iowa State professor Riney-Kehrberg said, as the toxic debt and other collateral damage of the Farm Crisis continued to spread in new ways.

Bernard and Karen Reisinger were Jim's cousins who farmed on hillsides lining the highway toward Sauk City, Wisconsin. The son and daughter-in-law of Herman, Jim's uncle and Albert's brother, their family had survived decades of challenges—starting of course with Herman being trampled by the horses and finding a way to be a successful businessman and farmer in the years to come. The 1980s required resilience of the next generation. Facing high interest rates as the Farm Crisis wore on, Bernard and Karen slashed expenses and focused everything they could on making debt payments. They had long raised beef cattle and pigs, in addition to milking cows, to hedge against times when the milk price was low. With painstaking care, they shepherded those resources—once available to buy more land when they needed to—to make it through.

"We just hunkered down and did what we had to do," Karen said. "Everybody says, 'Well how did you make it?' You just do."

Jim and Jean, lucky enough to have not acquired debt before the crisis hit, were proof that every farm was vulnerable in this time. In their first few years of marriage, they were still digging out of a financial hole—both from that first dry year of 1976 and from an infection called mastitis that hit more than half their herd. The illness spoiled their milk and cost money to treat. If they took another hit, it would come at a time when a financial lifeline would be hard to find with farms worth less and loans hard to come by.

There were other weights on their hearts. Jean had become pregnant in 1977, then lost the baby in the first few weeks. Saddened but surprised in the first place, Jim and Jean realized they wanted to try to have a baby again—only to lose their second baby after a few months. They went to the doctors and eventually learned they both had fertility issues that made them less likely to conceive and more likely to lose the baby when they did. Jim and Jean both tried various treatments, and Jean became pregnant four more times. They lost each baby. With each miscarriage came questions from friends and family. Both Jim and Jean wondered if it was their fault—too heavy of a job in the barn, a chemical in the farmyard, a bump on the tractor.

After the sixth time, they threw themselves into creating a home for another kind of child. Jim and Jean had signed up for adoption early in their struggles and now they decided to finish the inspections and paperwork. There was a room off the kitchen, which they'd built in place of the porch where Jim had watched his grandfather's horses and machinery go down the road nearly thirty years earlier. They kept it decorated for a baby, complete with a crib they weren't sure they would ever get to use. There was a rocking chair where Jean would sit and think about what it would be like to have a baby. Each month she went into the room, changed the sheets in the crib and cried.

Then one day in the dead of winter in 1985, Jean received a phone call. It was Catholic Social Services. "We have a baby for you," the social worker said. "You can come tomorrow."

It was a baby boy—a fourth generation of Reisinger men, who would join the farm his parents had fought to keep from the moment they were married. *Perhaps one day*, Jim thought, *he would take over.*

***

The Farm Crisis entered its final stages as I was learning to walk. I was born on November 20, 1984, to a mother who knew she couldn't care for me and instead put me up for adoption. My parents Jim and Jean brought me home to the farm a little over three months later in February of 1985.

For nearly four years, until my sister came along in an adoption from another family in late 1988, it was the three of us. The farm where I took my first steps—from the soft carpet of our living room to the rough gravel of the farmyard to the barn where my father worked—was beginning to emerge into an entirely new world.

In 1985, music icons Willie Nelson, Neil Young, and John Cougar Mellencamp put on the first Farm Aid concert, raising money for American family farms in what would become an annual event and permanent nonprofit organization,[105] and contributing to the rising awareness that was spurring government action. After years of wrangling between the two parties in Congress, President Reagan signed the Agricultural Credit Act in January of 1988 to stabilize the farm lending system. The legislation was a compromise between a Republican White House and Democrats controlling Congress. Reagan called the remaining Farm Credit System—a government-established program that allows tax-free loans by private lending institutions—a private-sector source of financing for farmers,[106] as he signed a bill that provided funding and reorganized a system that some in his party had considered a wasteful part of the problem. The bill also included reforms that Vogel's successful class-action lawsuit on behalf of farmers had fought for, offering farmers in financial distress fairer hearings in disputes over debt.[107] The legislation provided assistance to a good deal of the distressed farmers who remained, but tension would continue between the Reagan administration and advocates who had fought for farmers, over proper implementation of the law's protections for family farms. Meanwhile, outside the halls of government, the American economy was growing.

The crisis was finally ending, but the damage was lasting. Although consolidation of farms was an ongoing trend by now, foreclosures and forced sales played an outsized role in the more than 14 percent drop in the number of farms from 1982 to 1992.[108] By 1984—before there was even a sustained national conversation around long-term solutions to the crisis—farm debt had crippled private lending institutions across the heartland, with earnings at agriculture-focused banks dropping 50 percent since 1980.[109] That's on top of the distressed federal programs that teetered until the Agricultural Credit Act stabilized them.

The remaining farms were often larger and produced a narrower range of goods. Specialization was a trend that had taken root decades earlier as farms worked to compete in the growing American economy by focusing on those crops and products where they could make the most money. However, Riney-Kehrberg said the Farm Crisis dealt farm diversity a further blow—many crop farmers or dairy farmers, for example, just couldn't justify raising alternative crops, or pigs and beef on the side anymore. They felt they had to focus on only their highest-profit products, rather than a diversified mix. The lack of farm diversity removed a hedge for farmers (such as selling a herd of hogs when the price of their main commodity was low) and limited sources of food for consumers, since many farmers previously sold their side products locally as well as on the larger market. In the end, experts and historians from a range of perspectives agree, the consequences of the Farm Crisis went far beyond wiping out those farms that couldn't cut it. Farmers were constantly reminding themselves of the need to compete in the ongoing march toward greater efficiency and higher production. The cost of this crisis was something else entirely.

"That's not weeding out the inefficient," Riney-Kehrberg said of the Farm Crisis. "That's a wholesale slaughter."

Many farms that remained were also fighting to survive in a world where innovation was leaving them behind. New ideas on growing crops and raising animals helped family farms shift from subsistence farming to a stable industry, survive decades of economic depression, and compete in a changing economy. And as noted before, it had always, to a degree, made less labor and fewer farms needed as productivity surged. However, heading into the late 1980s and early 1990s, farmers would find more and more of the technology that helped farms grow and subsequently achieve scale. This technology was just too expensive for many small and midsized farms to adopt.

My parents experienced this firsthand. As part of the battle in their early years against the mastitis that was spoiling their milk, they installed a pipeline system that pumped the milk directly from the milking machines on the cows' udders to the milkhouse to cool. It was a significant innovation that eliminated the hard labor of hauling pails of milk, and improved sanitation. It was also one of the last major investments in milking innovation that made economic sense for them, unless they wanted to take out massive debt to become an operation with far more cows.

As the future dimmed, the past began to slip away completely. One day, just as I was old enough to remember, the old barn on the original Reisinger homestead down in the valley began to creak and sway. It was brittle, from years without the heat and sweat of animals. In an instant the beams gave in, and the barn collapsed. All that was left of the proud building—where our family had first found a way to make a living decades ago—was a jagged pile of old lumber. Snapped beams, faltering frames, and torn siding leaned into the hillside, the stone foundation and surrounding ground littered with the splintered dreams of years ago. There was nothing to be done now but burn it. The fire department came soon enough and set fire to it, trucks arrayed around the yard, firemen hustling from one spot to the next with their hoses at the ready as I looked on with my dad. Standing there watching the blaze, the smoke billowing around the pantlegs of his overalls, was my grandpa Reisinger, Albert. He wiped his nose and looked back at his son and grandson for a moment, then turned away and watched the barn burn.

CHAPTER 7

A TALE OF TWO FARM KIDS

Coping with the Quiet Disappearance of the 1990s

My first memory with my dad—before the smoke of the old barn in our valley burning into oblivion—was in the barn on the upper farm, where we both grew up. It's a barn still standing to this day. I was three years old, sitting on a pile of shelled corn in a wheelbarrow my dad was pushing back and forth across the manger in front of our family's milk cows. Light shone from the long overhead lights, and the heat of animals filled the barn, so that everything was golden and warm, the cows maternal and hungry before milking. With the girls mooing and the wheelbarrow squeaking, we rolled from one cow to the next, feeding each of them by hand. My dad was tanned on the arms and neck, and strong. He thought nothing of hauling wheelbarrows full of corn up and down the length of the barn, the added weight of his little boy along for the job. At each cow he plunged his large metal scoop into the pile and dumped her share of corn out into the manger. I did the same with a little plastic scoop, dipping into a pail of mineral that sat with me in the wheelbarrow. Sprinkling each cow her ration of nutrients like pixie dust from Neverland. Every so often, my dad's scoops would dig enough corn out from beneath me that it would give way, like the sands of time, and I'd tumble—one way or the other—as he worked the wheelbarrow handles just so, to balance the load and keep us rolling.

This is where we learned about the world. Me, and my sister, too, after she came along. Working with our dad, in whatever way our little hands could muster, in the barn and farmyard. Laughing as he hung us from the barn beams by our pants. Screaming as he squirted us with milk from a cow's udder. Begging him, as he tried to get his work done, to tie us up with baler twine just one more time, to show him how we could escape no matter how tight he pretended to bind us. Watching as he and my mom did chores and tested milk quality and talked about crops together. Drinking whole milk from a pitcher my mom dipped straight from the bulk tank in the milkhouse then carried to our kitchen table where breakfast was waiting for us all to eat together. Coming back to the barn at the oddest of hours to help pull a calf if its mother was struggling in labor, feeling it slide to the ground, my dad clearing its mouth and nostrils and watching, waiting to see if it would take its first breath—or fall lifeless.

"Come on gol' dang you," he'd say. "Come on now."

We learned, too, in the fields beyond the farmyard where my dad would drive his old pickup, down through the valley, up onto sunny slopes where he had mowed rows of hay to make. Reaching down, he'd feel the fallen alfalfa with his hands, then look at the sky, deciding when it would be dry enough for him to come back through with the tractor to bale or chop his latest crop.

Work and weather and life and death. We learned each of these lessons, there in the dreams and safety of childhood, and each was destined to slip not only into the realities of adulthood, as all things do, but also into the peril of a vanishing way of life. This would be true no matter how badly we might wish it weren't so, and laid bare with harsh honesty as my sister and I took our different paths. Paths that began in a Neverland that would one day depart from its natural law and disappear before our eyes.

***

American farm country in the late 1980s and 1990s was a dream-world, an imaginary land in so many ways, not simply because of the innocence of childhood. And not because the fruits of a strong and relatively stable economy were not real, because they were. Farm life during this time was a dreamworld because it *felt* like a respite from the tumultuous decades that came before. Yet, for the hard-working families of the heartland that helped feed our country for centuries, it was a time of great danger and, for many, unseen extinction. As the economy of a modern America and global trade system grew, farms already battered by decades of decline lost more control over their own destinies than ever before. Even as they recovered from past crises, they also slipped, one by one, into the endless pull of getting bigger or falling by the wayside. A world of increasingly large farms producing most of our food, or increasingly small farms requiring jobs off the farm to make it, emerged. The farms in the middle, like our family's— once a major driver of our food economy and a hallmark of American identity—made up the largest share of the disappearance.

"What we end up seeing is kind of a dual system of agriculture," said Paul Lasley, a rural sociologist and professor emeritus at Iowa State University. That system was one with ever-larger farms producing most of the food, he said, and small farms that families couldn't depend upon for their entire living because the profits were too small, if they existed at all. Left in between was a hidden force that almost everyone who has closely studied it describes as a "hollowing out of the middle."

And this slipping away, of large and small farms further away from one another, and of midsized farms out of existence, happened as most Americans—including many recovering farmers—experienced a new wave of opportunity. The tradeoffs facing American agriculture, that constant pairing of opportunity and peril farm families had known from the beginning, were in some ways more closely linked than they'd ever been. Free trade opened more markets across the world to American farmers, while introducing new and often unforeseen risks. A more sophisticated food supply chain accomplished more than ever for the American consumer but demanded more than ever for farm families to adapt.

All this happened as the American farmer carried the scars now of seven decades of disappearance: the loss of mixed agriculture that enabled the shift from subsistence farming; the two decades of off and on economic depression so much deeper than many knew; the departure of farm kids, so important to farming's future, to the good jobs and bright lights of urban life; times of broad prosperity after World War II that left an unbelievable number of farms behind; family farms' very own economic catastrophe during the Farm Crisis of the 1980s; and the change in technology that would continue to handicap small and midsized farms, no matter how competitive they were capable of being, for decades more. Now these forces compounded atop one another.

The disappearance was also more invisible than ever before. America didn't see what was happening partially because of the opportunities of free trade—United States exports to Canada and Mexico nearly doubled in ten years as a result of the North American Free Trade Agreement[110]—and partially because a sophisticated food system was delivering a modern miracle. By 2020, Americans were only spending 10 percent of their money on food, down from 40 percent (yes, nearly half of what they had) in 1900.[111]

The more dramatic economic crises of years past still had lasting effects, but with recovery underway, they continued more quietly. The pace of disappearance was slower—sinister in its quiet patience.

Consolidation continued through the nineties to the turn of the century, with America losing about 8 percent of its farms in the twenty years from 1997 to 2017, a slow and steady pace compared to other eras both before and since.[112] But the hollowing out of the middle—fewer midsized farms between the large and small farms—drove a sharper loss beneath the surface than anyone realized, part of a broader transformation of our food system.

This loss of midsized farms is surrounded by miraculous advancement, as well as controversy and grinding hardship. Those farms that answered the economic call to get bigger, armed with scale and cutting-edge technology to produce more food at lower cost, emerged as the dominant source of our food supply. By 2012 the number of large farms with at least two thousand acres had nearly doubled in twenty-five years, while the number of midsized farms with one hundred to 999 acres fell by nearly half.[113] Farms once able to manage a few hundred acres, or milk a few dozen cows, could now handle thousands of each with less people breaking their backs to do it. It's part of what's enabled our modern food system—every food you could imagine available in every part of the country—even as new challenges remained on the horizon.

Other farms, in the meantime, opted to remain small and turned to off-farm income to make a living: starting side businesses pouring concrete or fixing tractors, or pulling shifts at local factories, construction sites, retailers, and more. These families worked multiple jobs, all while operating a hobby farm that didn't make money, or one that could only generate supplemental income as they struggled to operate a successful business. The number of these small farms also increased—some being families buying or leasing small plots of land in the hope of creating something new, in addition to those with land from prior generations. But these farms struggled daily, and their output wasn't nearly enough to make up for the loss in midsized farms that had once powered our food economy.[114]

These midsized farms were caught in a vice. Too small to make a profit, the rural historian David Danbom said, but too large to leave time for a job off the farm, they went from providing our food to fueling the disappearance of the American farmer. And in doing so, they became the clearest example yet of the land rich, cash poor dilemma farmers face. Farm families know it is an honor and privilege to own land—especially if that land is passed down debt free from the work of prior generations—and some people argue that makes even the most humble farmer wealthy. But more and more farms, especially midsized farms, were facing a growing paradox as the land they owned became highly valuable but increasingly incapable of supporting a farm that could turn a profit. The only way to generate massive wealth was to sell it, which so many farm families never want to do. Keeping it meant grinding out a living. Even those lucky enough to have land in their family were often making payments to the prior generation under land contract—as noted previously, the passing of the land needing to generate new income for the current generation and retirement income for the previous one.

As this dilemma deepened, the day of reckoning was coming when the trends driving the disappearance of our farms, and other economic changes, would endanger America's food supply during global disaster.

Until then, the heart-rending result was a slow-moving national crisis that we began to lose sight of. The sharp economic upheaval gone, the hopes of a new economic dawn in its place, and the hidden consolidation all clouded our reality, leaving families like mine in a dreamworld filled with beauty but where something isn't quite right—a subconscious feeling of a nightmare in the offing.

***

It was a tale of two farm kids.

I was always small for my age. One of a few ways I'd find I was destined to have a harder time following my dad than I might have otherwise. But from my toddler days on, I insisted on wearing a baseball cap—just like him. I rode in the tractor with him for hours and followed him around the farmyard. So, when he handed me a rope and told me to hold on, I listened. At the other end of it was a calf, big enough to carry the weight and force of a full-grown cow to a four-year-old boy my size. We were moving our calves from their individual hutches to the calf barn where they'd grow until they were big enough to join the older cattle. It was my job to hold onto this one and keep it from running away as my dad closed the pen. The calves were rowdy, bucking in their hutches, clanging against their metal paneling and jumping. My dad turned away. I felt the halter rope, rough between my little palms, and gripped it tighter. Then came a bang. The rope pulled tight, and I was gone—the calf bolting across the farmyard, with me in tow. I tried to run, my little legs motoring over the ground, but the pull of the rope was too swift, and soon I was on my face, the calf dragging me across the gravel and dirt. When my dad caught us, I was scraped and dirty and distraught. My hands were burned raw from refusing to let go of the rope. But even at age four it wasn't the harrowing experience, or the pain, that made me most upset. My shoe, I cried out in anger, had come untied.

My sister, Malia, had more love for animals, and wouldn't have worn shoes if my parents hadn't made her. In fact, she proved that— and so much more—when she was just two years old. It was winter, and my parents were milking cows together in the barn. They had managed to work outside while I was a baby, listening on an intercom next to the old barn radio so that one of them could run up to the house when I woke up. When Malia came along, they tried the same, hoping we'd both stay in the house, with my sister in her crib until their work was done. The air outside the barn was cold, and they could see the snow on the ground outside as they strode back and forth from cow to cow. Then, on one trip across the driveway from one cow to another, they looked out the barn door and saw my sister, somehow out of her crib, toddling in her diaper, on the snow-covered ground outside to join them for milking.

This was my sister and I from the start—a difference not only in how we reacted to the farm, but in the sense of expectation that farmland tradition placed upon us. For as long as I can remember, I had the sense that I was supposed to do as my father had. Perhaps some of it was instinctive as the eldest son, learning over the years what each eldest son did before me. However, it was also there in the way my dad directed my work—not always patient in the way he was with others, wanting me to anticipate what needed to be done next, hoping I'd understand. It was there, too, in the way my grandparents and the old timers around town talked.

"Now you got a son," Grandpa Albert said to my dad. "Now you got somebody to take over the farm."

My sister, four years younger, remembers seeing my dad directing me, relying on me, day after day, as she longed to be part of the farm in the same way we were. She was welcome in the barn, but not always required in her younger years. It was in these subtle but clear differences that my sister and I would both struggle, as farms like ours fell into greater peril—me emerging as a son facing an expectation I wasn't sure I could meet; Malia as a daughter without the same expectation even though she'd grow to want nothing more.

There were innocent times, before the weight of tradition set in on us both: the little red wagon we would use to haul hay bales and pails of milk to the calves, one of us pulling the wagon, the other steadying the load to prevent the disaster of overturned cargo too heavy to reload ourselves; times we'd scuttle into the calf hutches to shoo the calves into the sunlight so we could feed them without getting pinned against the wall as they frolicked; hours of rumbling over rolling fields in the tractor with our dad, Malia taking what had been my spot on the armrest at my dad's side, and me hanging on to the back of his seat; those hot summer days of making hay, now with hay wagons carrying a jumbled heap of bales that shot one by one out of the baler automatically, like a farmland cannon. We'd climb to the top of the pile and ride the highest bales down to the wooden floor so our dad could hoist them off the wagon on their journey to the haymow.

Malia found a fearless joy in animals: at age three, she ran toward a family of rabid racoons hiding and hissing by our dad's silos in the early morning. "Kitties, Daddy, kitties!" By the time she was four, she had her own pet cow. I found my joys not in the barn, but in the adventure of growing up in the country. Tying a rope in the rafters of the haymow to swing through the dusty darkness, escaping to Old West hideouts in the woods. I carried a pocketknife my dad let me have at the age of eight, with more wonder than I've had in any inanimate object since.

We had glimpses, too, of days gone by—clues to how our way of life was different. Grandpa Albert wore overalls every day of his life, absent the occasional Sunday gathering special enough for Grandma Ann to make him put on a pair of pants and suspenders. He would sit in his dim living room in town, pouring cheap beer into a glass and sipping it while I sat on his workshoes and we watched game shows. His siblings would visit—Herman with the prosthetic leg, or Sister Bede smiling in her black-and-white nun's habit—and talk about the olden days. Sometimes when we were alone, Grandpa Albert was wistful, talking about his stern upbringing, telling me there ought to be more love in the world than he felt in his life before we came along. Other times he was jovial, calling me "Smart Eagle Bird" when I'd guess an answer on the TV.

"You're going to fly over top of all of us," he'd say, his hand leaving his beer for a moment in quiet flight. "Way, way up here, Eagle Bird." Now and then he let me have a sip of beer, if he was sure nobody was there to give him hell.

While Grandpa sat and reflected, Grandma Ann never stopped moving—quilting and sewing and banging around in the kitchen. She loved to bake with my sister and make sure everyone was fed. Now and then she'd yell for Grandpa to go down in the basement to grab some canned goods for a meal she was making or for our parents to take home when they picked us up. Grandma had shelves upon shelves of canned goods—tomatoes to peaches to pickles—stowed away for hard days she had no doubt could return.

She enjoyed few forms of relaxation. One was to join us in the evening when *Wheel of Fortune* came on. Another was to play cards with me and my sister. She argued about the rules and laughed when we beat her and let us drink more pop in one day than she'd allowed our dad in all his childhood. But she never once let us think life was easy. Grandma Ann kept score for every card game, scratching her tallies on a spare piece of paper. She played for keeps because she knew the world would do the same.

"I'm not gonna let you win," she'd say. "What good would that do?"

I got glimpses of days gone by with my dad, too. On fog-laced mornings, back in the cup of woods where Grandpa Albert had pastured cows behind our farmhouse. When the bellowing calves I had to help feed and the busted machinery my dad had to patch could wait, he'd take me hunting for squirrel and rabbit—just as he'd done to clear his head as a young man and to bring home meat in those first spare years on the farm with his new bride. These were warm days of boyhood, long before I was old enough to carry a gun or understand the harm the world could do. In those days my dad was so tall and sure to me, passing over his land in a pair of worn work shoes like a giant ambling over the earth. He had the time to teach and was patient, such that if I stumbled and fell headlong into the leaves, he would turn and hold a finger to his smiling face to remind me again to be quiet. There was nothing, not even his stature, that could dwarf the size of those woods or the place our farm held in the world.

Yet, as each year passed, I grew not only in my love for our way of life but also in my frustration at falling short. Reading more books by the day and imagining how things could be—from daring exploits in the fields and woods, to visions of how I'd do things once I was my own boss—came much easier than tending animals or running machinery. While Malia won over her testy pet cow, I had one slam my wiry frame into a cement wall. The experience made me wary of walking in front of them, but there was little choice; feeding the cows before milking was my job. Another time when I was ten years old, my dad stationed me in the haymow while we made hay to push the haybales off a series of elevators—one conveyor that carried them from the ground up to the little window at the top of the barn and another that ferried them to the place we wanted them in the hay-mow. The work progressed until I was pushing the bales off the second elevator at the right time pretty easily, and could turn to the book I'd brought with me to get my mind off the monotony and heat. I was immersed in a far-off place when I heard the elevator rattling and my parents yelling. The hay bales were bottlenecked and falling in all directions, even backward out the barn window to the farmyard thirty feet below.

I was luckier than some who grew up like I did. My dad wouldn't hit me if I broke a piece of machinery nor would he have too much to drink if life became too difficult. I felt the impact of each of our shortcomings in other ways. From early on, he came running when we had bad dreams or fell in the farmyard, and he always told us he loved us. But as I got older and our conversations turned from fun and laughter to tasks and trouble, a distance built. I could see, by his hurried hand motions and the strain in his eyes, how it weighed on him that farming did not come to me as naturally as it did him.

But he could see my heart wasn't in the work—going all the way back to my reading in the haymow—no matter how hard I tried. Over time, my dad simply said less to me. He was proud of me doing well in school, but soon enough I was learning subjects he never did, leaving us even less to talk about. There wasn't much room for me alongside my dad's endless work. I'd see him talk happily to hired men over the years in a way he didn't with me, and I'd get mad. Then, after arguing or yelling, I'd feel guilty for being angry. My mom did the best she could to shield me—encouraging me to think about college and to keep working with my dad, never seeing the two things as at odds.

"To really know your dad, you have to work with him," she said.

We each tried to show our devotion. We negotiated a wage for me as early as third grade, and for years I rose early to help before school. My dad taught me how to drive a skid-steer (a small piece of machinery with a big loader bucket out front that could turn on a dime) so I could load and mix feed for him. We continued to hunt together—squirrel in the early fall, deer in the November snow. But too often I found myself thinking of the failures over the successes—the shed I accidentally rammed with the tractor instead of the new machinery I could run, the deer I missed with him watching instead of the ones I brought home.

Finding myself falling short on the farm but doing well in class, I turned more toward reading, friends, and school. I had learned over the years to compensate for my small stature with my mind, quickly learning all I could, quoting from movies and cracking jokes, telling stories with the flare I'd learned from books. I was adapting socially to make sure I wasn't ignored in the world like I was at home.

Malia found her own way, too. The unruliness that led her to the barn at an early age also led her to rebel young against my parents, and she spent more time on her own as she got older—playing with the animals, drawing alone in her room. She was taller than me by the time I was in middle school, and the standard bickering between siblings was made worse by people mistaking her for being older than me, or my dad complimenting her for "being a trooper" on the farm in ways he never told me. I picked on her to make myself feel bigger. My desire to fit in led me to sports, though I struggled. First was wrestling, where my slim and lanky build left me weaker than stockier competitors, losing for years before finally achieving a winning record in high school. Long distance running on the cross-country team—discovered when my wrestling coaches saw me outlasting stronger competitors in the third period—was where I had more talent. I trained on the steep hills that had defined our family's plight and came to understand what a little determination could do. What I failed to see was my dad's contribution to those lessons, living like he did.

The desire to please him persisted, even as I found my own way. When I was old enough, my dad signed me up for tractor safety, so I could drive tractor on the highway before I got my regular driver's license. We took weeks of evening classes together. Finally, I was reading about something he valued, and we talked endlessly—the way tractors and other machinery functioned, the dangers of our work, ways we could save life and limb. On the big day, I aced the written test, but struggled with the final phase of the drive test. I was too short to keep my foot on the clutch and see behind me at the same time as I backed up a wagon. I got nervous and frustrated, trying over and over to pull the tractor ahead, line up the wagon, and then ease it back into the parking space. Finally, the instructor called it quits. There were no stretches of highway separating our farm, so I could still drive tractor in our farmyard and fields. But I had failed, and we never talked about it. There was little good to say.

There would be more failures—and more things left unsaid—as our family hurtled through a world swallowing up farms like ours. The dream turned more and more toward the sense that something was wrong—the fear beneath the beauty.

***

Men and women like my parents experienced the 1990s feeling an odd disquiet. During the good years, farmers could put money away to guard against the bad years, or invest in their operations with extra cash or new debt. During the bad years, there was a growing sense not just of a rougher patch but also of the feeling that farms of a certain size just couldn't make it anymore. Our farm was one of those putting away money when we could; in the good years, those taking out debt surpassed us, and in the bad years, they went broke trying to pay it off. Meanwhile, we persisted, life slowly getting harder in a world leaving us behind. Farming was becoming impossible for many, just beneath the surface of success.

The surge toward free trade offered both boom and bust. Stephanie Mercier worked for years as a top advisor in the Senate during the negotiation of major trade deals. Now an economist and rural policy historian working with the Farm Journal Foundation, she saw first-hand in those formative years the strategy and hours put into opening new markets to American farmers. While there were big trade deals in prior decades—such as President Nixon's grain deal with the Soviet Union—Mercier said the United States had largely assumed the ability to sell American surpluses overseas. In the nineties, it became a broader economic and geopolitical strategy to improve American prosperity. This meant higher prices as American supply was met with greater demand for decades on end.[115] The opportunity gave groups advocating for farms and many farmers themselves reason to be supporters of free trade—then and now.

"More open markets is always something that farmers like," Mercier said. But there were trade-offs. While both political parties embraced free trade, Mercier said, organized labor warned that big trade deals gave advantages to countries that could produce more cheaply in part by casting aside workers' rights. For farmers, opening foreign markets to American goods also meant opening American markets to foreign goods, which brought more goods into the United States and at times brought down the price American farmers could get for tomatoes, beef, or any number of other products.[116] Farmers were competing with countries that had lower labor standards and lower costs. Many economists—including those arguing free trade remains worth it—acknowledge that global trade also favors some farms over others. Large farms can keep up with ever-bigger food processors, as our agriculture and food industries strive to keep up with global demand under massive trade deals.

On top of those trade-offs, there is always the possibility of a large foreign trading partner becoming an adversary—meaning that just when Americans depend upon another country the most, its leaders can begin to take advantage of us. That was a threat that would take root long before it was too late to stop.

Meanwhile, the global marketplace combined with additional industry pressures to completely transform America's food system. Navigating the demands of large worldwide markets drove an even larger and more sophisticated supply chain, contributing to further consolidation in our agriculture and food industries, as with the rest of the American economy. Those industries supplying farmers with materials they needed for production, and those buying farm products to fuel the broader food economy, would consolidate from the 1990s through the 2010s.[117] By 2020, over a dozen of the major industries supplying or buying goods in our food economy had consolidated to the point of having a few major players left standing.[118]

The shift put the ongoing American debate over "how big is too big" on steroids. Industry advocates point out this consolidation is not unique to America's food and agriculture industries—it happened all across the American economy, meaning they were responding both to the global and domestic demands for food, and economy-wide pressures that had most industries growing and consolidating. Even more efficient companies were offering even cheaper and more miraculous products, from more resilient and specialized seed for farmers, to every imaginable new food for consumers, they argue. And yet, critics note, fewer companies eventually face less competition to influence their prices and service in the marketplace. Eventually, farmers were simply finding fewer places to buy from and sell to, and taking whatever price they got. Mary Hendrickson—an associate professor of food systems at the University of Missouri who has painstakingly assembled the levels of consolidation all across our food system—calls this *constrained choices*. And farmers became less able to make changes in their operations to create efficiencies—say, cutting costs—because modern farming required less adjustable costs like labor and more "intermediate costs" like chemicals and energy, where they had no control over prices.[119] Such forces leave farmers with less market power than others they do business with, Hendrickson said, buying what they need to produce at higher prices and selling their products for lower prices.

"Am I against big?" she said. "Not necessarily. I'm against the explicit use of power."

Farms had long guarded against this by joining co-ops, where they could band together to buy goods and services and market their products. But the challenges were growing, and even large farms were often the little guy. Supporters of free enterprise continued to point to low prices and more products lining the stacked and varied grocery store aisles. Critics raised a wide range of concerns, from food that is overly processed and less healthy, to environmental risks like contamination and pollution of air and water, as larger companies became responsible for more of our food production. Eventually, concerns from across the political spectrum, including from free-market advocates who saw competition waning, would emerge. But in the 1990s the problem was pushed aside. The opportunities and demands of both free trade and consolidated American industry combined now with the forces affecting farms from past decades, to drive the partially concealed consolidation of the nineties.

My dad navigated these years fighting to hold on and questioning whether his children deserved his fate. In 1992 he bought 220 acres next to our valley from an Illinois businessman, taking the rare step of debt owed to someone outside the family, under a land contract to pay the seller off gradually. The acreage meant we could produce more crops with equipment we already had and bring a dormant farm once run by my dad's aunt and uncle back in the family. The Reisinger farm was now three farms once run by separate family members, totaling nearly six hundred acres. And yet, even as my dad doubled down, he struggled with the idea that it was all for naught. He began to think about other ways to make a better living, and whether his children deserved more opportunity. At one point Grandpa Roman Ripp—my grandpa on my mom's side, who had become a successful businessman after growing up on a farm himself—was involved in the construction of a small hotel in their hometown. He asked my parents to get involved. Thinking in part that it would be a good way to have income off the farm, like so many farmers were doing with side businesses or second jobs, they mustered what money they could to put toward a minority stake in my grandpa's family business in 1996. It was money that might have otherwise gone toward the milking parlor my dad had been considering for years, as other farms expanded their dairy herds to keep up with a changing world.

Once, standing below the barn in the afternoon sun, my dad mentioned Grandpa Albert wanting to be a priest and wondered aloud if he himself ought to have been a truck driver. He'd have loved to see the country on the open road. But they both had to take over farming, he said, and he loved the work and being his own boss. I see now, years later, he was wrestling with the choice he'd worked to give me. Trying to offer his blessing for whatever I might do, without saying out loud that I might not farm. But all I heard then was his commitment to the work I struggled with. The sun descended toward the tree line, and we walked to the house in silence.

Our family saw the changing industry—and a deepening debate that would even pit farmers against one another—from my dad's pickup. Rolling over the winding roads rising and falling with the hills of southern Wisconsin, we'd drive through farmland changing before our eyes. Midsized farms like ours or smaller, once operating independently, were now newly marked with the roadside sign of a bigger local farm buying up yet another neighbor. Others were already claimed by past eras of decline, their barns fading from bright red or white to the neutral gray of wood aged by wind and rain. Some others were still in operation and taking out debt to build milking parlors—be they sleek metal buildings or converted wooden barns—to take on a few hundred animals or more. Some others still tried their hand at cash cropping after selling their cows or leased their land to other farmers working their fields. Here and there were small farms looking for a niche, some run by local families, others by people from Chicago or the Twin Cities trying to escape city life.

"That was a nice farm," he'd say about one farm or another. "Now what's gonna happen?"

Now and then my dad would raise a finger off the steering wheel in greeting to an oncoming pickup, sometimes whether the driver was familiar or not, whether the driver was a farmer operating a farm like ours—or one bigger or smaller—or had lost everything. There was no separating the owners of the large farms from those midsized, small, or dormant. Sometimes we'd season the conversation with complaints of massive farms in far-off lands—especially California, which overtook Wisconsin in milk production in these years,[120] and went on to call itself home of the "happy cows" to both acclaim and controversy.[121] But we knew there was more to it than just blaming someone who was thriving while we struggled, even if we couldn't say what.

Now and then we'd see one of those weathered gray barns had blown over, just like Great-Grandpa Alois's had when I was a little boy—a toppled heap of busted lumber where once a family's livelihood stood.

***

I stared at the ground while Ed fed the hose into the gas tank. It was 1999, and I was fourteen years old, and I'd done something I should have known better not to do: Rushing to finish chores on a cold winter day, I'd swung my dad's skid-steer up to the gas tanks on our farm and filled it up with unleaded gasoline instead of diesel fuel. Now Ed was left trying to siphon the gasoline out of the tank, sucking on the end of a plastic hose, hoping he could draw it out without getting it in his mouth. I had known him for years. A tall, wise-cracking mechanic who grew up on a nearby farm and milked cows for extra money on the rare day my dad would take off. But this was the first time I was embarrassed in front of him. He was here to milk each morning and night, and I was supposed to help him while my dad was sick, and now this. The plastic hose filled, and Ed jerked his head away and spat gasoline on the frigid concrete.

My dad is sick, I thought. With what exactly, and for how long, I wouldn't know until our family talked about it years later. But I knew he'd had surgery and that I had to do everything I'd done working with him and more. Ed was here to milk, like the men who'd come to milk when Grandpa Albert had broken his back, and like them he had a family and work of his own. I was here, like my father had been for his—except there was a mismatch as Ed and I stood there, our warm breaths rising in the frozen air. Although I was older than my dad when he stepped up, I was uneasy taking on this responsibility after years of struggling to become the farmer he had—years of carrying pails heavier than they ought to have been, years of animals less trusting of me than him, years of more than my share of tractor mishaps and broken machinery. So many things I might have known if I'd been a little better, tried a little harder, paid a little more attention when my dad was healthy. Like how you don't run gasoline through a diesel engine.

Fuck, I thought. *You should know better than that.*

"I'm sorry," I said.

"Well." Ed smiled, the gasoline draining from the hose. "I bet you won't do that again."

There are many things from that winter I would not do again. But stepping forward when my dad needed me is not one of them; I was grateful then, and am grateful now, that I could help. I rose each morning before the sun without fail. I prepared the cows and equipment for milking, cleaned their udders for Ed, and milked when I got far enough ahead. Then I'd do all the other chores, feeding the livestock, cleaning the barn—leaping from tractor to skid-steer and back for one job after another until the work was done. Then I was back at it in the evening, with school in between.

Each morning when chores were done, I'd walk up the hill toward the farmhouse, watching the sun already risen, climbing higher now over the barren winter fields, and wonder if today would be the day my dad would come back to work. There were meals dropped off by local families and prayers for him in church and on phone prayer chains ringing from one household to the next, and other families telling me how important my work was. But my dad remained sick. And the cows kept mooing for feed, and the calves kept bellering for milk, and the tractor kept roaring, and I did my work and took a breath each morning, watching that sun, hoping, and waiting.

And then one day my dad was back—tall and sure and ready to work, but different. For years, he ran from one job to the next, bounding up the hill to the machine shed, leaping in and out of the tractor in the farmyard and the fields. Now he walked steadily and deliberately, but slower than before. I kept working with him, doing much of what I'd done with Ed, my dad taking on some of the tasks and accomplishing even more as we worked full-time alongside one another. I knew he wondered, with all I'd done, whether I would take over the farm. That flame of hope, lit fourteen years before when they

140

first got the call their adopted baby was a boy, dampened over the years as I grew up, was now rekindled and dancing in the back of his mind—not quite out in the open, not yet spoken of, but there again.

One evening, I was milking with my dad when my Grandpa Ripp walked into the barn. Grandpa Albert was too frail by then to make the trip to the barn often, but my mom's dad grew up in the Depression just like him and talked often of the farm his family lost. Standing there with my dad, he began to wonder aloud about my future. Maybe I would take over the farm, working like I had, or help run the hotel, seeing how good I was becoming with people. As I strode from one side of the driveway to the other, moving to clean the next cow, I heard him say what my dad wouldn't.

"Look at him go, Jim," he said. "He saves you a lot of steps, boy."

"I know it."

I could hear in my dad's voice that hope—for the first time since he caught me reading as a kid in the haymow—that maybe his son would take over the farm someday after all. I smiled to myself, the compliment hot on my cheeks, then felt it fade. Leaning there against the milking cart, my grandpa and dad wondering what my future held, I stayed quiet. I could not bear to tell them I already knew it would not be on the farm.

CHAPTER 8

THE CENTURY OF RECESSIONS

Losing Our Way in the Wake of the Great Recession and Beyond

One January 5, 2010, under the glowing dark blue sky signaling the earliest moments of dawn, I finished packing my car and drove out of the farmyard. My car held all I had: clothes and books and posters from my college days, all crammed in the trunk and piled high in the backseat, so full it blocked out the windows and rearview so that all I could see was the road ahead. I told myself that suited me just fine, headed where I was. Yet, as the car began to roll, it had the effect of making things disappear as I went. The sensation of it settled—gentle, but persistent—over my mind and upon my shoulders and down into my chest, as I pulled out of the farmyard with a kind of finality I had never felt before. I drove slowly at first, over the snow and gravel crunching and popping beneath the tires, past the tall red barn where I'd learned to work, past the white farmhouse on one side and my dad's shop on the other, then out onto the paved backroad. As I made my way down the hill, I picked up speed, tracing the curving downhill I knew so well toward the county highway.

With speed came the excitement of my journey, but I couldn't shake that feeling of something final as I went. It was early enough still that few people were awake, outside of my family and those few neighbors who still farmed. The further I got from them, the more I felt like not only the only person awake but also the only person alive—alone, traversing the snow-covered earth from my home to my future with nobody to join me in my journey. I said a prayer for home and accepted then that I was on my own. I sped along the curving county highway, to the long straight road where American flags adorned the power poles and snapped in the roadside winter wind as the sun came up, to the loping state highways until, finally, the highways filled with other vehicles. I hit the Interstate and was on my way.

I was bound for Nashville, Tennessee. Although the feeling of finality lingered, its warning faded all too soon. Before long, I was singing old country music with the windows down and the heat on blast, punching the gas harder any time the roads were clear, and picturing how life would be in a city like Nashville, a place where thousands of people my age were flocking, and where my career as a twenty-four-year-old journalist was ready to burst forth after surviving two years of layoffs in the Great Recession. Despite its big city trappings, there was a history—as the home of country music—that I thought sure would keep me grounded in my roots no matter how far away I was. You couldn't have told me I was going to lose touch—that I was leaving behind something that would never be the same, even though I knew damn well by then what was happening to farms like ours.

No warnings would have gotten through to me because of what I was trying to leave behind: those times of failing my dad. I wanted to escape the distance that arose between us, the growing guilt that too often came out as reckless abandon or anger, and, most of all, a moment I was so ashamed of it would take me years to face it. I didn't want to look in the rearview mirror because that moment was there, looming nearly seven years back in the frozen farmland behind me, and awaiting me if I had looked myself in the eye in the rearview mirror. It was too terrible of a thing to stare in the face, so I didn't. Much better to look forward, with the sky clear over the howling Interstate as I hurtled south, and think about the life I was headed toward instead of the home I was leaving behind. But looking away wouldn't work. The problem with leaving home behind is that it's not just a place you come from—it is who you are and with you wherever you're going. Turning from it makes it far too easy to lose your way.

***

The two recessions that defined the early 2000s in the years before I left home—the brief recession of the 9/11 era and the deeper Great Recession of 2007 to 2009—dealt a secret blow to the American family farm, far different from the rest of the country's hardship. It was not a crisis of a collapsing industry, although farmers faced their share of economic devastation, but of deep disorientation that would knock American agriculture off course at a crucial turning point. Family farms began the twenty-first century fighting for a brighter future after decades of economic crisis, demographic shifts, technological change, the opportunities and threats of a bigger global economy, and other forces that had created the disappearing American farmer. A new path forward, one that could help them rise above the decades of disappearance, was within their grasp until the two recessions in the first decade of the 2000s hit. The result was initial economic shock, a frenzied recovery, and a fateful shift—away from an industry trend of family farms creating specialty foods, which could have saved many farms if it hadn't fallen by the wayside. American agriculture lost its way, just as it was finding a new path forward.

Both recessions led to initial economic shocks that put farmers in a dangerous position. Those who depended upon off-farm income, a larger number now in the era of small farms only partially supporting families,[122] faced layoffs and pay cuts in the recession years. Meantime, direct threats to income on the farm—from those selling grains to those selling vegetables, beef, milk, or any other number of agricultural commodities—came and went like crosswinds on an already dangerous road.

One clear measure of price drops in this era is the prices received ratio, which tracks the prices farmers receive compared to a base price the government sets. That base is used to make decisions about government policy, but the ratio is also one of the more complete measures of price changes over time.

The brief recession in 2001 came when prices paid to farmers for their goods were already low, and stunted a climb that had begun prior to 9/11.[123] The Great Recession brought another tumble. Throughout 2007 and 2008, prices for agricultural commodities climbed from the mid-seventies (which means 70 percent of the base price targeted for that year) to the mid-nineties, nearly reaching the 100 percent level farms can only hope for each year. Then the deepening of the Great Recession in the fall of 2008—the same quake that sent shockwaves through the country's housing market—took commodity prices down into the 70 to low 80 percent range for much of the next year.[124]

Those prices came as both farmers and consumers weathered the worst nationwide economic downturn since the Great Depression. Starting first with the tanking of the housing market that had been rising for decades,[125] the financial vulnerability of the Great Recession ripped through the rural and urban economy alike: making homeowners suddenly unable to afford their mortgages, leaving lenders struggling to stay afloat, crashing into industries affected by the drops in consumer demand or availability of loans, driving unemployment to a peak of 10 percent, and creating the longest economic downturn in over half a century.[126] Farmers faced faltering off-farm income, with the hard-hit sectors of manufacturing and construction accounting for 29 percent of off-farm income in 2007.[127] Any farmers with debt were also at greater risk of getting in trouble, with struggling lenders looking to clean up their books. Both the number of farmers struggling with debt and losses to agricultural lenders increased in 2008 and 2009.[128] Then there was the risk to any farm family that happened to have a mortgage on a home or an investment account they'd squirrelled away for retirement.

However, the falling income and rising bad debt weren't as dramatic for farmers as for the rest of the public. The falling prices that followed the economic devastation of the day were simply initial shocks. What came next was a furious recovery that both got American agriculture back on its feet and led it astray. The stronger prices—which returned by fall of 2010 or earlier for many farmers[129]—were driven in part by increasing demand for American crops and products abroad. That demand came especially through exports to China, which skyrocketed 200 percent from 2007 to 2012, reaching nearly $30 billion.[130]

That's the threat we didn't see, focused as we were on recovering prices. In the 1990s, prior to the years of recession, American agriculture had begun to deepen its focus on what's called *value-add products* used in our food industry, said Jason Henderson, an agricultural economist who serves as vice president for extension and outreach at Iowa State University. Value-add products are the variation of corn used in corn tortillas, the premium eggs or meat worth the extra money to the consumer, or the milk going toward the growing array of American specialty cheeses—niche products produced by small and midsized farms and businesses, sometimes setting their own prices in regional markets, as opposed to the usual bulk products sold on the global commodity markets. However, when the recession years hit, Henderson and other experts who've studied the era agree that America lost track of value-add agriculture. While the niche didn't completely disappear, what could have been a healthy balance between bulk commodities and specialty products took a hard turn toward bulk commodities, in a frantic effort to meet global demand and keep prices high in the wake of economic recession.

"Through the 2000s, there was so much income and support coming from the commodity-based side," Henderson said. "Those niche market opportunities slowed down."

The rebellion against bulk commodity dominance unfolded just down the road from our farm, at the cheese factory that bought our family's milk. Bob Wills, the owner of Cedar Grove Cheese factory—just a short stretch from where Great-Grandpa Alois worked when he came to America—was mainly selling Colby cheese in the early 1990s, generally to a small number of large customers. He was destined to learn firsthand how depending upon large amounts of just a few products could devastate businesses like his, and the small and midsized farms where he bought milk.

The lesson luckily came years before the Great Recession, when a large customer dropped him. The little cheese factory, with the blue walls and the busy workers making cheese by hand with stainless steel equipment, now had boxes of cheese stacked to the ceiling. With production costs and cheese towering overhead, Bob hit the road, calling all over the state. He had to find a way to unload his cheese and make something else that someone would buy. His livelihood, as well as that of his employees and area farm families, depended upon it.

"Panic was setting in," Bob recalled years later.

What he discovered changed his business and could have saved more farms like ours if the broader food industry had taken heed. Bob's frantic search landed on a food company that needed a special soft cheese used in holiday gift boxes—if Bob would make that cheese, the buyer would purchase his inventory and sign a new contract with him. The cheese was the first of dozens of specialty products (value-add, in economic terms) Cedar Grove would churn out in the decades to come: organic and hormone-free cheeses, an obscure form of Brazilian grilling cheese now popular at tailgate parties, specialty variations of classic cheeses blossoming in new directions, and more. Bob felt it was fitting for Cedar Grove to build an innovative niche. The prior owner had fronted the money for local farmers to install bulk tanks in their milkhouses to cool milk more efficiently, because he knew they'd be better suppliers.

Along the way, Bob found he could pay his farmers—like my parents—a little more for their milk. That gave them a better shot to feed their families, stay in business, and avoid the natural shift toward selling their land to build houses and retire comfortably, rather than risk losing everything one day. He wanted to save them from giving in to the pressures of becoming land rich, cash poor.

"One of my goals had been to help the farmers resist the development pressures," Bob said.

The problem was that too few in the industry were innovating in this way, especially during and after the two recessions of the early 2000s. If they had, it might have helped break the trap of owning land so valuable if you sell it, but harder to make a living on if you keep it. It was a world where farmers were price takers, both for the materials they bought and the goods they sold, rather than price makers, and couldn't make enough money on bulk commodities to turn a profit on the extremely valuable land they were sitting on. What many farmers were left with increasingly, as the industry got bigger and made it harder for more farms to make it, was the age-old cycle where they tried to produce more in good and bad years—the former to capitalize on the high price; the latter to make up for the low price by selling a higher volume. All this surplus of goods, of course, helps drive the price down, the adage of "farmers producing themselves out of prosperity" getting worse by the year. Many of the specialty-food makers who could help break the cycle, such as small cheese factories like Cedar Grove, faced the same pressures as farms—to get bigger or sell to bigger competitors, or risk one day not being able to make it.

Of course, there were still all the other reasons for farms to go by the wayside, built up over decades, plus the very first threat all farm families face: the physical danger and wear of the work. It was in this era of tighter margins and economic uncertainty that it all became too much for our family. My dad had wrestled with doubts throughout the nineties, cheering the good years and lamenting the bad ones that were tighter than they used to be. When he got sick the winter I stepped up, it pushed him over the edge. The doctors had originally gone in to fix digestive issues causing severe bleeding, but found cancer and undertook a fiercer operation. That health scare not only left me helping run the farm that winter of 1999 but also left my parents questioning whether the years of physical strain on the farm were too much.

In summer of 2001, during the first of that decade's two recessions, they decided to sell the cows. We talked as a family about the tough economics of making a living on such a small farm, my dad's health, and how we could turn more attention to our family's other small business. After a string of setbacks at the little hotel, my mom was now working as manager, and my dad was helping as handyman, sometimes pulling the night shift before going home for morning milking. The more I heard about those reasons for selling the cows, the more I felt that maybe it wasn't because of the fears—my parents' and my own—that I would never take over. My dad would still work the farm on the side, raising beef cattle that required less attention and doing the fieldwork to sell his crops, while our family ran the hotel. We'd have a new start.

We never could have predicted what would happen next, although we should've known the farm without milk cows wouldn't be enough then—for my dad emotionally or the farm financially. For nearly two years my dad wandered the farm and worked with my mom at the hotel. He was quiet, but not in the work-driven way of years past. It was a deflated quiet, hiding beneath the brim of his cap as he fed his cattle and worked his fields when he could. He was no longer a farmer, he felt, but a replaceable hotel maintenance man who puttered with a few cattle at home. I didn't understand what he was going through and told myself he'd come out of it. With the milk cows that required hard labor every morning and night gone, and the farm being one of two family businesses, I felt freer to follow my own path. I knew my family had doubts about a writing career, from their questions about how someone could make a living doing such a foreign thing. I decided it was time to prove everyone wrong.

There were few signs, outside of my dad's depression, that going back to milking was the thing to do. The milk price had fluctuated for years. The recession of 2001 followed by the broader uncertainty after the terrorist attacks of September 11 did little to calm our fears for the future. We knew the march toward farms getting bigger to survive was continuing, even if we didn't know all the reasons that had developed over the decades. We also didn't know how much worse it was going to get. While economists of many stripes argue worldwide commodity sales are needed for growth, they also say it needs to be balanced alongside the specialty foods and products America could have embraced. The bulk commodities farms like ours were depending upon could only take prices so high, and they would favor larger farms with greater scale as world demand grew.

That's when our family doubled down.

***

I'll never forget that white tablecloth. The moment of shame I wanted to leave behind when I headed for Nashville years later would stay with me because of that tablecloth. It was rare for our family to sit at such a table, so smooth and bright with cloth napkins to match and the multiple forks and spoons of a formal table setting. Yet, it was all the more striking for how I would become lost upon its sheer white surface. Stumbling wounded, sullying it with my anger, looking for answers in the void.

It was spring of 2003, and my parents had brought us here to talk about the farm and its future. I was eighteen. After graduation in a few weeks, I planned to study journalism and political science at the University of Wisconsin-Eau Claire. I had hoped my dad would see that what we'd all agreed upon, about the future of the farm and the other ways we'd make a living now, was true. It had freed me of so many things I'd struggled to live up to and let me work at the hotel, where I learned to talk to people from across the country. I looked forward to college without feeling like I'd let anyone down.

Malia was fourteen. Opposite from me in so many ways then, she was tall for her age and had played on a traveling basketball team that would put her on a fast track to play varsity as a freshman that fall. Up until then, Malia was unsure of what she wanted to do—in the way most teenagers are—while I followed my new path and my dad wrestled with how to farm without a successor.

Then everything changed over that fine white tablecloth. My dad said he and Malia had talked and were planning to get back into milking. My parents were going to take some of the money left over from the sale of the cows less than two years earlier, to buy back part of a herd and combine it with some of the heifers we still had. They were going to build a new herd together. I asked why, and what was different from when he decided a few years ago—because of his health and the way farming was going and the things we'd found instead—that it was time to move on from milking.

I could feel myself getting mad, arguments of logic rising atop a deep mass of emotional illogic boiling inside of me. My dad tried to explain how he missed milking. I countered that all the reasons we'd sold were still true. He said Malia was interested in it. I told my sister she'd better be ready for the long haul if Dad was going to depend upon her enough to buy the cows back. At that point, I realized I was yelling. I was angrier than I should have been, for more reasons than my family—or I, at the time—understood. I was shocked and torn and drifting, everything on that bright white table before me blinding and deafening like the moment after a gunshot. My dad tried again to explain, but I stood and walked out.

The best I could describe it then was I felt "like the rug has been pulled out from under me." What I didn't say was the question that rose in my mind, beneath the anger: *If my dad sold when I was a teenager, and bought them back when Malia came along, didn't that mean he'd sold them because of me? I wasn't good enough.*

The idea was like a swarm of locusts invading a field—the first thought or two coming in like the early insects flying on a curious wind, followed soon enough by the swarm bursting upon the earth. Before long, the swarm was so strong it had overtaken the green field of my mind where my love of family resided. All the times my dad felt conflicted about whether his kids should farm, all the times he encouraged me in school, all the times we talked about the tough economics of farming, all the times we considered the promise of running the small business of the hotel instead, and all the worries over his once-failing health—all real things that had driven the decision, covered over like the sun blocked out by the swarm. Any whispers of truth were drowned out by the deafening hum of the invasive presence.

Life for my sister and I now followed two diverging paths. Meanwhile, Grandpa Albert had fallen and was struggling to recover from a nursing-home bed. Although we saw by his loving face that he recognized us, he said little. He survived until I went off to school in Eau Claire, dying within days of when the first eldest son in our family who didn't farm also became the first son in our family who went to college.

I was scared and struggled to find my way in the city, surrounded by people from so many places, but I loved my classes in literature, journalism, political science, and history. It was a world where arguing in class was rewarded. Eventually, I found my footing in the college party scene, learning to drink well enough in dorm-room pre-parties and basement keggers to at least keep up. I spent my few idle moments doing shots and beer bongs and laughing my fears and guilt away.

My first job writing—which I pitched to the editor of my mom's hometown newspaper, the *Waunakee Tribune*, after Grandpa Ripp introduced me—began summer after my freshman year, leading to a string of jobs at the student newspaper and increasingly bigger professional news outlets each summer. I drove around talking to people, learning about their worlds, and writing about what I found. Here, my wits and words, more so than my small stature and clumsy hands, were assets.

As I turned further away from the farmyard, my sister journeyed deeper into it. My dad and Malia started their days at four in the morning now, milking and working together every morning and night as three generations of Reisingers had done. They faced an early setback that first winter when Malia got sick. The first doctors couldn't explain her debilitating fatigue, headaches, and dizziness.

"There's nothing wrong with you," one local doctor said. I had never meant to doubt my sister's ability to farm, or the challenges she was facing now, but my questions about whether she understood the kind of commitment she was making, after the winter I worked while my dad was sick, left her feeling my skepticism. That, blended now with the mysterious sickness, made her feel the doubts of me and others even more deeply, including whether she was really sick. By the time doctors at Mayo Clinic in Rochester, Minnesota, figured out that it was a nervous system illness they could treat, Malia had quit basketball, a sport that had been her main source of confidence and direction.

Farming with our dad became her comeback. Stepping back into the barn, basketball behind her, Malia walked among the rows of cows and began to tell herself it was time to stop caring what people thought. There was something else waiting for her, in that warm golden light bathing the backs of the cows she'd loved all her life, that had never been there for me. As she progressed through high school, working with our dad each morning and night, they found they loved the work in the same ways. Although she never lost her independent streak, she'd also become more introverted, matching our dad's quiet workmanlike habits. Meanwhile, our dad had things he wanted to teach her. He'd already lost the chance to teach one child and would not let the distance build with another. Each morning, he walked into the barn to smile and check her coffee, determining whether she'd drank enough of it to want to chat. About halfway through milking they'd begin to talk, and he'd tell her his ways, more clearly than he had when I was coming along—of how to handle a jumpy cow, how to see if something was wrong with an animal, and what the weather meant for the workday to come.

And Malia showed him her own ways in return. Early on, they had a Jersey cow that couldn't see, nicknamed "Bat" for her blindness. Part of our dad would have been content to leave her in the barn with whatever humble feed was convenient, but Malia wouldn't have it. She led the blind cow out of the barn to the cow yard, where the other cows ate and roamed as they pleased. Bat, Malia decided, deserved the same. It became a ritual each day. There in the farmyard air, be it bright and clean under the sun or dim and hazy under clouds, Malia helped Bat to her food. Then she would leave her to eat and loaf, until it was time to lead her back into the warmth and safety of the big red barn the kindly cow couldn't even see.

Malia joined me to party at college, and those little kids pushing the red wagon together returned, in the joyous dark of those drunken nights. In between sneaking her into bars and laughing over dropped bottles of liquor, we became friends. She was smoking by then—a harsh brand that impressed even my partying friends—and I admired her for becoming her own person. She was rebelling against our parents, like me, but doing it on the opposite path. Rebelling, you might say, against me too. I realized we were the same. We were both trying, in our own ways, to prove the world wrong: me as a farm boy far from the Ivy League trying to make it as a writer, her as a young woman in a man's world taking on a burden I knew the weight of all too well. We began to see ourselves as living different but parallel lives over the years, and we started to root for each other. I became her biggest defender, and she became my link to a home I loved but just didn't think I fit into.

Our friendship blossomed just in time for life to move faster, and as my career began to take me further from home—to my first job a few hours north, and eventually to my next job in Nashville. Our mom's parents died in the summer of 2007, depriving me of Grandpa Ripp, my mentor, and Grandma Ripp, who was a great supporter of my education and writing. The loss left Grandma Ann, still leather tough and speaking her mind as she pleased, our only link to the generation that had farmed in the Depression. I took my first job after college at a daily newspaper on the cusp of the Wisconsin Northwoods, making enough to pay rent on my own. Drinking was by now my main activity in my free time. It mixed well with a love of old country music I'd stumbled upon when Johnny Cash turned up, singing about things I understood from home, alongside the protest music of Bob Dylan and Neil Young that friends introduced me to.

Malia was farming with my dad and thinking about how to keep doing it into the future. In summer of 2008, she learned she was pregnant. Our family rallied around her. Even Grandma Ann, who a generation earlier had such tough standards for our mom under the hot sun of the farmyard, was far more excited about the great-grand-child to come than she was worried about the surprise circumstances. Steven Albert Ederer-Reisinger—the fifth generation of farming Reisingers, named in part after Grandpa Albert, of the second generation—was born January 20, 2009.

My dad and I found tentative paths toward each other. There was pride in his voice when I turned down the money he offered me as the winter heating bill in my drafty apartment taxed my budget. I was working in a job that required me to understand all viewpoints of an issue; it helped me understand how my dad buying the cows back was only him doing what he loved, just like me. Once, he and my mom even came to the newsroom to visit me at my work. The Great Recession had deepened by then, leading to multiple rounds of layoffs across the community that I was lucky to have escaped, working as hard as I could to be worth every penny of my salary. Before long, I had a new assignment: traveling to farms and small businesses and factories and homeless shelters to tell the stories of the people surviving the economic collapse. As we walked the newsroom, phones ringing and the police scanner crackling, one of my editors paused to talk to us and made an offhand comment about my work ethic.

"You can tell he's a farm boy."

My throat hitched; it was the first time I'd felt close to my dad in years.

But it wasn't enough to withstand the economic hardship or my misfit feelings. As the recession continued to impact the local community where I worked, I took my cue to begin looking for jobs elsewhere. That's when I settled on Nashville, and the beliefs I carried with me on that momentous car ride south—that it was a place where a farm boy could remember his roots, where a young journalist could find work in a growing city, and where maybe a writer stuck between those two worlds could find his way.

***

While I drove off to Nashville to leave my farmland troubles behind, my family prepared to face theirs more deeply.

Their return to milking cows was not unlike my journey south. On one hand, the excitement of new possibilities propelled them just as it did me. My dad was healthy and diving back into the job he'd loved. And now he had one of his children at his side. On the other hand, they were fighting for a path forward in an industry deeply off course in the wake of the Great Recession. American agriculture was proud but battered—bruised by decades of upheaval.

The dependence on large foreign trading partners—again, something that was tied to positive economic opportunity, if balanced with domestic specialty products—was intensifying. With trade spread across so many countries, this wouldn't have had to be a serious problem. America after all had free-trade agreements covering twenty countries as of 2022,[131] holding the possibility for risk spread across diverse global economies facing different challenges at different times. However, there was another factor that would become a massive controversy and growing threat: the dependence, specifically, on China.

Midsized farms like ours continued to disappear, and small farms continued to struggle to support a family. What's more, farms like ours were increasingly becoming "small" rather than "midsized." Measuring this, in an era where it was harder to detect as the industry slowly shifted toward larger farms beneath the surface, is difficult. University of Maryland researcher Jim MacDonald and his colleagues developed one groundbreaking way—recognized even by economists with different views of the various causes of consolidation—by which one measures the midpoint size of farms. The examples are striking and plentiful. In 1987 the midpoint size of a farm raising wheat was 404 acres. By 2012, the midpoint size was 1,000 acres. The midpoint size of a herd of hogs and pigs went from 1,200 animals to forty thousand in the same period.[132]

The trends driving these changes meant our family's farm was on a path that was not sustainable economically, even with the burst of momentum that came with my dad and sister farming together. Some farms had years of record profits as recovering prices carried them forward from the initial shock of recession. But it wasn't always so for midsized and small farms like ours, operating on a scale where rising costs quickly ate up gains in income. The herd my dad and sister built up of around fifty cows would have been close to midsized at one time, but as farms and their midpoints grew, my family's herd was consistently on the smallest end of the spectrum. Our acreage was bigger than some of our neighbors, after my dad built it to six hundred acres. However, it was hard to make a living from crops alone, with so many states having more wide-open acreage than Wisconsin.

While these large economic forces pressed down, my parents' off-farm income wasn't panning out like they'd hoped. A series of unexpected challenges contributed to the hotel having a rough start, which was underway even before my parents got involved. As it would turn out, the hotel would largely fund my mom's salary as manager, about $38,000 per year, and was otherwise shaping up as an investment where they'd be lucky if they broke even. My family's time was now split and increasingly stretched to the limit, between a farm with even tighter profit margins and a side business that was struggling.

The structural changes now long underway and getting worse—for family farms and America's food supply—would require a much deeper rebirth of American agriculture, not just the recovery of the broader economy from the Great Recession. Unbelievably, despite those devastating forces piling atop one another not reaching an end point, we were still surviving.

***

For the more than five years I lived across the country, Grandma Ann wrote to me almost every month. Grandpa Albert had been dead for a decade. Dozens of letters, piling up in the desk drawer where I saved them—telling almost always of the weather, to make sure her farm boy in the city remembered its whims that had directed our family's course for generations. She also wrote about the goings on around town she thought I'd like to know: the latest fish fry, the faces she saw at the brat stand where she worked to keep busy, the most recent funeral of someone she knew. But the letters also spoke of my dad, of the fieldwork and changes on the farm. And, of course, she wrote about my sister, and little Steven, admiring Malia and wondering how she took on all she did. Sometimes her letters soothed, telling me of things I missed most. Other times, I felt I should be there, as she told me her fears of my dad working so hard, as she had of course taught him to do. Since moving to Nashville and traipsing around the country, my love of home had grown stronger. I had come to joke that I was a "fallen son of agriculture," expressing both my separation from, and unbreakable bond with, the heartland. I questioned each day whether I was meant to return home, or love home from a distance.

Honest as they were, there was much more to know beyond my grandma's cross-country letters. Malia had gone to cosmetology school after she had Steven, to build a skill for off-farm income while also continuing to work with our dad on the farm. My dad was getting older, in his sixties now, as the farm's margins continued to tighten. My grandma's letters were a lifeline to all this, as I struggled with being away from home and realized the strengths and vulnerabilities I'd inherited and carried with me, no matter where I went.

I began to understand one of the strengths first in the small newsrooms of Wisconsin, then in the booming streets of Nashville with construction cranes overhead and country music always blaring from the honky-tonks, then in the hallowed Capitol hallways where I

worked as a speechwriter and spokesman to a US senator while split-
ting my time between Tennessee and Washington, DC. I learned I
had a special ability. It was an ability handed down by Alois to Albert
to Jim to me: a farmer's work ethic.

Seeing that I shared my father's level of determination helped me
grow up, not to mention work my way off the night shift at my first
job after college. It's what allowed me to be on the scene when
Tennessee had its first bank failure in the wake of the Great Recession.
Driving there on a Friday tip from a source, I was almost to the bank
when a string of cops flipped on the blue and red lights behind me.
Realizing they were seizing the building for bank regulators, I
punched the gas and got to the parking lot before they did, scribbling
in my notebook as the authorities careened up to the bank doors. And
my father's determination is what got me to the world of public policy,
where my stories caught the attention of advisors to a biparti-
san-minded politician named Lamar Alexander, who liked to hire
aggressive reporters as press aides.

I had inherited vulnerabilities, too, some more obvious than others. I can't remember how many times I drank before work in my early
days. But I remember the first time: there in the dingy kitchen of my
Nashville apartment, stopping on my way out the back door, chest
thumping with stress and turmoil, seizing the refrigerator door and
slamming a beer. I never went to work drunk, but those moments
happened more than I'd like to think. Along with the all-night happy
hours several days a week, the weekend benders, and reckless behavior that so often comes with hard drinking. I told myself it was just to
take the edge off the stress, but it was only part of it. Drinking also
helped me avoid thinking about my guilt over not farming, and it
took me years to acknowledge that I'd developed a problem. Although
I straightened up some as my professional responsibilities grew, particularly after realizing the risks I was taking in DC, it was a problem
that persisted for over a decade, from my college days to my early

thirties. I'm lucky that I didn't slip further into it, allow any relation-ships to get destroyed, or let it hurt someone else or undo everything I was working toward in life.

Yet, even as I grew up and eventually cut down on the boozing, my life remained a wild one as I carried those things that had led me to drink in the first place. From my party days in Nashville to my life on the road between Washington, DC, and Tennessee—thriving on work and little else along the way—I often found myself walking a line between the world I grew up in and the faster one I'd found. It was a line I felt few others understood. I felt all I could do was keep on the move. It had all begun to take on the hue of so many of the country songs that seemed to be the only thing connecting my pres-ent with my past. My anthem at the time was Merle Haggard's "Ramblin' Fever" about sticking to the road no matter the cost in life. *If someone said I ever gave a damn, they damn sure told you wrong/I've had ramblin' fever all along.*

Then one night, I woke up not knowing where I was. It wasn't just that momentary lapse we all feel after an odd dream. Nor was I drunk. I'd begun to taper my partying by then in search of cleaner living. This was a deep confusion, one that kept me from remembering—for how long in the dark I couldn't tell—the basic contours of my life. Laying there in the pitch-black bedroom in Nashville that I'd forgot-ten was my own, I tried to sort the pieces of my life as the shifting ceiling came into focus. I was unmoored, a place a farm boy should never want to be. Until that point in my life, my roots had kept me very aware of where I was—either at the farm deciding where to go instead, or somewhere else with the farm as my reference point. Before, I was always a specific direction and number of miles and emotional distance away from home, wondering if I'd go back. I was lost.

Several months later, the feeling I'd had in the dark of that Nashville bedroom began to make sense. I had worked to sort it out, listening to the bands play at night in Nashville, walking among the Capitol Mall in DC, and traveling in between. Finally, clarity came as I was visiting Wisconsin, driving the final stretch home to meet my second nephew who had just been born. It was the same straight backroad I'd driven five years earlier on my way south, only now it was March of 2015, and the last of the winter's snow was melting and freshening the soil along the roadside. The wind was calm, the flags hung from the utility poles gently rolling as the sun set, and suddenly I knew then what I was feeling. It was time to come home.

CHAPTER 9

HOLDING ON

Surviving Economic Upheaval and Trade Wars, 2015–2020

The green alfalfa blew in the wind as the helicopter's turbines began to whir, the clover leaves exposing their undersides, lighter and softer and vulnerable. Gusts rolled faster over the field, and then all at once we were up, above it all. The field beneath us and the farm where I grew up and the hundreds of acres around it unfurled like a map over a table, only it was so quick you didn't see the map's edges—just the picture there, of our world as we knew it, green and rich and rolling. And then the world turned, and we hurtled through the great blue sky toward the valley where our family first settled to build a life in America.

Unlike a plane, the helicopter left little between us and the world below, so that it felt like we were flying in a dream—over the fields where Alois and Teresia worked with the woodland flanking their toil on either side, over the slumping homestead where Grandpa Albert grew up, up the hill he climbed to carry our family into the middle class, over the trees and fields toward the farm he'd paid off and worked with Grandma Ann. Then there—over that last hill, past bands of green alfalfa and golden corn—sat that white farmhouse where our dad grew up, and he and our mom raised us and worked toward our family's brightest days. The proud red barn and outbuildings all around it stood surrounded by trees and rolling hills in every direction.

I was Eagle Bird, flying up high like Grandpa Albert said I would. Only I wasn't alone. In the helicopter with me and the pilot were my dad and nephew Steven, six years old then and smiling round-faced in awe of our family's world. Out there, in our world, was my sister, the key figure in it all continuing, working the farm, raising her kids, and charting her course.

We hardly talked in the headsets we wore, but it was for lack of words, not desire to communicate. We exclaimed over the plunge and climb of the hills beneath the soaring chopper, murmured at the sight of the fields and farmyards we'd grown up working and playing in for generations, turned to address one another in broken nonsensical phrases that we somehow all understood in our collective awe. This was our farm from above in a way we'd only seen in pictures. The old tradition of pilots offering aerial photos to local farm families came alive on this day, thanks to a helicopter pilot my dad had met.

It was the summer of 2015, not long after I had returned home— this time not to visit, but to live. And the greens and golds and blues of that day offered just one of the many ways I felt I was living again in color, having seen my years on the road and in the shadow of the US Capitol all fade into a dull gray of loneliness. After more than five years away from Wisconsin and years before that pursuing my career off the farm, I'd come home to work for my home-state US senator. Even then, in those early days of my return, I could clearly envision how my career and my home could finally be in the same place. I would dive into the public policy world in my native state with this first job, perhaps moving on from politics eventually, maybe building a business, and doing my own writing. I could have my work and my home, and no longer have to choose.

Or so I thought.

What I didn't know was how hard my family had been fighting—and how much harder we'd fight in the years to come—to keep the way of life to which I was returning. I was aware of the fight, and this latest job with the senator was less about politics and more the latest manifestation of an ongoing, unfinished labor: to make my work a worthy substitute for failing to help carry on our farm myself. It started with finding my way to writing in the first place, to pursue a profession with the same passion as my dad did his. Then came reporting on the stories of others struggling in the economy, from farmers to small businesses, and then helping to communicate public policy I hoped would help places like where I was from. Perhaps someday there would be something even bigger and broader to try to honor my roots. I was a little wiser than when I'd left, but focused on proving myself. A rough beard always covered my boyish face by now, and I was quick to smile or laugh or argue—depending upon what the moment called for, in a fast world that was scary unless you found a way to navigate it. Along the way, I'd lost the understanding to see how much harder life was now for those still farming, like my dad and sister.

Trading between helping my dad with milking, chores, and field-work, Malia was working both on the farm and also at a salon by then, earning the off-farm income she needed to support her growing family. She still had the same big blue eyes and sweetness she'd had since we were little, but life's challenges had given her an edge to use when she needed it; her tenderness was now for quiet moments with her two boys. There was Steven, a cheerful farm boy who loved his grandpa and tractors in equal measure (likely because those two loves were so often paired together). And there was Malia's new baby Roman, named for our Grandpa Ripp on my mom's side.

My dad was sixty-three, happy to be working with his daughter, but getting slower. The limp he'd had since I was little was more pronounced. Both knees were going, from years of kneeling to milk cows and leaping off tractors. He had employed one hired man or another over the years to help him milk and join in the heavy work, especially when my sister was at her other job. And my mom, still cheerful with the gift of gab but getting older, too, had taken on work caring for elderly people after helping her dad and mom in their final days.

My parents had sold the hotel where she'd worked as manager, finding that after the rough start that predated their involvement and the years of recession, they would only break even after all the money they had poured into it. The money that had gone toward the hotel had once been destined to help our farm modernize for the future. Grandma Ann, the last member of our family from the olden days, still played cards whenever I visited, and she still played for keeps.

But there was far more waiting on our land below as we swept over it, challenges that would test our farm and family and even our sense of who we were—and what exactly it was that my dad, mom, sister, and I we were fighting for, each in our own way.

***

My return home in 2015 came just in time for a shocking era of economic strife for family farms. With the long recovery from the Great Recession picking up and giving way to an explosive economy in the years to come, farms that weathered the recession well had reason for high hopes. Instead, as the American economy would go gangbusters, it became clear that family farms—especially dairy farms like ours—were in deep trouble. The rate of the disappearing American farmer would spike to alarming levels as the country finally took notice again of a crisis with nearly century-old roots. The vulnerabilities spurring the crisis, both old and new embedded in the lush fields of the heartland, would reveal a completely changed industry—one driving a food supply capable of modern miracles and terrifying catastrophes alike.

The sudden economic shock would come to light during America's politically explosive trade war with China that began in 2018, but the crisis ran much deeper beneath the surface. The forces of disappearance from past decades—even as they'd become quieter in recent years—left many farms more vulnerable than they might have been during sturdier times. They would fuse with newer problems, with dairy exemplifying the peril, leaving farms wide open to the shrapnel flying across the globe when the trade war began.

One problem was that farms were seizing economic opportunity that would again prove fickle. Christopher Wolf, a professor of agriculture and economics at Cornell University, said in the years before the trade war, more American dairy farms were starting in places like Michigan, trying to take advantage of high commodity prices. This represented opportunity but was also tied to the whims of large international players like China. The next problem emerged, Wolf said, when margins got tighter for dairy farms with the boom in Greek yogurt leveling off in 2015. The American consumer craze had made milk a valuable component in a specialty-food product, driving farmers to expand, then settling back down. The warnings from economists who were saying America needed many specialty food markets, instead of a limited range combined with an overreliance on global commodity markets, were now on full display. Specialty yogurt had been a boon, but we needed more such markets as opportunities came and went. All the while, increased production from farms in Europe and New Zealand—chasing the same high prices as American farmers—hit the market, eventually depressing prices globally and yet again increasing the pressure for individual farms in America to get bigger to survive.

Other farms faced similar pressures. Much of livestock farming had also expanded, according to agricultural economist Scott Brown from the University of Missouri, with beef, pork, and chicken production rising nearly 12 percent in three years to 95 billion pounds in 2018. On top of that, Brown said, years of higher-than-average crop yields for family farm staples like corn and soybeans put enough supply on the market to drive down prices. From milk to meat to grains, farms battered by economic upheaval since the 1920s now battled trends defining modern American farming: good times followed all too rapidly by tight times, dependence on commodity markets driven by undependable foreign adversaries, a value-add specialty-food sector too narrow to offer lasting alternatives, the double-edged sword of international trade, and of course the ongoing economic pressure to get bigger or get out. All this set in before the trade war.

Family farmers, and by extension the Americans they fed, faced this burgeoning crisis in a far different state than they did the Great Depression or the 1980s Farm Crisis. It's a fact, and an irony for small and midsized farmers: Farms had long been disappearing, but the industry was not shrinking. After decades of economic pressure, what remained were large farms trying to weather the tight margins through economic scale, and many midsized and small farms that no longer could. In many cases, rural researchers say, these struggling farms were just as efficient, pound for pound, as their larger counterparts—but unable to make it without the ability to spread costs across large operations or the size to negotiate. Those factors transformed dairy, like they had other kinds of farms. From 1987 to 2012, the midpoint size of dairy farms in America went from 80 cows to 1,025 cows.[133] That's in contrast to other agricultural sectors, like broiler chickens, which had undergone consolidation decades earlier. But once the consolidation kicked in, it quickly made dairy defined by much larger farms.[134]

Dairy farming had been more resilient in allowing farms of all sizes up until that point for many reasons, ranging from government intervention to market factors. Bob Cropp, a professor emeritus at the

University of Wisconsin-Madison, said dairy had one of the stronger forms of price supports, with the federal government buying surplus to keep prices high into the 1980s. That changed as Congress ratcheted down the price support, he said, and eventually replaced it with programs like government-backed insurance—those previously referenced programs that farmers pay into, then receive payments from if the milk price drops below a certain point.

Then there was the market. Dairy farmers were more likely than some other farmers to have a wider range of places competing to buy their milk—small cheese factories and specialty cheesemakers like Cedar Grove where my dad sold our milk, co-ops of farmers banding together to market their products, large dairy processors, and so on—counteracting food industry consolidation by giving dairy farms more options.

And the fateful technology shift that favored large farms over small and midsized farms hit dairy later in some ways. Farms like my dad's were benefiting from technology that was still economical for small farms—like automatic take-off sensors on milking machines—even as innovation trended harder toward larger facilities.

But now the times had caught up with dairy too. America's march toward bigger and better in our economy had plunged the country, and our family, into a deep and evolving dilemma. The debate over the concept of the "factory farm" raged on. Critics paired concerns over the food industry creating increasingly processed foods with a range of recriminations aimed at the country's largest farms, from their environmental impact to the living conditions of their animals. Defenders of the food and agriculture industries continued to note the affordability of any imaginable food stocking shelves and gracing restaurant tables, arguing farms were responding to consumers' needs while remaining committed to animal welfare and environmental stewardship.[135] While farms struggled, these debates and battles over government support for farms intensified. Our farm participated, as most farms like ours did, in government insurance and other available programs, finding over the years that neither the government, the market, nor the innovations we were able to undertake could fix the fundamental issues making it harder to survive.

For farmers, the concept of a "factory farm" is complicated and controversial. The reality is that 96 percent of America's farms remain family farms,[136] from the smallest hobby farms to many of the largest and most professionalized operations. There are debates from many directions about the government's thresholds for what counts as a farm, and a family-owned one. Some farms are corporate owned or may involve investors mainly looking for tax benefits or subsidies.[137] Yet, the data still indicates most farms of all sizes are genuine family operations—with the large ones growing bigger to keep up and provide fathers, mothers, sons, and daughters with an income and health insurance, along with employees.

Today, like decades ago, farmers and their families don't always fall into neat political boxes. There are groups with progressive roots like the National Farmers Union that echo food, animal, and environmental concerns, while arguing the same forces causing those issues are leaving small family farmers in an impossible situation.[138] On the opposite side of the coin are groups like the American Farm Bureau Federation, representing farms of all sizes, that defend the agriculture industry's environmental record while advocating for policies that can open more markets and against regulations it warns make farming even more expensive.[139] Both organizations—sometimes at odds, sometimes united on specific issues—work hard to have local farmer membership direct their policy priorities. Meaning, they reflect the lives of farmers on the ground.

Farmers face these debates every day, whatever their size. Over time, farmers like my dad evolved away from blaming "the big guys." Casting aside new farmers, often from out of town, trying sustainable food practices also didn't hold up over time. Our drives through the countryside watching midsized farms disappear—cursing places like California with their larger farms and rolling our eyes at "hippie farms"—shifted toward simply rooting for farms of any kind to keep going. Nobody cares more about their animals or land than a good farmer, whatever the product or crop. We watched, year after year, as the landscape of American farming dramatically changed, all because of the same kinds of challenges we were facing.

"It's hard," my dad said. "I just want to keep the farms going."

Our family's rooting for any kind of farm to keep going became even more intense as the crisis surged. It's harder to separate farmers into camps when America's Dairyland is losing farms at the rate of three per day.[140]

***

My sister didn't have time for any bullshit. She was a skilled welder by then, one of the many trades a farmer picks up, and had patched and pounded machinery for years to get it going again when breakdowns halted work on the farm. So, when she needed a part that required going to town, she went in herself. Her footsteps were the same as any farmer, that gruff whisper of dirt grating beneath work shoes on a smooth floor. Yet, when she asked a guy for help finding the right spot, she got a response my dad or I never would have.

"Shouldn't a man be getting it?"

That was far from the only time she confronted being a woman in the profession of farming, more a man's world than so many of the industries that had female trailblazers by then. There were the salesmen who for years drove into the farmyard and spoke only to our dad—never acknowledging my sister at all, let alone talk to her as she helped make decisions. There were the various farmers and farmhands who wouldn't take her phone calls seriously or joked about her being a girl when the heavy work was underway. Rarely, did she encounter openly hostile sexism; more often it was small indignities that piled up over time—each one trying to tell her she wasn't supposed to be there.

She had faced a variation of this for most of her life—the expectation that it wouldn't be her who would farm. Nobody in our family ever told her a woman couldn't farm. Our dad was overjoyed when she stepped up. But, as the second eldest she didn't face the same expectation I did early on, and there was no shortage of loved ones and strangers alike surprised that a girl might take over. As she took the reins, she saw not everyone was as happy as our dad to see her farming. Of course, the logic made little sense, in a world where generations of farm women had done the work of men—our mom, grandma, great-aunts, and great-grandmother among them—long before the urban economy was recognizing the value of women. However, the women of generations past had done it as wives and sisters, less often as lone successors, and had rarely if ever spoken up. Eventually, Malia decided she didn't care what people thought.

"If people can't respect me," she said, "I'm not doing business with them."

Still, the barrier remained, one of many she'd face as a young farmer. There was the challenge of surprise motherhood at age twenty. Maintaining the balance working for our dad, milking in the mornings, and caring for her family while going to night school and then having a second career proved taxing on her. And unlike our parents, despite eventually finding love, she would never go on to have a partner who farmed alongside her. One early morning when she was still in cosmetology school, as she drove to the farm for morning milking after classes the night before, she nodded off.

Waking up to her front wheels hitting the ditch, Malia swerved back onto the road and knew—the shock of fear spiking, then lingering long after—that she couldn't continue like this. She still did evening milking and other work, but it was her first step back from a life she'd tried to take on in full, and it would exemplify the growing challenge she faced of fighting hard for both farm and family over the years. As time went on, she had not only her second son, Roman, but a third son, Paxton. Over the years she balanced caring for her boys, doing hair for supplemental income, and farming. Malia ceded some responsibility when she had to, to my dad and a string of farmhands who came and went. She never stopped farming—always joining in the fieldwork and other responsibilities—but nor could she devote all the time our parents had while farming together. On top of it all, better pay at the salon meant she had to work more hours there. At one time or another, she also took jobs as a mail carrier and bartender to make ends meet.

Once again, my sister and I found ourselves on different paths that somehow brought us together. While she balanced growing family responsibilities and stitched together a living, I was isolated and focused almost completely on my overwhelming career. Working for our home-state senator and then home-state governor, I also started my own business and began to focus on clients involved in bipartisan issues and a range of industries, eventually charting my way out of partisan politics. I'd like to say all my free time went toward family and working on the farm as I careened across the state trying to build a stable career, and I'm grateful for the amount that did. But my drinking, tamed some during my time of growing responsibility in DC, had picked back up—stiff drinks and dark barrooms taking the edge off my lonely, stressful life. For years, between working and partying, relationships came and went, as did plans I'd had to propose marriage before things didn't work out. I had learned the difference between being on my own and being alone, and it helped bring me home. But I was far from housebroken.

I was also self-medicating a problem I'd only partially conquered— what I viewed as my failure to farm. Realizing that writing and crisis management were my replacements for cattle and tractors, I'd begun to see ways I was like my dad after all. We had admitted things, which helped. I said I felt he'd sold the cows because of me, and I was wrong to get mad when he resumed milking. On a road trip together, he admitted that his years of relative silence reflected what I'd always felt—that there was a time he'd been angry when I didn't want to farm and my sister was too young to take my place. His honesty about those issues helped me believe him more fully when he said he was proud of me now.

"I felt mad because 'I don't have nobody to step in, to do what I want to do,'" he said. "But as you grow older, you get wiser." I began to remember the other reasons he'd sold—tough farm economics, his once-failing health, and the hope of the hotel—as he told me more about them. I even began to enjoy farm work in a way I hadn't since I was a little boy, finding that rumbling in a tractor on my day off eased the stresses of my job and felt like a return to better times. The core of the issue was still there, though, and it lasts to this day: the doubts about me farming came at a time when my dad might have otherwise put in a milking parlor or other innovation, if he'd felt I would have wanted to farm. I began to say I didn't farm because I was no good at the things my father did. My parents began to say it wasn't that I lacked the skill, just that I wanted something else. It was a small disagreement in which we spared one another's feelings. The compromise became saying my gifts were elsewhere. To this day it's one I believe on good days and tell myself on bad ones.

There were other sources of guilt forming beneath the surface. After years of renting small apartments on humble salaries, I'd begun to make decent money—just as I saw how truly hard farming was becoming. My parents were finding their later years more financially strapped. My sister was working hard but couldn't afford to work on the farm alone. The time when our family banked money in the good years to weather the bad years, and saw opportunity in other small businesses like the hotel, faded to tough years with few options.

Despite my success, I found there was little I could do about it. I was helping where I could and making enough money to save cash, but not enough to overcome the challenges facing farms like ours. Every time I jumped in a tractor to join in the fieldwork, hauled feed with the skid-steer, or helped move cattle, the joyful return to my roots also reminded me of my limitations. The biggest change I could have made to help more—quit my career to join the family business— would have meant wages for another farmhand, and a subpar one who'd have been miserable to boot.

What we were experiencing was the way farms become land rich and cash poor. We all knew we wanted to hold onto the land. But we were wrestling with what was happening. Our farm gave my parents a good middle-class living, helped put me through college, and provided my sister a shot at her own dreams. Now, it was struggling as farming got tougher. Absent a solution, like so many farm families raised on hard work curing all, we blamed ourselves. Our parents wondered if they'd gone wrong somewhere. My sister tried to figure out if she'd ever find a way to take over and make the farm successful again. I began to question if we could have made different decisions twenty years earlier. If I had wanted to farm, would things have been different? Did we miss our chance? There was no way to know.

***

The national media headlines screamed:

"They're trying to wipe us off the map." Small American Farmers Are Nearing Extinction.[141]

Such news forced our country—however briefly—to look the disappearing American farmer in the eye. It was a frenzy from 2018 through early 2020 that reflected both the real economic pain of farmers, and the schizophrenic nature of our national conversation. Farmers felt left behind for decades by then. Despite their place in our national mythology, the modern struggles of family farms had only truly seized the national conversation twice in nearly four decades—now, during an international trade war, and during the Farm Crisis of the 1980s. The whimsical commercials that recalled a happier time, and the many stories in film and literature of farmers overcoming adversity, were by now just America telling itself it hadn't been stamping farmers out of existence for decades.

After dabbling with initial tariffs against China, President Donald Trump announced tariffs on all steel and aluminum imports on March 1, 2018.[142] The announcement was the first in a string of serious moves that had him acting tougher with US adversaries and allies alike, and led to retaliation from other countries that limited American farmers' ability to sell abroad. Like so many moments of the Trump presidency, it was a move that completely upended the national conversation—scrambling our politics from the halls of Congress to the fields of the heartland. Democrats, who had long wanted better protections against countries with lower labor and environmental standards (and therefore lower costs), criticized the growing trade fight as reckless.[143] Republicans found themselves caught—between traditional conservative arguments in favor of the economic opportunity of free trade[144] and the fact that some of the working-class support shifting toward Republicans was driven by Trump's tough trade stance.

The reaction of individual farmers varied widely, like any issue, but two facts began to exist at the same time: Farmers were facing economic pain, while also cheering someone finally fighting back. Polling showed farmers viewed the trade war as a matter of short-term pain for long-term gain and that government assistance offsetting the impact was easing concerns.[145] Farmers had long felt they were getting screwed, from rising bills to the notorious "middle man"—a stand in for anyone taking an unfair cut of farmers' income. China was high on the list, after years of unreliable buying—purchasing massive amounts of American farm products until farmers were captive, then dropping them—and a range of cheating on trade standards.

Part of the reason the politics were scrambled was that the economics were scrambled. Economists of various stripes and policy experts from across the political spectrum had long agreed China was not operating aboveboard, violating intellectual property rights, manipulating its currency, and holding farmers hostage with erratic buying that could sway world markets. Christopher Wolf, the Cornell economist, said other countries were also messing with America. Canadian farmers, insulated by a system that sets a stable price in part by limiting foreign imports, were *dumping*—selling at an artificially low price—excess dairy proteins they couldn't otherwise sell, he said. The actions of these Canadian farmers were driving down prices of the goods being sold by American farmers. The problem with suddenly slapping tariffs on these countries, Wolf and other economists said, is that in addition to increasing the cost of imported goods for American consumers, it led to other countries retaliating with tariffs that made American farmers' goods harder to sell in foreign markets. From 2017 to 2018, American agricultural exports to China plummeted more than 60 percent. Ultimately, countries including Canada, China, Mexico, Turkey, and members of the European Union retaliated against America too.[146] Falling sales to China alone were enough to exacerbate the tough market conditions that had set in before the trade war.

"They're just so big that they can do that," Wolf said. "China's big enough to move the whole world demand."

I had begun in recent years to see how completely our political system was failing families like mine, despite the efforts of many good people I met working in the public-policy arena. Once in early 2014 I was walking past the Capitol to work—so far from home, in the suit and tie I had to wear each day—when I called my dad to tell him the news. Congress was close, after years of gridlock, to passing a bipartisan Farm Bill. Instead of my dad, I heard my nephew Steven, almost five, answer back in his little voice, thick with the accent of midwestern farm country.

"Yah, but is it a good farm bill or a bad farm bill?"

I laughed as I slipped from the shadow of the Capitol to our office building, but the question stuck with me. The truth was I didn't have a good answer.

After moving home, the contrast between the political world and the real world with my family became stark. It really wasn't a partisan matter. The best I can say is that I felt myself becoming as alienated from our political environment as many Americans. Nationally, I saw both parties failing us—Democrats losing touch with rural areas in what is now a well-documented trend; Republicans running short on new policy ideas for how to help the rural Americans they'd won over. Campaigning in 2016 and 2018 took me to dairy breakfasts, factory shop floors, schools, small businesses, and community festivals across Wisconsin—a rare chance to learn all corners of my home state.

Yet, in between those campaigns, and also during the 2018 election cycle, I saw how working on bipartisan policy issues and completely nonpartisan issues facing midwestern industries was good work and less toxic. All the while, I found myself coping more on the farm or in the woods or by playing with my sister's kids—all things that helped me feel closer to the real fight for our way of life.

As 2017 and 2018 raged on professionally, I took deeper refuge in a new relationship. Rachael was a journalist, from California of all places, and she had a ready laugh and a free way about her that made me know I wanted to marry her someday. Grandma Ann lived long enough to know Rachael, who instinctively called her "Anna," resurrecting in her last days the given name she had as a little girl. When Grandma died in February of 2018, it was after living out her final months on the farm with my parents. My dad drove her casket to the cemetery—as he had for Grandpa

180

Albert—on a flat-bed wagon behind the old Super M tractor she'd made hay with years ago. Rachael helped me grieve and brought a calming presence that helped me reconnect even further with my family and our way of life.

And yet everywhere I saw signs of our way of life under siege, just as I saw what it was truly worth. By late 2019, farm bankruptcies had skyrocketed 24 percent in one year and reached their highest level since 2011 just after the Great Recession.[147] The state hit hardest: our native Wisconsin, America's Dairyland. Although it was a sharp increase, the numbers were just one small indicator of the loss; many others were families selling when they wanted nothing more than to keep going. Once, when making calls on behalf of a client to talk with rural families about Wisconsin's challenges, I stumbled on a farm family I'd grown up knowing. The mother on the phone told me she couldn't talk because there was nothing good to tell—they weren't sure how much longer they could hold on.

In January of 2020, President Trump signed the United States-Mexico-Canada agreement, a rare bipartisan bill that updated NAFTA.[148] Though it restored trade relations with new protections, America's headlong charge toward free trade dating back to the 1990s was halted. Supporters of free trade have argued that America is missing out on economic growth, including for farmers who could have new markets in more countries,[149] yet both political parties have since stood by a tougher trade stance to protect American interests. Tensions with China continued into the administration of Trump's successor, President Joe Biden (who hewed more closely to the position of organized labor and preserved or added to many Trump-era trade practices).[150]

Improving prices and easing tensions gave farmers more room going into 2020, but the economic crosswinds that made farmers so vulnerable heading into the trade war threatened to return any time. China would remain both a massive buyer of American exports and a major adversary.

***

The sky was overcast as I walked among the buildings with my dad. We sat for a while under the tent where the auctioneer, in his jumping cadence, announced each cow, while handlers brought one animal after another through the series of gates for the crowd of farmers, cattle buyers, and onlookers to survey. A farm family my dad had admired for years was auctioning off their cattle and selling their land to a neighboring farm. My dad bought a cow, doing his best to show his support. After a while of watching others do the same, he got up to walk the farm, and I went with him.

We wandered the farmyard and into and out of a big metal shed with machinery parked and old tools lining the wall. He talked as we walked, about our family's history—back to the days of his childhood, and of Grandpa Albert, and my great-grandparents. I asked him questions about them, and soon enough our conversation slipped back and forth between family history and the business of modern-day farming, until it was all one. Both of us found something there. For me, a father sharing the kind of stories that had led me to writing over the years. For him, the interest of a son he thought had moved on from his world. I saw more clearly than ever what we shared: a proud heritage that was ours no matter how different we were. Even though it was not raining as we walked, it felt at any moment it might—the day gray and sad but swelling with change.

We grew closer throughout late 2019—at the auction, working together to prepare the site for a cabin I was planning in the woods out back of the farmhouse, talking about the farm. One day my dad called me with a question that changed everything. I was in my office a few blocks from the Wisconsin State Capitol. Though life was still dominated by work, the job at a consulting firm I'd joined was more stable and less tied to the demands of the political world—I worked feverishly all week, then spent every weekend with Rachael or at the farm. Seeing my dad calling randomly on a weekday, I picked up to hear his voice, raw and urgent: "Do you think I should sell the cows?" I was unsure of what to say. Having no idea what was driving my dad's question, what my sister thought, or the right path forward, I replied that I thought we needed a plan. Maybe, I said, if we worked through what we wanted as a family long term, we could figure out whether to keep milking or whether to try to keep the farm going another way. He asked me if I would help with a plan. My chest swelled; it was the first time in years I'd felt truly useful to my dad.

I started that day, setting up discussions with him and the rest of the family to hear what they thought, doing what I did so often in my day job—write a plan to navigate the challenges ahead. So began my rejoining the family business, and with it, the breaking of a chain of denials I'd carried for years. The first denial was at the age of sixteen, when my dad sold the cows the first time and I told myself he'd be fine raising beef cattle on his own. Then, when I became angry at the idea that it was my inadequacy that led him to sell—those locusts that still flitted about my mind—I told myself I'd never wanted to farm, because it was easier than thinking I couldn't. As my sister proved herself, my denial shifted to telling myself the farm would be fine, even though I knew the problems for such a small dairy farm remained. All the while, building one denial upon another, I'd avoided true responsibility and let vague guilt take root. Fully facing the farm's problems in the modern day now shattered that last, most dangerous denial—that ultimately the farm would somehow be fine—and forced me to face a simple truth. I would never feel okay, about my dad or my family or myself, if I didn't try to help find a path forward for the farm.

My sister was ready to fight for the farm harder than ever before too. She had built up some financial stability and was full of ideas for where to take the farm. We embarked on a plan to turn things around—my sister steering more hours toward the farm even though other jobs could pay more, me volunteering where I could between work and everything else. I learned just how much harder farming was becoming financially, just how hard it was to afford reliable help, and just how difficult it was to sort the tangled emotions of a family business. In our early meetings, we discussed options from a plan I'd written from everyone's input and resolved to keep milking, with Malia becoming more involved in managing the farm. She implemented new breeding practices to improve our cows' pregnancy rate—one of many problems costing the farm money—and protocols for animal health. Gradually, we worked toward Malia making more per hour on the farm and began to rely less on hired help, mainly hiring temporary relief milkers for the remaining times of the week when Malia had off-farm responsibilities.

We'll never know what would have happened if COVID hadn't hit. The pandemic shocked us as it did all families, each of us working through how to navigate one another's feelings about the health risks and restrictions, the economic fallout, and the changes to daily life. In time we figured it out, but the strain on our family—both on the farm and on our relationships—was only just beginning. My sister and dad struggled forward each day—Malia trying to keep working with the kids home during school shutdowns, the work taxing my dad more than his younger days. People were scared to do basic things like meet up for a job interview, so it became harder to find good hired help. In fact, the workforce challenges we were facing would become a complicated tangle for many farmers, improving somewhat as the temporarily unemployed looked for work during the ongoing economic shutdown that spring, then worsening as so many dropped out of the workforce or found other jobs. Along the way, Malia learned in summer of 2020 that she was pregnant again. This time, it would be a daughter. It was a happy moment that nevertheless had all of us wondering how she'd do it all.

Then one day, my sister felt the tears coming. She and my dad were sitting in my parents' garage. It was a quiet spot, free of the bellering cattle and roaring machinery—a place where they could meet to plan their work and look to the future. Except today Malia only saw questions about how they could go on—milking morning and night, our dad slowing down, her exhausted with another young child on the way, COVID exacerbating all of it, the farm barely making it.

"I want the farm to succeed," she said. The tears came gently, not a sobbing breakdown but a well of emotion reaching the surface. "I know you want to milk cows."

But she just couldn't do it anymore, that immovable, grueling morning and evening commitment of milking. She tried to explain she didn't think they could continue with the physical strain and all they were up against. She shared how she wanted to be present for her kids in a way milking didn't allow. She offered ideas for how the end of milking didn't have to mean the end of farming—how they could raise other kinds of animals and crops, all more flexible types of farming, perhaps a brighter future. But no matter how she said it, the tears staining her cheeks, she felt like she was letting him down. Just as I'd felt all those years ago.

And in that moment, our dad felt himself letting her down too. He listened but said little. When she was done, he stood up and quietly walked out without reassuring her that they'd find a way forward. Most of all, he failed to tell her he knew she was right. He admitted those things later, long after he'd walked out into the clean farm air, sat alone in his shop, and answered his daughter's cry for help with solitary tears of his own.

CHAPTER 10

COVID CRASH

*Our Food Supply in Crisis and the Modern-Day
Dilemmas of American Farming*

The ambulance plowed down the highway through the hard Wisconsin winter. It was bound for Madison, where there were more doctors and more beds and—when it got bad enough—more ventilators to keep the oxygen streaming through ever-more patients arriving to the hospital in droves. In the back of the ambulance was my dad, a severe case of COVID-19 closing in on his lungs. He didn't know what they were doing to him there or what they'd do when he got to the hospital. He didn't know if his wife or their eleven-year-old grandson, or anyone else he'd been around the past several days, were okay. All he knew was he could barely breathe and his heart was pounding. The phone rang and somehow he got hold of it, and he answered. It was me—calling in blind hope that he'd pick up, refusing to let the last time we'd talked be the last time we talked.

"Dad? Dad what's happening there, are you okay?"

The whine and shake of the ambulance fell upon our voices, letting our words get through to each other only in fits and starts. My dad was panicked, heaving, and crying out in between us trying to understand each other. I realized, by the torture of his feverish breaths, that he didn't think he was going to make it. Somehow a calm came over me, and I stopped and listened as he told me all the final things—what he wanted us to do and to know, before he was gone. He told me to find out if Steven was okay, to make sure my sister knew it was COVID so she could get him out of school and to the doctor. He told me to take care of my mom and sister. He told me yet more things lost somewhere in the madness of it all, my calm fleeting now with the full realization of what he wanted me to do. His breaths became more labored with each passing moment, and then he trailed off. I pleaded with him not to leave me there with that burden, alone.

"Dad, you have to fight," I said. "You have to fight for your kids and your grandkids, and—"

"I can't hear you."

"No, Dad, you have to—"

"I love you."

"You have to *fight*!"

I yelled the final words as the phone went dead. I texted him that I loved him. I ran across the wooden floor of our apartment to the Christmas tree in the dining room, found the ornament with the photo of me and Rachael smiling, and took a picture and sent it to him. I rifled through my phone and found another of our whole family, including Malia's boys and her pregnant with her little girl, all of us posing for a family portrait with a Holstein calf in front and the lush green hayfields rolling behind. I hoped all the while something would make him remember what he had to live for before it was too late.

When I'd wrung myself out of everything I thought might give him the will to survive, I found myself out on the porch of our apartment, facing the throbbing afternoon sunlight reflecting off the snow-covered rooftops of our neighborhood. It was December of

2020, and all was quiet then. I asked myself what I would do between now and when I had kids, so that they knew—if I ever got sick—that I had done everything in my power to be with them for as long as I could. And when that was done, I said a prayer, picked up my phone, and started again to call my family, one by one, to try and carry out my father's wishes.

What it took—for our family and our country—to get to the point of such crisis would reveal so much about modern-day agriculture. And facing the impact of the COVID crash on our economy would reveal what we need to do if we want a reliable American food supply.

***

The COVID-19 pandemic put farms like ours on a journey that would tear through the heartland and put on terrible display the deep vulnerabilities of the modern American food system. There was, of course, the immediate shock of the death toll, as well as the fear and distrust that the pandemic bred among many Americans—from our political debates to the dilemmas every family faced over how to navigate the situation.

The economic toll, meanwhile, would hit the entire country in sudden and uneven ways. One of the least understood and longest lasting would be the toll on our food economy. The unique blow to farmers, accompanied by a catastrophic shock to the broader agriculture and food industries, would increase yet again the pressure on America's vanishing farms. It would reveal the many ways our food system leaves every family in our country vulnerable—despite its many remaining miracles—to another food crisis.

Although in many ways the debates over COVID—how we handled it and how to view it now—are still ongoing, there are some unassailable facts. The economic shock that occurred was the sharpest we'd seen since the Great Depression. As COVID spread and deaths spiked, governments responded by locking down industries, and unemployment skyrocketed to levels well past those of the Great Recession: more than 14 percent in April of 2020, with many industries, states, and demographic groups far higher.[151] The recession associated with the "Great Lockdown" was also the shortest in American history,[152] with economic decline ripping through the country in the wake of the virus, and then easing within a few months as America and other countries adapted and reopened industry. Governments in the United States and across the world also pumped massive amounts of money into the economy through direct spending, stimulus checks, temporary loans, and more. Yet, the pain lasted much longer. Although the actual shrinking of the economy—the technical definition of a recession—had ceased, a long and rolling economic crisis continued. Different variants throughout 2021 and 2022, the shifting habits of the American consumer, key industries suffering ongoing disruption to their operations, adjusting global supply chains, and skyrocketing food prices, all contributed to the multifaceted food-system catastrophe that unfolded.

The obvious and well-documented example of how COVID affected our food economy is the meatpacking industry, but the issue went far deeper than that. Meatpacking remains an industry where a large amount of on-site, hands-on labor is required, and infections among employees working in close quarters—as well as the country's response to control the virus—temporarily devastated the industry,[153] shutting down parts of a key link in our food supply chain.

They were not alone. Similar shutdowns occurred across other parts of the agricultural and food industries, just like the rest of the economy, disrupting the food supply chain from the farm gate to the dinner table—manufacturers of all kinds of goods needed in our food economy, distribution centers that gather and distribute goods, the trucking industry that carries so much of our food from coast to coast, the shipping industry that exports farmers' products (and imports foreign food to accompany our domestic supply), and on and on.[154] The disruptions meant consumers saw food prices increase because of less supply—even as farmers saw the prices they were paid drop as the backlog halted some food-product purchasing and as demand in restaurants and other public places fell.[155]

The result across much of our food economy was devastating dilemmas for everyone—from the disappearing American farmer to the distressed American consumer to the many industries in between. With parts of the supply chain disrupted, some farmers found themselves unable to sell their goods, while at the same time families across America found many foods scarcer and sometimes more expensive or unavailable altogether. The holdup on moving perishable goods through the economy was crushing, financially and emotionally, for those involved: millions of animals were slaughtered in the first few months of 2020,[156] and 5 percent of the nation's milk went down the drain in just one month,[157] in addition to various crops that went to waste. Farmers also saw skyrocketing fertilizer prices throughout 2020 and 2021 because of a wide range of factors.[158] The end result was farmers facing higher prices at a time when they couldn't sell their goods—or if they could, often for far less. And this occurred as the American consumer grew more desperate for the modern miracles of our food system to continue. Those broken links in the supply chain suffered massive losses and tried to recover by getting the government to rule them essential and able to operate. Then the initial economic shock abated, and demand from consumers spiked—even though many of the disruptions to the global food-supply chain remained. These conflicting factors made the economic crisis worse in some ways, even as it subsided in others.

Farmers were among those deemed essential, but there was no granting a reprieve from the hardship. My sister continued fighting to get to work each day with her kids home from shutdowns, and my dad continued to shoulder the work of a much younger man, while hiring good help kept getting even harder. Together they worked alongside a string of hired hands we had throughout the year—until our dad got sick in December of 2020. And these challenges were on top of my sister getting up to milk cows at three thirty in the morning, while pregnant, with my mom stationed at Malia's house in case the boys woke up before she got back. Missing work, at the farm or salon, was money she didn't have to pay bills and feed her kids.

I found myself walking in a different world from my sister and struggling to help. My work could be done from anywhere that a phone and computer could work—a privilege that made earning a paycheck possible no matter what COVID did to my day. It also allowed me to pitch in at home, driving out each week, not only to spend time on the farm but also to help take care of my sister's kids on weeknights when I could. Even as I dealt with my own challenges at work, as the company I worked for tried to help clients getting hammered by the crisis, I told myself I was fortunate. I had to do more to help my family get through hardship far worse than my own. I ended more than one day with enough booze to keep the world at bay.

There were some moments of relief and beauty as our family drew closer. After months of work with my dad preparing the site, in May of 2020 we finally stood up a cabin—built off-site by Amish craftsmen—back in some woods I owned behind the farmhouse to spend even more time back home. The stained pine wood was honey brown, with a porch and a bench commemorating Grandpa Albert and Grandma Anna. Inside I began to collect items that tied my various walks of life together—books and deer antlers and photos of good memories.

While my sister and I battled our different challenges, we remained unified in our fight for a long-term path for the farm. After Malia told our dad she didn't think they could keep milking in summer of

2020, she and I got to work on a new phase of the plan: finding life after milking for our farm, as well as our family. Our dad had accepted what she'd said without ridicule. But his inability to reassure her about the future—because of his own honest uncertainty—left her working to show how the farm's finances could work without a monthly milk check.

Malia brought the ideas and farm know-how, while I brought experience in strategic planning and business. She saw a world that harkened back to the mixed agriculture of our roots, when farmers like Great-Grandpa Alois sold many crops and products, in search of enough winners to make a go. We could use the facilities that had led to award-winning milk production to instead raise heifers to join the milk herds of other dairy farms. We could use the tender loving care Malia had shown our milk herd to raise beef cattle that were fatter, happier, and healthier than consumers could find elsewhere. And we could raise a range of strong crops on our fertile, rolling acreage.

While she developed these ideas and figured out the finances of a new operation, I worked with her to develop a business plan for the farm and set my parents up on a retirement plan. If this was going to work, it would not only have to keep the farm operational but generate the kind of income to help Malia buy the farm and allow our parents to retire with financial security.

In this way, our generation faced challenges unlike any of the previous three. Alois and Teresia had survived severe hardship and labored under debt for decades. Albert had paid off debt and climbed up through economic bust and boom alike. Our parents Jim and Jean had survived their early lean years and the turbulent global economy to buy the farm and give us a good middle-class living. Malia and I hadn't lived through depression, and we had modern comforts and choices none of them had. But we were now trying to find a way to transfer the farm to the next generation, as all of them had done, at a time when milking cows at our size and scale was no longer a bright future but a dimming past. Our dad awaited our plan, saying only that he worried about the numbers.

There was more there. Although he tried to remain open-minded, he was becoming quiet and frustrated, just as he had when it became clear I wouldn't farm. When we finished the plan, he didn't read it. Instead, he wandered the farm, working and worrying about far more than the numbers. We had discussed the plan some, and so he knew its basic ideas. He also knew that it still lacked a way to use his barn since heifers and beef would spend time in other parts of our farm—in other facilities or outdoors. He looked at the big red barn and thought of how it would become brittle without the heat of animals and fall to pieces, just as Alois's barn in the valley had. He thought about his mornings and how he would no longer rise early to milk cows like his grandparents and parents had done before him. Less knowledgeable about the farm than my sister but used to fighting for a path forward, I pushed him to read the plan—first persuading, then pleading, then yelling through the phone. It was worth nothing but my shame later. He couldn't hear my arguments any better than he could my sister's dreams. He couldn't see the ways that raising animals of all ages and crops of all kinds could fill his days like his smaller side operation hadn't the first time he'd sold his milk cows. He couldn't bring himself to evaluate the numbers. He couldn't do these things because he worried about losing not just his job but also a place that was his home, his community, his heritage. Everything. His purpose—preserving our way of life on this land—hung in the balance.

Our father's doubts were by then part of an epidemic of another kind, which gave him good reason to worry. Farming had initially been a growing source of entrepreneurship when Great-Grandpa Alois came to America and settled in the valley, but the American farmer had now been disappearing for nearly a century. From the 1920s to the 2020s, America lost more than 4.5 million farms. It was a more than 70 percent plummet, averaging roughly forty-five thousand farms per year.[159] Everything in my dad—from the time he stepped forward as an eight-year-old boy to today—had grown up in resistance to letting our farm be next.

Then came the morning, in December of 2020, when the cold winter air became too heavy in his lungs. He had to sit on a haybale, trying to catch his breath. It was the moment when all of it—our father's faith, our farm's future, and our family's unity—would fall into danger as he fought for his life.

***

I leapt into Rachael's car and tore out of the driveway to set things right.

It was just a few hours after my dad had gone to a testing site, barely breathing, and we learned he had a case so severe it warranted that ambulance ride to Madison. COVID had by then proven a fickle enemy—a mild annoyance for one person, a life-threatening illness for another. Our family had experienced that like any other. Depending upon the day and the circumstances, we were at turns worried about our health, frustrated at the limitations on life and work, and often both things at once. However, now our dad was sick with the kind of COVID that cut through any political or social notions—raging past the stage of a cold or light phantom illness to a serious threat that forced everyone to face what it would mean if he didn't come back to us.

And now, the sound of my dad's labored breaths in my mind, I was in full crisis mode. After my brief moment of calm, the frenzy of enacting my dad's last wishes set in: checking on my mom, trying to reach my sister, trading information with everyone, striving—as best I could—to piece together a strategy for the family. The problem was that my first talk with Malia had done little to ease my concerns. Malia was away from the farm getting estimates for a home she was building and had responded in brief conversations that she would handle things with Steven. Having passed along my dad's message on getting him out of school and knowing it might fall to our mom to pick Steven up, I wanted to talk about how we would make sure that if one of them had COVID, they didn't give it to the other. Our mom, sixty-eight then, was the most at risk, and I had medical instructions to keep her separate. But Malia wasn't answering me on next steps.

Not sure what else to do, I got in the car and sped through the snow-covered countryside toward the farm, hoping as I went that my sister would pick up one of my calls or I could get there soon enough to figure out a plan. Meanwhile, Malia was trying to get back home herself and figure out what to do: how to get Steven home from school, where he could stay that would be safe for others if he was infected, and how to keep the farm going with our dad sick. All the while, I was calling with more problems. When I finally reached her, the call was like an explosion. Somewhere I realized that I was yelling, and she was screaming. That's when I saw myself: barreling down the road at untold speeds, fighting with my sister, neither of us trusting the other, when we needed to more than ever. I apologized and told her everything would be okay if we could just talk once I got to the farm.

The agreement we worked out would change our lives forever. I volunteered for our dad to stay with me and Rachael if he got out of the hospital—so that he could remain separate from our mom until he wasn't contagious and so his care wouldn't become a burden while my sister ran the farm. Malia shared her plan for how to keep the farm work going, and we figured out a way our mom could stay separate but still be a help to Malia if Steven got sick. Just how random COVID could be, even varying from person to person in the same chain, was not clear then. It would be a while before Malia and I would talk about that day and realize how similarly we'd actually felt.

But we'd come together, and we each had a job to do while our dad fought his way back to the farm.

The sky was dark and the ground slick with ice when the hospital cleared my dad. I had hauled his favorite recliner in the farm's pickup, and Rachael and I had carried it into the small spare room in our apartment with his clothes and other belongings. He could barely walk, and his breathing was easily taxed, each step into our apartment a test of his fledgling recovery. What followed was two weeks of caring for my dad. There was a regimen to monitor his oxygen and other vitals to make sure he didn't backslide. In between work, we prepared him meals, made sure he was comfortable, corresponded with the hospital, and found our way forward. At night, I'd wake up and open his door, listening to make sure he was breathing.

In the middle of the night one evening, his oxygen level fell so far that I had to rush him into the hospital on nurse's orders. As I parked the truck in the darkness, my dad readmitted to the hospital, a man walking his dog yelled to make sure I didn't back into another vehicle. I almost leapt out of the truck to fight him. A farmer like my dad would have seen I was just trying to make a tight space and held out his hands to show how much further I could back up. But my father wasn't there. And even if he did come back, I was realizing—moment by moment—that he was no longer invincible.

The hospital cleared my dad again, and he returned to the little room in our apartment, but no matter the ups and downs of his recovery, Malia had to keep moving without him. Now she faced all the same challenges they had on the farm, on her own. Fortunately, we had good relief help for milkings by then. Malia also called on close friends for help. It was a circle of support that recalled the olden days: the threshing crew banding together with Alois for harvest, neighbors coming to milk while Albert's back healed, older farmers giving our newlywed parents hay to make it through the winter. The thing about a farm in a precarious situation is that there's always another challenge piling on. Early on a few cows went down sick. One morning, Malia was testing cows, an extra monthly step to milking where a farmer collects samples to ensure quality, when a cow gave birth to twins outside. Malia ran through the cold damp air to our skid-steer to help gently move the calves into the barn where they'd be warm, but a bolt had fallen out of the skid-steer's safety release, and it wouldn't move. The sick cows and the testing procedures and the newborn baby calves were all waiting. There was little to do but yell.

"Fuck this!"

Still, she kept at it. Each morning my dad kept getting a little better, and the chores kept getting done. As his recovery continued, my dad became more aware of what was happening around him: me sharing each next step from the doctors as Rachael and I continued his care, Malia texting him about how well the farm was doing despite the challenges. He coined a saying that his son was taking care of the farmer, while his daughter was taking care of the farm. Finally, on the morning of December 23, 2020, I drove him back to the farm in time to be with my mom for Christmas Eve.

We were all grateful—for his recovery and for each other—but things were different. His severe illness brought with it an early form of "long COVID" that meant chronic fatigue, weak lungs, and other health complications. Feeling the vulnerability in his chest and limbs made him uneasy. My dad and I had more than one moment, often back at the cabin in the woods behind the farmhouse, where we talked about his newfound vulnerabilities. One day, a tractor pulling a manure spreader jackknifed on the way into the valley and careened into the ditch—off that same steep road that had imperiled vehicles ever since our family had first settled there more than a century ago. Our dad, usually more cheerful than most when tractors got stuck, worried aloud now about how they'd ever get it out.

"What are we gonna do?" he said. "What are we gonna do?"

"You're gonna go home," Malia said. "I'm gonna make some calls."

His lungs were straining in the cold, and he knew she was right. He stepped back as Malia called a big truck, a wrecker capable of towing semis, to hook a chain to the manure spreader and pull it backward up the hill. Our dad said Malia was the only person he'd trust to steer the tractor as the wrecker pulled. And so Malia climbed in and helped jimmy it out of the ditch, then drove it down the ice-laden hill it had failed to make the first time, and the day's work went on.

Life went on, too, and it was in these early days of seeing his limitations that he accepted Malia's ideas for the farm. It was time, he told her, to sell the cows.

***

As we prepared to renew our family's four-generation gamble with a different kind of farming, it was becoming clearer than ever just how deep the vulnerabilities to America's way of life—our food system and our broader economy and culture—had become. Each vulnerability is tied, in some fashion, to the disappearing American farmer. And each represents a place where we can, and must, find solutions that defy the current debate.

First, there were the clear problems with our supply chain, acknowledged by industry proponents and critics alike, even if their views of the root problems and future solutions were different. From the farm to the dinner table, each link in the chain faced a challenge where food was wasted because it couldn't move through the system.[160] Some argued it was because of government restrictions in the face of COVID, others countered it was a lack of safety preparations for a public health crisis, and others simply labeled it a blameless "black swan" event with countless dead ends nobody could have predicted.[161] Challenges to the food industry would continue and evolve into fierce debate. The defenders of various parts of our food system argue that, in fact, the global supply chain held. They cite the unpredictable nature of COVID and note that food processors acted quickly to implement effective safety measures and continue to feed America.[162] Critics say the crisis showed many of the ills of large consolidated industry, including the risks of big facilities spreading disease among workers and animals alike, while arguing the race for efficiency has led to a lack of redundancy[163] (for example, where a food processing plant going idle has invested in back-up operations or can be backed up by another operator).

Whatever the merits or demerits of our supply chain, the impact of the disaster on farmers, companies, and families was clear. And protecting our food supply against a similar disaster is just one of many dilemmas we must solve imminently, many of which existed long before COVID. Some of the challenges facing our food system result in deep debates, while others are problems we can all agree upon. All exemplify the desperate need for solutions after decades of turmoil.

For example, divisive debates over the environment are raging, with critics contending that bigger farms are contributing to climate change and industry pushing back with steps they're taking to protect the environment. However, farmers and environmentalists should be able to find a mutual interest in solving certain environmental issues, like ensuring an abundance of good water and the quality, durability, and longevity of soil. On the issue of limiting pollution, large farms are certainly producing more animal waste, but Nichole Anderson, an assistant professor of animal behavior and welfare at Texas Tech University, noted that large farms also can afford biosecurity technology more capable of protecting our environment than ever. (Proponents of small-farm innovation that stalled in the twentieth century might ask, what kinds of technology piloted by big farms can be affordable for small farms too?) In other words, the fact that farmers and environmentalists alike have reason and the ability to preserve the land for future use can be a path toward solutions, if we take it.

Other issues offer even more room for consensus. Take, for example, the issue of foreign adversaries buying up farmland—a risk to our food supply and national security that also existed before COVID and is part of the broader problem of having our farmland in fewer hands. In basic terms, it's become easier for foreign adversaries to buy it up. This is not to say all foreign investment is bad—like any industry, some farmers say friendly countries can provide crucial backing, while others would never dream of it. Some economists also note that foreign ownership stands at a little over 3 percent of farmland, still a small and inconsequential amount. However, the pace of foreign ownership, increasing 15 percent to 43.4 million acres in just two years,[164] is worrying both sides of the aisle, with many arguing that it's becoming too easy for foreign adversaries to buy in. In one of the rare ways Congress has acted,[165] initial protections against Iran, China, Russia, and North Korea have been established and can be built upon.

Then there's the issue of rural economic decline. A rising farm sector drove economic growth for small communities like where my family settled, and now the loss of farms, loss of people, and loss of other jobs along the way is a rampant, self-reinforcing problem. In place of rural prosperity is a growing collective hopelessness, as reflected by a rural drug crisis fueled by skyrocketing fentanyl deaths,[166] farmer suicide rates that put agriculture near the top of at-risk industries,[167] and more. Amid this loss of hope, the rural-urban divide has become one of our country's most stubborn political divisions, contributing to a world where we aren't disagreeing on ideas but on our differences as a people.[168]

Each of these problems—the resiliency of our supply chains, the environmental sustainability of an industry that depends upon the land, the physical security of our farmland, and the economic and cultural vitality of our rural areas—is solvable if we recognize a simple but painful truth: The disappearance of the American farmer has left us a less durable, less sustainable, and less secure food supply— and an economy and culture in crisis.

Take, for instance, the core issue of how we feed ourselves. Scott Brown, the University of Missouri economist, said he thinks the large players in our food industry responded well to a crisis nobody foresaw, but COVID still showed the dangers of having a small number of large players at so many parts of our supply chain, because there weren't enough routes to get products from the farm to the dinner table. Experts of various stripes note that having farms of various sizes supplying more of our food through a range of distribution channels would mean not as much of our country's food is impacted if one big distribution center, or shipping company, or processing plant faces disaster. Whether America decides it's time to change, Brown said, is unclear.

"If we have another big shock that shuts down, then this discussion about size I think becomes more critical," he said. "If COVID is one and done, we go back." While COVID was the largest-scale shutdown, history shows that disease among animals and other disasters have forced mass destruction of food and other problems for years.[169] The price of eggs again came under threat in 2022 and 2023 from bird flu.[170] So why not guard against it?

Beyond building the will to address the problems with our current food system, there's sorting out the right solution. The farm part of the solution may not be as simple as "big" vs. "small." It's true COVID showed the ways "big" wasn't always best during COVID. Critics of our food system have long said big facilities—from farms to food processors to many other industries—are breeding grounds for disease.[171] But Anderson, the Texas Tech professor, said similar to environmental issues, both large and small farms have advantages for resiliency. Big farms that have an outsized impact on the availability of meat when they have to slaughter their animals can also more easily afford to cull their herds of sick animals, she said, and employ the most advanced health techniques. The acknowledgment of these trade-offs—the potential for less widespread impact of disaster in the case of many small farms, and the potential for more advanced practices in the case of large farms—comes from an expert whose area of study is the health and happiness of the animal. Whether a farmer or farmhand is doing the right thing for their animals or anything else, she said, is more about the person than the type of farm.

"I think it depends upon the individual's moral and ethical stance," Anderson said.

Therefore, all of these issues—whether they involve farmers as champions of what is possible or as targets of criticism along with the broader food industry—mean there's value to there being more ways for farms of all sizes to be part of our country's solutions. Even if you have an objection to one kind of farm or another—say you value small farms' contributions to our society over those of big farms, or you think small farms are permanently obsolete—we still have the reality that large farms supply much of our food by keeping up with big players across the economy, and many small farms remain in existence, fighting for a way forward. We can't turn back the clock, and for the sake of all of us—large farms, small farms, and consumers at their dinner table or favorite restaurant—we can't let the disappearance continue indefinitely. The answer is having an economy where we have a diversity of farm sizes (large, midsized, and small) all making a more meaningful contribution to our country's food supply, and helping to solve the other economic and cultural challenges of modern America. Harnessing innovation to make large farms and our broader food system more sustainable, and more farms of all sizes viable, is the only realistic path.

Whether we can make more farms viable, and address the crisis of the disappearing American farmer, is a question our family was about to face more painfully than we ever had.

***

My sister had a system for when it got brutally cold outside. For our people—midwestern dairy farmers working morning and night through hard winters—cold temperatures were nothing new. They'd long been freezing the water our cows drank, busting pipes in our barn, and taxing the constitution of human and animal alike. Yet, this was an especially harsh winter, blended with the hardest of times.

Our dad was back working, but still recovering—those long-COVID symptoms still present, mixing now with a Vitamin B deficiency and further deterioration of his knees. His ailments left him with nothing to run on but the sheer determination of a man who had known cows in the barn all his life. My sister was seven months pregnant, her energy levels falling and discomfort rising as she consulted with doctors on how much longer she should work. And so, Malia took extra comfort in hanging her heavy coat over the compressor in the milkhouse, letting it warm before she ventured back out to brave the cold.

It was the long, hard, final winter of milking as our family searched, through friends and cattle jockeys and random word of mouth, for someone to buy our cows at a good price—a price good enough to give our new way of farming a strong start and let us hold our heads high. The heightened hardship sent us all reverting to our old ways. My dad had accepted it was time to sell, but he was putting his head down and burying the emotional loss to come. My sister hoped to show him a bright future but still harbored feelings of her own that she'd failed him. Our mom, who'd undergone brain aneurysm surgery, was less able to help than before, but she soldiered on, helping with Malia's kids as much as she could while worrying for them both.

And I was finding more ways to help but still as guilt-ridden as ever over not being able to do more.

Moments of love and loss alike accompanied the brutal winter. At one point during what looked like a lull in the difficult times with my dad back on his feet, I embarked on a winter road trip across the country with Rachael, fulfilling our hopes to see her family for a belated Christmas. We made it across the snow-covered Great Plains and through the Sierra Nevada Mountains to sunny California for a few days, only to be stranded when my car broke down in the wintry foothills of the mountains on the way back.

The upshot was us staying at her parents' house another week, just as the temperatures back home in Wisconsin dropped to some of their worst depths. I felt a stab of guilt even deeper than usual, wanting to be back to help my family, but my sister smoothed some of it over with a gesture that reminded me of where I came from and the bond my sister and I had built: In the middle of all the farm's challenges, she recognized my troubles enough to offer to drive across the country with the farm's pickup truck to help.

Finally, after months of dashed hopes, my sister found a buyer who met our price—a moment of finality we all recognized, at the same time, in our own ways. Malia and our dad spent their last moments milking and talking to and walking among the cattle, working together in the barn. Rachael and I walked the farmyard with my dad, hearing him recount some of the deepest family history that would eventually become this book. We got together for final milkings: our whole family all at once—working and laughing as our mom told stories of her and my dad dancing in the barn to the Grand Ole Opry on the radio—and my sister and I, each alone with our dad. Friends who had pitched in during tough times came to help or visit and show their support.

On the day the cows would go, my dad stood on a hill overlooking the back of our barn. It was March, that time turning from winter to spring when the snow is gone, but the earth hasn't yet woken back up. The cowyard spread below us, the cattle milling about in their final moments on our farm. Beyond its edges rolled the fields and old pastures on out to the woods where my dad used to escape as a young man, considering the weight on his shoulders of the farm that would one day be his.

I looked at the land bright under the sun, but not yet fully green, then back to him. His face was resolute leather beneath the brim of his cap, softened ever so slightly with the knowledge of the loss to come. His thick beard had weathered, somewhere, from gray to a stark white. Older now, wise as I'd seen him. Carrying in his mind and heart both pride for his animals and grief for their departure. He bore more nobly than ever that special weight that comes with standing for something that will soon be gone.

The trucks and trailers emerged on the road out past the driveway and rumbled into the yard, long and powerful, creaking and clinking with hints of the tumult to come. We assembled in the barn—the cattle jockey's crew, hired hands, me, my sister, family friends, and my dad—and began the sad and chaotic work of loading the cows. Starting first at the back of the barn, we drove the cows forward in groups with that blend of physicality and care needed to move a large group of animals that are stubborn but nonetheless beloved. Nudging and prodding and pushing and clapping and yelling. The noise drowned, as we went, those sounds of memory we would rather have let fill the barn forever—of the cows mooing low, of the milker pump blaring, of children running and laughing.

Before long there was nothing but the loading. And although there were no electronic cattle prods, nor an angry handler in the bunch, it was terrible in its finality. Each group of cows was another page of a century-long story nearing its end, turning with the deep and decisive sounds of the trailers filling. The boom of the cows' hooves into the trailer, the heavy creak of the metal beneath their weight, the clang of the trailer doors closing one by one. As we went, we found more and more cows breaking ranks—doubling back, as though they did not want to go—forcing us to turn them again and again toward the front of the barn to leave their home.

I turned amid the struggle and saw my dad standing in the back. He had started his morning walking up and down this very barn driveway, his hands clasped behind his back, weeping over his final moments with his cows. And he would return again after, weeping over their absence. Yet, in that moment, as the cows bellered and the handlers yelled and the trailers sounded, he watched quietly, declining to join in this task of loading his cattle. It was perhaps the one chore he had ever accepted, in all his life, that was not for him to do. Instead, he stood there in solidarity, with those bravest of cows that refused to go.

After the loading, we stood in the yard to watch the trailers go down the road. It was the same spot where Great-Grandpa Alois's machinery had clattered past after he sold the lower farm in the valley and where Grandpa Albert had looked as a young man, out the window of the farmhouse before he left for morning chores with booze coursing in his veins; now it would forever be the spot where my dad watched as our family's milk cows departed for good. He talked, to anyone who would listen, about how good the cows had done for him that day—3,900 pounds of milk, more than almost any other day—as though they had known what was coming. But now he stood there alone, hunched in his heavy work coat, and waved an open hand to all that was lost.

CHAPTER 11

THE ROAD TO REVIVAL

*Finding a Modern Path Forward through the
Lessons of the Past*

And so there we were, my dad and I, on that sacred ground. Back at the cabin we'd completed before he got sick, on that forty-acre parcel atop a cup of woods behind the farmhouse where we both grew up. It was that land where I had escaped the work that I'd done since I was old enough to walk, work that I was starting to value more than most things in life. I turned from the woods where I had struggled to follow my father's path years ago and took in this moment with him now.

We all lived this way of life, where a farm is not just a job but also our home, our community, our heritage. My dad most of all. His calloused hands hung off his knees, his strong but aging back barely holding him up against his sorrow. The sun still glowed across the honey-brown wood of the porch, and the trees still whispered of those things we had lost. And my father's tears still fell, like the rain that sometimes comes even as the sun shines.

I said it again.

"We have a chance to keep the farm going now, because of you, Dad."

It felt thin, hearing it again, and I was unsure if he would believe it over the sorrow of his cows going down the road. I said more.

"We don't have any debt, and you got a good price for your cows. Now we can go forward."

It was less about him believing me, more about him even hearing me. I could feel that unspoken specter—the hopelessness that had led farmers like him to take their own lives—hovering over us, crowding into his mind like a final storm that we couldn't see gathering over the land, darkening this day despite the shining sun and our family's hopes for the future. We still had our land, and we knew that was a privilege. And we had my sister's plan to take what we had left and find a new path.

But my dad thought only of failure. We understood on some level, being a stubborn farm family, each blaming ourselves. And yet my father's burden had a heavier weight, and he returned to it over and over. How, after a century of our family milking cows on this land, he was the one to sell them. How he was unsure, after a lifetime of rising before the sun, of what he would do tomorrow. How as he sat on my cabin porch, walked his empty barn, or looked out upon the land, he was uncertain of his purpose. Uncertain of who he was now. Thoughts came like dark storm clouds. *Why should I even be here?* So many farmers, across America and right down the road, asked similar questions before doing things that couldn't be undone. And now he was considering doing the same.

But he didn't. Instead, we talked, and after a while he stood and ventured into the sunlight coming down through the trees. In the days ahead, he began to think not only of what we had lost and the family he feared he had failed but also of his grandchildren. Most of all, his grandchildren: Steven, a young man now old enough to drive tractor. Roman and Paxton, the two younger boys running about the farmyard. And Malia's little girl due in April of 2021: Harlie Jean, to be named in part for our mother, the woman who helped him carry the farm forward. He began to see that no matter what happened to the farm, the farmer would still be needed. It was the same force that drove our family for more than one hundred years: the next generation. *I got grandkids here.* He began to repeat it to himself. *I got grandkids here, and I gotta teach them things.*

Soon enough, my sister offered new reasons for hope. Less than a month from the sale, she was in the empty barn, preparing it for the future. Instead of milking cows, Malia said, they would raise the smallest calves they would buy to build our new beef operation there, giving them a warm barn in their youngest days, just as they had when we milked, before turning them out into more space. We would need to make some updates, she said, and we would keep them dry and comfortable with lots of straw like in the old days. She was over eight months pregnant, and her refusal to let it stop her was as much about family as it was the farm.

"I don't want an empty barn," she said. Here she would start our animals off with the kind of love they would only get on a family farm, and a level of care that can be difficult for many small operations to provide. Along the way, she would ensure our barn had new life, the warmth of the animals keeping it from becoming brittle and falling to pieces, as Alois's barn once did down in the valley.

In addition to beef, she shifted our farm toward custom raising heifers for other farms—becoming a supplier to dairy farms, rather than a producer of dairy ourselves. She also remade our crop operation. Instead of raising crops mainly to feed the dairy herd we used to have, she planned to sell more. She and my dad would still grow hay, corn, and soybeans, but also begin to consider other crops. We began to shift, in ways large and small, away from the dairying that defined our farm for more than a century and toward the kind of mixed agriculture that first gave it a start—to the days when Alois and Teresia raised many things, searching for what could best put money in their pocket and food on their table.

As time went on, I saw that the answers to the future were indeed in our past—not just in those woods where I had my first deer hunt but also all over this land. Our return to the mixed agriculture of our roots once again offered both opportunity and peril. The opportunity was coming through new customers and more than one way to make money as a hedge against misfortune, just as farm families did before specialization became so intense. The peril was coming through uncertainty over which ideas would work and which would drive our farm closer to the edge. But now, unlike Alois and Teresia's time, we had lessons from a century of disappearing farms to guide us.

And that raised a question we all must confront. Not only our family, but our entire country—together.

***

Will we make it? Deciding whether we want to continue on the path that has given us the disappearing American farmer and all the consequences is the same as considering that generational question. It's the question facing farm families like ours, from those early days of survival to the challenges of modern-day farming and beyond. It's a question, too, facing America. *Will we make it?* Or will we continue with a food system that is capable of modern miracles but vulnerable to devastating disaster?

It's a difficult question because of the stakes and the many obstacles we must confront along the way. If we want to change course, we must find a way to challenge the status quo and make it possible for more farms to be part of the road to revival, rather than statistics in an ongoing downward spiral. Absent a way to do that, in many ways, the choice seems impossible. Choosing between a system that delivers any food imaginable to any corner of the country efficiently, safely and—for most of its history—cheaply, and one that guards America against supply-chain breakdowns, limited natural resources, foreign adversaries, rural decline, and the suffering of millions of families working to feed us. And the decision is made even more difficult by the fact that our guiding principle of cheap food has betrayed us. That system producing food for a lower share of family income is the same that's faced price hikes well beyond other rising costs in our economy. The cost of food saw the largest increase in forty years in August of 2022,[172] easily outpacing the fierce inflation at the time. It's a hard fact experts attribute to COVID's supply-chain disruptions, the war in Ukraine, bird flu affecting chicken and egg production, and more. At the same time, returning to a system of more plentiful small farms we idealize in our national mythology would not only mean turning back the clock but also mean, according to economists, that it could contribute yet again to higher prices if those farms can't operate as efficiently.

Maybe there's a better way—a way to have both the modern miracle of a global supply chain and a strong network of farms of all sizes, competing in a variety of markets. A system where some farms supply global commodities markets—still a helpful facilitator of trade and baseline pricing—and some supply local and regional markets that become a more regular part of how we feed ourselves. Maybe there are some farms that can supply both commodity markets and local food needs. It would require, of course, that large and small farms aren't all chasing the same opportunities, and there are many things that would need to change for that to happen. And yet, if this is a system that can exist, it offers a new way for farmers in this country to persist, and a way for Americans to have more choices every day, and greater access to food when disaster strikes.

There are those who say it can't be done, that we lost more than four million farms in the past century because of unavoidable needs for economic scale. But that ignores the farms we still have and the choices we can still make. Nearly two million farms remain in this country,[173] almost all meeting the government's definition of a family farm.[174] The largest of them drive our food economy, but 93 percent of them are still small or mid-sized farms looking for a path forward.[175] As with other government data, it's subject to definitions and assumptions that lead to debate over how many operations ought to qualify.[176] But that doesn't change the fact that America still has millions of resilient families, trying to farm. Many of them are on their way to being land rich and cash poor, and many of them already are.

What if more of those farms could be profitable businesses? Not hobby farms or sources of supplemental income, but growing businesses with new entrepreneurial possibilities, as they were when Alois Reisinger first settled in that valley deep in Wisconsin. Imagine the power of that happening at a time when data shows America's desire for healthy, conscious eating, which more regional food economies would support, is here to stay in a post-COVID world.[177] That renewal would also come at a time when revitalization of regional rural economies is more possible than ever in the wake of COVID, with more urban workers able to live and spend money in rural areas by working remotely, and more rural workers able to take advantage of remote work opportunities in addition to traditional rural jobs. In fact, from 2020 to 2021 rural population gains exceeded urban gains for the first time in decades[178]—a rural resurgence similar to farm kids fleeing urban squalor during the Great Depression, except this time in an era of opportunity where it can mean more rural customers, entrepreneurs, and workers.

Joby Young, executive vice president of the American Farm Bureau Federation, said the past few years have illustrated deep challenges, and farmers continue to battle as much uncertainty as ever. Yet, he argued America's renewed focus on how we feed ourselves is also an opportunity.

"There's a lot of new interest in where food comes from," he said.

"The rest of society is eager to hear from farmers and ranchers about what they do, and how they do it."

And so, we stand on these issues as if on a precipice, able to see and address these problems or fall deeper into them. The stakes could not be higher: our ongoing ability to feed ourselves, and the health of our broader economy and culture.

The time to act is now. Although food prices eased in 2023,[179] there's reason to think we'll be even more vulnerable to price spikes and other threats if our problems go unaddressed. Although economists say farms have gotten more efficient for decades, we're now in a place where productivity has slowed, said Jim MacDonald, the University of Maryland researcher who has spent years uncovering the wonders and worries of technology for farmers. That's a stark warning, because it means the affordability of our food could vanish, even without external forces like supply-chain disruptions that could return any time.

"If this doesn't turn around," MacDonald said, "then we can expect real food prices to rise, rather than remain constant."

Solving these problems requires that we face the hard truths—found in the history of the disappearing American farmer—that can unite rural and urban, right and left, farmer and consumer, defender and critic. These solutions will have to make economic sense for the farms that remain, as well as for consumers and others in our food economy, if we want them to work.

One key component, and prime example of the challenge, is the need for the growing local food movement, and dormant regional economies, to become far more robust. Our large, sophisticated food system—driven in part by the large farms that had to keep up with even larger suppliers and buyers—and other farms need to coexist and compete around different market opportunities. Some smaller farms might serve as suppliers of services to larger farms, like raising young livestock. Many more would need to provide new goods to other industries, like hemp for textile manufacturing or specialty foods to American households, via farmer's markets, farm-to-table restaurants, specialty-food sellers, direct sales to consumers, permanent outdoor markets, and other alternatives. A dynamic industry like this will also require enough opportunity to encourage new local market infrastructure to grow; many farmers in the heartland have a co-op or other commodity grain buyer to sell corn to, but no buyer or distributor for artisan vegetables or specialty wheat.

Some farms would make it, and others wouldn't. We can't (and shouldn't) guarantee the survival of every farm, and there will always be the uncertainty of weather, disaster, and other uncontrollable factors. As we've established, some level of disappearance was inevitable. There is only so much farmland, so early 1900s America couldn't keep adding new farms forever. Afterward, farms—as well as others in the agriculture and food industries—were always going to be competing and undergoing some level of industry consolidation as some did better than others. Yet, one thing seems certain: We don't have to keep making choices that wipe even more farm families off the map.

The fact is our country has made decision after decision that stacked the deck against a more economically diverse farm sector. Farmers who found niches during the days of survival moved on from mixed agriculture. Much of the country lived in an excess that all Americans paid for—farms uniquely so—in the Great Depression, and shifted far more fully than we realized from a rural economy to an urban economy that left farm communities languishing. Industry and government favored some players over others and began to leave behind more farms no matter how efficient they got. We chose which kinds of technological innovation to place a premium on in our economy. Both political parties supported using food as a weapon abroad, just as economic catastrophes of our own making were unfolding at home. We plunged into a modern economy increasingly defined by global forces and large industry, with too little regard for how we should preserve fair trade and real competition. And in those moments when we had the chance to save our farms, the desperation to survive was so deep we couldn't see them. In other words, while consolidation is a significant part of our disappearing farms, it's only one small part in a decades-long devastation driven by a range of forces outside our control and by seeds of decline we sewed as a country throughout our history.

The real problem is not the growth of some farms and the death of others, but the lack of rebirth that should always come next in America. It's tempting to pick a villain. Blame the big farms if you want, but they got that way trying to survive. Blame the big suppliers and buyers that leave even large farms the little guy, but then again, they're doing what we all do—reacting to the incentives of the market—and keeping up with bigger players across the rest of the economy. You probably could find good cause to blame the government. (And Nixon, Carter, or any president since. Why the hell not? Depending upon the policy decision you pick, you may have a point.) But that's imperfect, too, given how government under both Republicans and Democrats have made bad decisions for decades and that all of us have a say in what the government does. Some people want to also blame the consumer for demanding cheap and convenient no matter what. But that's not really the choice the consumers are making, because many don't see the alternative, outside of the occasional farmer's market that doesn't have the affordability or options they need. After all we've gotten wrong, the problem with blaming one person or group is that it avoids the deeper answer: We all did it.

In the critically acclaimed HBO crime series *The Wire*, creator David Simon portrays the city of Baltimore's problems not just as the actions of individuals but also as a result of what he calls broken institutions. Cops, drug users, dealers, business owners, unions, educators, journalists—all of them are complex humans acting rationally within a system that incentivizes the same damaging ends.

The rural economic version of this is what's called the "commodity trap." It's a trap farm boy and economic-development guru Chris Gibbons knows all too well, watching the decline of the rural Oklahoma community where his family began their farm in the 1890s. Recall that a commodity, which defines most of our agricultural economy, is generally a product that has become so uniform it no longer has any difference (e.g., corn grown in Wisconsin vs. Iowa), usually sold on an exchange (like the Chicago Mercantile Exchange, which allows for the trading of commodities like the New York Stock Exchange does stocks). Gibbons, founder of the National Center for Economic Gardening, said this destines rural communities for devastation if it's their only path.

Gibbons's theories, which have helped revitalize rural communities across the country with real economic growth, operate on simple economics. All businesses, he notes, run on how high of a profit margin they can make, and how much volume of a product or service they can produce. High margin/high volume exists in the economic blink of an eye—a gold rush—while low margin/low volume is a dead business, Gibbons said. What remains is high margin/low volume (say a tech company rolling out a unique product nobody else makes yet) and low margin/high volume (where not only farms but many businesses reside, with the end point being a commodity). Most businesses operate somewhere within those two sectors of a unique product and a commodity, he said. Some slide around in between being unique and commoditized (say, a restaurant just like any other, except for that rare dish nobody else can perfect).

Our family's story, like so many, is of sliding into the commodity trap. Milk wasn't a unique product when Alois Reisinger first laid eyes upon our valley, but Wisconsin's niche as America's Dairyland was on the rise—farmers, researchers, and advocates finding ways for our state to stand apart. Wisconsin farmers led the way in milk for drinking, cheese, cream, and more, while experimenting with other products and crops to keep innovating. Yet, as dairy became the dominant industry in Wisconsin and grew elsewhere, it became standardized and part of a much larger supply chain. The game for dairy farmers shifted from doing something new to perfecting more of the same for a lower price, Gibbons said. And that price was determined by a far-off market exchange, like today's Chicago Mercantile Exchange, that made much more commerce possible but lessened the farmer's chance to negotiate. Finally, farms got so efficient, the only way to compete was to consolidate with one another.

"It squeezes everybody out; it automates," Gibbons said. "It's a systems issue."

It's easy to think there's no way out of a system like that. But that's why we have to remember the untold history of the disappearing American farmer, one our country has made worse—and can therefore make better—with economic, political, and technological decisions. In a world where so many farmers are so committed to a way of life that is so unworkable in this country, imagine what we can accomplish if we agree on making it work again. We could find ways to resist the pull of more and more farms becoming land rich and cash poor, and to enable new opportunity for those who already have. Gibbons says the way to do that is innovation: farms, small businesses, and rural communities constantly finding ways to offer something unique. Among the dozens of agricultural economists, experts, farmers, advocates, and others I've talked to, those who believe there's a way out often say that's the only one. I believe there are solutions to help make this happen that emerge from the history of the disappearing American farmer—solutions that can help create an environment where those working on farmland innovation have a better shot of pulling it off. How to do this is what families like ours have to explore—and what everyone, rural and urban alike, must support—if we want the American farmer to survive.

***

My sister looked at the empty free stall barn and saw possibility where our dad saw pain. The free stall was a shed he built onto our old barn years earlier, one of the final major improvements we could afford as margins got tighter. It was once a simple but important innovation that gave our milk cows another place to roam when they weren't in the barn—shelter from weather, access to food and water, a dry place to lie down. Now with our milk cows gone, it stood empty. The pigeons that had flown in and out of it for years were the only remaining sign of life. Alone now, they gave the free stall the feel of a shuttered church any time a visitor drove them flapping from the rafters and out the door.

Malia knew it could be more—part of a broader reorientation to accommodate heifers for other farms. We didn't need the iron dividing the free stall into lanes and stanchions, or the cement curbs, all of which gave our milk cows loose areas to bed down as they pleased. If we tore out the iron and poured cement to smooth out the floor and spread dry, warm cornstalk bedding, that would give the heifers plenty of space and all the shelter they would need. And if we made some new fencing, eventually we could even connect the free stall and the cow yard outside to the cow lane running past old pastures, to a corral up the hill. With a little money and a lot of work, Malia's idea could catapult another of our new businesses, offering a place for quality care of animals that would become milk cows on other farms.

The problem was getting our dad to agree. As he saw it, the free stall was destined either to hold milk cows or sit empty. Our dad had joined the ranks of aging farmers fearful of change. He was filled with hard-earned wisdom and doubt. Change is always hard, but especially so for someone fighting his whole life to preserve something that felt endangered from the start.

Our family, and our country, must break free of false choices to make change. For our family, breaking free of the false dilemma of our free stall barn—one of doing the same or doing nothing—was one of many decisions we have had to navigate, large and small, to find new products, markets, and customers. For America, there are false choices all around us, but the central one is that we must pick between a global system delivering our food in all the ways we're accustomed to, or the local farmer's market as a novelty—the subject of a Sunday morning stroll for the extra food-conscious, but not a serious industry providing our country's food and other specialty products. If we are to reject that false choice, we must reject the many other false choices of the past and look for a place where our boundaries as a society (political and otherwise) are being redrawn. Only then can we marshal all our resources—private industry, academia, government under both political parties, farms of all sizes, and consumers of all stripes—to create the sustained private-sector innovation we need for a more durable, more sustainable, more secure food supply. This sort of sustained private-sector innovation would require ways for small and midsized farms to innovate as well as large farms do, a government that helps open more trade opportunities for our current food system while protecting legitimate competition for everyone operating in it, an agriculture industry ready to reorient itself, rural communities that are thriving again, and consumers who are ready for more lasting change. This is a huge and complex problem that took decades to create, so fixes won't be easy or immediate, and there's a good deal that's unforeseeable still. But there are opportunities to fundamentally change our thinking and create a path toward clearer solutions:

1. Start a research and development revolution

Technological innovation in this country has made the impossible possible—and the unknown suddenly obvious and crucial to advancement—countless times in the history of our country. This is true of society at large, be it the printing press or the personal computer. It's also true of farming with hybrid corn that multiplied yields exponentially, tractors and irrigation that made far more land farmable, methods that made dairy farming a unique niche for America's Dairyland, and more. Now, artificial intelligence (AI) and other tech place us at a crucial crossroads.

The problem is that research and development resources are sorely lagging. Combined with the way technological innovation has needlessly left behind smaller farms, the stalling R&D means many haven't benefited from the kind of advancements that could make them newly economically viable. One of the best measures of innovation driven by R&D is Virginia Tech's *Global Agricultural Productivity Report*. It shows that growth in total factor productivity—the amount of additional productivity achieved with the same or fewer resources— has declined by an average of 43 percent globally since 2010, with the United States being a major source of the drag after decades as a global leader in innovation.[180]

R&D represents an opportunity for a new consensus on American farming: a solution that the many farm groups who disagree on other issues are unified on and that both sides of the aisle can support. The need for more innovation can be partially remedied by private-sector companies focusing on R&D that can include farms of all sizes— maybe not the first inclination of large companies looking for large partners, but in their interest ahead of another supply-chain crisis. Privately funded university research can also help.

Government is an important source of funding for laboratories and universities researching unknown frontiers where private entities can't, and such funding is at its lowest level since 1970 when controlling for inflation.[181] The fix gets tangled in disagreements over spending priorities and endless examples of wasteful government spending by both parties. However, properly focused government research has long fueled private-sector innovation—from jet engines to the Internet[182]—meaning, with the right accountability, there's room for bipartisan agreement.

Technological breakthroughs can give farmers more options beyond getting big or getting out—if we make innovation for farms of all sizes a priority in ways we've failed to in the past. Take AI. Researchers say it may mean more large farms operating driverless tractors, with one worker watching a bank of screens. But AI is also capable of creating small driverless vehicles for jobs like spraying fields, which some economists say could be *scale neutral*, meaning affordable and practical for smaller farms too. There's another opportunity for gene-editing technology, which edits the genetics of existing crops—rather than the more controversial practice of engineering new life—to make them growable in more places. This could mean a whole new generation of crops, economists say, grown in different climates by all kinds of local farms, rather than shipped across the country.

Then there is sustainable aviation fuel—which researchers say can draw on corn and other agricultural products and waste[183]—creating a new market for many farmers and providing economical clean energy. One thing we need to bear in mind is the financial limitations of many farms that have become land rich, cash poor. The innovation for midsized and small farms will need to be affordable and efficient enough to quickly recoup the up-front expense through cost savings. That way, farms can justify funding transitions to new technology with whatever savings they can muster, a (hopefully) small amount of debt, or the sale of used machinery or a portion of land that doesn't compromise their whole farm.

Scott Irwin, a prominent agricultural researcher and professor at the University of Illinois at Urbana-Champaign, said the potential for innovation is explosive. The only question, he said, is whether we'll steer technology to benefit all farms.

"I do think there's potential room to grow businesses in a different direction, not just by pure scale," Irwin said. "I think we are on the cusp of a huge technological revolution."

Events like World Dairy Expo and Farm Technology Days—to name just two examples in my home state—have kept technology front of mind for farmers. A research and development revolution could spread quickly if we agree to set it off.

2. Remake government policy around competition

Government under both political parties has long shown support for America's farmers, and yet both parties have failed farmers—and therefore everyone who eats in this country—throughout our history. What's lacking is a unified principle to guide us, beyond the simple desire for cheap food, that can take us past bipartisan affection into a total transformation. It's a complicated picture, but there are some simple truths. The left's usual answer, government intervention, has provided support but failed to solve the underlying issues, leaving the American farmer chasing subsidies around specific crops because of the sure money, rather than innovating. The right's usual answer, the market, has represented new opportunity but let the American economy become filled with global and domestic industry so large that the American farmer is left endlessly chasing bigger scale to survive. What we need is government policy that makes it easier for farmers to chase new entrepreneurial opportunity in a fair marketplace. There's a wide range of policy reforms that can do that, touching everything from tax reform to regulations, but there are at least two areas ripe for bipartisan cooperation right off the bat:

Targeted trade strategy: The American pendulum has swung from bipartisan support for free trade to bipartisan resistance. One path forward would be targeting trade barriers with individual countries to cut deals around a specific crop or product. Stephanie Mercier, the Farm Journal Foundation economist, said this strategy can open up new markets for American farmers, with fewer trade-offs than deals involving many products across many countries. Paired with tough trade enforcement that holds trading partners accountable without a trade war, this can be an effective solution; America's dominant global economic position still gives us plenty of leverage. Removing smaller trade barriers and enforcing current agreements may create room for progress while our political parties recalibrate on big trade deals. If we get to a point where the public trusts our leaders to cut larger deals again, perhaps they'll do so with a more nimble and resolute approach, based on the lessons of a more targeted strategy.

Balanced antitrust policy: Though worry over the presence of "big" in our economy has been a long-running concern of the left and a newer one for the right, both sides have an interest in this issue that could represent a new alignment in American politics. Capitalizing on this—and not taking it too far—requires both sides channeling populist anger in a productive direction. The left can't target every company in this country just for being big, both for practicality's sake and because economists say that would upend markets that farmers and working families alike depend upon. The right needs to complete its internal debate between free-market economists focused on economic growth and those conservatives wanting to fight corporate control. (There's a balance to be had on the political right, with the tipping point being competition—you can fight for low taxes and less regulation and still believe in preventing companies from restricting their own competition.) If both the left and right emerge ready to tackle this issue in a productive way, we can encourage meaningful competition across the entire American economy, giving more types of business owners—including farm families—a fair shot at competing, without restricting proper private enterprise.

There are other places the two parties could explore, such as removing barriers around emerging crops like hemp that can be grown on farms and used in a wide range of consumer products and materials. With both parties seeming to accept that some level of government support is necessary to guard our food supply against weather and other natural disaster, there are ways to reform subsidies: diversifying to avoid such heavy incentives around crops that don't always corre-spond to consumer needs, and ideas to ensure subsidies reach a broad base of farmers rather than becoming concentrated among a favored few. It's also legitimate to discuss what kinds of programs might be worthwhile to help cash-strapped farms wanting to retool for the future. However many issues we tackle, we can build upon our best policies and discard our worst if the equality-minded left accepts that government spending can't solve all of farmers' problems and the competition-minded right accepts that our global and domestic econ-omies lack fair and legitimate competition in some places.

Affordable food can remain part of the discussion, but the north star should be freeing farmers to capitalize on opportunity by ensur-ing a competitive marketplace.

3. Reorganize farms around new market opportunities

Farmers are among the most resourceful people you will find. Anyone who can learn to repair a tractor through trial and error and use baler twine to fix damn near anything is going to find a way to survive. But being under siege for so long has forced the industry to focus on pre-serving the status quo, rather than looking for new opportunity more often. Farmers need to find more ways to reorganize themselves—as an industry overall, and on an individual farm level—around how to find new market opportunities.

One industry-level example is Wisconsin cheesemaking. For decades, America's cheese industry largely made the same varieties, often cheddar, that could be sold for many uses and that the federal government used to buy to help control supply. But with its title as top milk producer under siege in the 1990s, Wisconsin launched its Master Cheesemaker Program,[184] part of a broad effort to fuel a new generation of private-sector cheese production. Today, it's the only such program in the country: cheesemakers creating a wide variety of cheeses used all throughout our food economy, giving small cheese factories a more robust industry to compete in alongside other players and supporting more places for farmers to sell their milk. It's one of the reasons Wisconsin remained a strong source of farms of all sizes for longer, as so many farms vanished—a sign that specializing to create a regional food economy works, but also that we need more such innovation to have a bigger impact.

There have been other examples, such as the rise in organic farming, agri-tourism, and other trends that have created opportunities that work for some but not all. What we need are more outlets, because reorganizing around new market opportunities is a challenge—it means farmers taking risks on new products and new ways of doing things that would be hard for anyone, with their livelihoods and so much more at stake. My family's experience exemplifies this shift as we retool our farm for mixed agriculture: raising beef for consumers, heifers for other farms, and a range of cash crops. Making this transition means changing our operations, but also the more difficult task of finding customers outside of the traditional market infrastructure.

Belinda Burrier knows all too well the challenges of making change. The farm she and her husband Dave run in Maryland grows corn, wheat, hay, and soybeans (standard commodities for many farms). But they also grow high oleic soybeans, a specialty variety used in a wide range of cooking oils and foods. They voluntarily led the way in their region on conservation practices that required time and money but reduced the erosion of their soil, leading to higher crop yields and better sustainability. Burrier, who helps the Farm Journal Foundation and others promote new practices, said innovation that meets a market opportunity is the key.

"We get a premium for growing it, so we grow it," Burrier said of the high oleic soybean. "It's one of the ways that you diversify."

As more opportunities like this become possible through an R&D revolution, reformed government policy, and new market opportunities, farmers can capitalize by injecting some additional experimentation into their operations—taking any small leftover earnings to invest a few acres in a new crop or a new farming method to see what it can become. This can also mean a return to farmers hedging against any one market taking a nosedive—as they used to do by selling a trailer of pigs in a down year—rather than having to double down on producing more of their main crop or product, no matter the price.

4. Revitalize rural communities

When a place loses hope, it's in need of both emotional and economic revitalization.

One place to start is recognizing the unique mental anguish of farmers who feel it's not just their job but also their entire heritage on the line as they work endlessly to save their farms. Simply advising "work-life balance" doesn't cut it with those stakes—we need to streamline the process for licensing mental health professionals and teach them about rural America, to unleash a new generation of counselors ready to save lives.

The Farmer Angel Network, a group that shines a light on farmer mental health issues and organizes a wide range of events and support, began in my native Sauk County after a beloved local farmer took his life. Randy Roecker, a founding member who fell into depression himself while fighting through the Great Recession, said farm families—a group raised to keep their heads down and move ahead—are talking about the issue more.

"We're bringing it out into the light," Roecker told me. "It's okay to talk about mental health now and the struggles we're going through."

More properly trained counselors could also help rural residents of all stripes with many problems, from losing their economic prospects to falling into our rural drug crisis.

On the economic-revitalization front, local communities can have an impact by finding the unique identity and products they can offer, said Chris Gibbons, the economic gardening expert who has helped rural communities revitalize. State and federal policymakers can help with policies encouraging rural small business growth and investment. There may be more opportunity to do this than ever—with many rural areas attracting new residents in the wake of COVID, there are more people bringing money into the rural economy and more ways rural residents can access the urban one. That means more customers, more economic opportunities, more ideas in both directions.

5. Vote with dollars and time in a whole new way

These solutions bring us to what we all can do as individuals, which boils down to one simple question: What are you doing to give our farms new opportunities?

This is a question we can all ask ourselves—as consumers and citizens—to guide our decision-making in a new food economy. It's a very different question than "what are you doing to support farmers?" or others like it, so that we can go beyond what we've tried before in this country—there has been no shortage of goodwill, government, or occasional purchases at farmers markets that show support but don't really change anything. If a research and development revolution is creating unforeseen opportunity, government is geared to preserve a meaningful marketplace, farmers are organized around new market opportunities, and rural communities are being revitalized, we'll still need people making more decisions than ever with the American farmer in mind. We can all help our farmers find new opportunities, our families new food sources, and America a system that can withstand disaster.

Consider for a moment the dilemmas of the local food movement. Though they're sprouting up in more communities, farmers markets and farm-to-table restaurants are still most prominent in cities with affluent, food-conscious customers. Other parts of the country lack robust options altogether, often in rural communities that don't even have a local grocery store—contributing to food deserts, ironically, in places with plenty of land to grow local food. We also have to respect that affordable food is a rational desire for all Americans. What we have now is a catch-22: a local food movement becoming more accepted but with too small of a presence—too few farmers in some areas, too few customers in others—to thrive and truly seem like an option to many consumers. The system has to change to allow the naturally growing desire for local options to flourish, which is why R&D making innovation possible for more farms, government policy removing barriers, farmers focusing on new markets, and rural revitalization happening are all part of the solution.

The next step is finding ways to gear all of our food decision-making toward new opportunities for farmers. Of course, those who can afford it and live by a specialty food source can do more of what they're doing. Those who can't afford it or don't have access can take incremental steps: balancing affordability and variety by deliberately pairing a standard grocery run with a stop by a farmers market or produce stand or local butcher shop. We'll all have to work to bridge divides. Proponents of the local food movement may have to become more accepting of and attuned to the foods many people want. And those people who are new converts to eating locally will need to accept alternative places to buy food and some of the trade-offs (happy surprises from unique local food vendors, but also seasonal limitations on some foods, at least until gene editing blossoms).

The result, if it is guided by giving farms new opportunity, will be growing and raising more kinds of local, fresh, natural, and sustainable food—and a new consensus around what we expect as consumers. Eventually, more customers at farmers markets, grocery stores that offer local specialty foods, restaurants with meaningful farm-to-table options, and other truly local food sources will make broader change possible. With technological innovation, government policy, and farmers' actions reinforcing this change, the market can shift toward the rebirth of regional food economies. This means a world where not only farmers grow more types of local food but also food buyers, distributors, and other market infrastructure sprout up to connect farmers and consumers in new ways. If enough people show they want new opportunity for our country's farmers, you can guarantee American ingenuity will give them what they want.

This philosophy can provide common ground in the debates over modern farming, too. It's true some farms make good money and some bad actors exploit government assistance—both scenarios fanning the flames of debate between critics and defenders of modern agriculture. If we don't make a change, no matter the ups and downs, many more struggling farms acting in good faith will continue to disappear. They may fall transitioning from one generation to the next, collapse under debt, or fail trying to lease acreage in the absence of land passed down. Freeing all of them to pursue new opportunities can give successful farms more room to live up to the ideals they were founded upon and struggling farms a chance to earn more than our admiration.

This philosophy also provides a principle for us as citizens. If we want a government that will back the American farmer in a new way—reorienting policy properly and staying out of the way of these other solutions—then politicians need to hear that from voters. The next time someone running for office (or someone on their behalf) walks by in a parade, knocks on your door, engages you online, or gives a local speech, ask this specific question and see if you get a thoughtful answer: What are you doing to give our farms new opportunities? If they need you to explain what you mean to get past answers you've heard before, tell them about the local sources where you buy food—or the lack of them—and what you'd like to see more of in the future.

***

As the months turned to the first few years of life after milking, I saw my sister blossom. The little girl who ran without fear toward rabid raccoons—believing them to be kitties in need of love—ran toward her role as farm successor with the same passion, paired now with a grown woman's sense of the dangers. Our dad agreed to update the free stall barn and make other changes.

As Malia took on more, she began to see what it would take for the farm's new finances to pencil out to profit. Each of her business lines—cash cropping, raising heifers, and raising beef cattle—hit the income levels she had projected, but the farm still faced expensive challenges as we transitioned out of dairy. She and our dad worked the fields, found new customers for our crops, and considered what else might be friendly to our soil. The heifers she was custom-raising for local farmers filled the space she had made for them. The biggest area of growth that remained was our beef business, where she worked to move past the occasional side sale to create a growing operation regularly selling beef to a variety of local sale barns, as well as local families, and—we could only hope—a new generation of consumers who cared where their food comes from.

One day in early 2022, my dad texted me a picture of heifers fat and happy, roaming our cow yard. The rolling hills of our fields were beyond, under a blanket of snow bright beneath the warm sun.

"Good to see cattle again," he said.

He continued to worry about high expenses and tight margins, uncontrollable weather, and other vulnerabilities as we transitioned from one type of farming to another, one generation to another. But he no longer worried about who would take over the farm. He could see her—the fourth generation to come after Alois, Albert, and him—working by his side. And he began to accept again the idea, declared by family and many local farmers, that he was a good farmer, one who made it when others didn't, to provide a debt-free farm so the next generation can try to beat the odds.

Malia began to talk with a kind of hope many had thought long dead. Somehow, when she thought of taking over when my dad was sick and other times she had done the impossible, she thought not of the hardship—as I did in my days of falling short on the farm—but of the people who have helped her. Her life started to embody that unique farmland spirit—a blend of the individualism it takes to dig your living out of the ground and the sense of community it takes to come running when a neighbor is in need. Hearing her gave me hope our farm can go on, even if the era that built it is over. Our dad agreed.

"I think we'll make it," he told me in quiet moments. "She's doing a good job."

As for me, I smile when I think of my sister achieving her dream of doing as our ancestors did while raising her own family. I think of the blessings of growing up in this place: our old cow dog running out to pasture to bring the cows in, on a simple whistle from my dad; riding as kids in the back of his old pickup with the sun setting, chanting, "Eighty-five! Eighty-five!"—the highest number on the speedometer—and screaming when he pushes it to what couldn't be more than forty on the uneven dirt road. And I still feel a tinge of guilt during the tough times. The only things that relieve the guilt are to try to help when I can, and to write by myself—in the clear fresh morning, when nobody else is awake but the farmers. Suspended there between the gratitude and the guilt is a mental picture of me and my father working together. I could tell myself it's a memory from boyhood before our paths in life parted. Or maybe it's just an idea of us never parting, as if in another life. But I know it is a picture of a very specific memory: our last milking together.

We are just days now from selling the herd. It's early and the hard winter has begun to give way to spring, the morning air just cool enough that our breaths rise like the gentle fog of days gone by as we work and talk, and I try to remember. The yellow barn lights shining overhead take on that golden hue of my boyhood, and the barn is warm again now with the heat of the cows, maternal and hungry, lining the barn on both sides. We journey among them together and do the morning chores, those I'd done from the time I was old enough to walk, until the time I was old enough to walk away. The old barn radio crackles, and out of it comes country music and in between local news—word of kids' sports and weather and commodity prices and obituaries, and then back around in another loop. The milking machines begin to pulse, and I feel again that old feeling of being unsure.

Although I've been helping again for years now with fieldwork, odd jobs, and the business side of the farm when I can, I realize at age thirty-six it's been two decades since I milked alone with my father. While I am not quite afraid, I am uneasy like when I first began to milk, and the cows don't know me well. I fumble the milking machines, finally dropping one, and bow my head. He sees—I know he sees—and I think of letting him down and then again of turning away.

Only this time, I do neither, and instead hold the moment close. I pick the milker back up and put it back on the cow, again and again. I embrace the uneasiness, knowing it is not just the feeling of being less than my father but also of holding onto something precious. My dad talks to his cows, and I watch him move from one to the next. Now and then he seems as strong and sure as when he was a young man, bringing his little boy along for the job. I see the herd is good and healthy with all Malia has done, the cows' tails tails swishing in the golden light. We continue.

I step between the warmth of each cow and think of my father and I, walking in the woods years ago, trying to find each other in the years since. That's when I realize it is all right to be unsure—of the world, our farm's future in it, and how I can live up to him. I am still following him, in my own way, carrying this special weight we share.

Somehow in this memory time bends, and it goes on longer than it did when I first lived it. I know of course as I look upon it that the cows are now gone, and that we are finding a new way. And yet I see us again and again, endlessly in the barn as we work and talk, and I try to remember—the yellow barn lights shine with an even more golden hue, the milkers pulse more softly, and the cows swish their tails with grace as my father walks among them forever. And the barn radio keeps playing its old country music—lying to us, sweetly, that it is still years ago.

EPILOGUE

When you grow up close to the land, you feel the presence of those who came before you. Sometimes you'll even believe in spirits of loved ones, hearing them in the wind as time passes around you. You'll sense them in the places you worked alongside them or the hillsides you looked upon together. You'll see them in signs of nature or the appearance of animals, too plentiful or oddly timed to ignore the notion that those who've passed live on and sometimes come back from the heavens above to comfort us.

The red-breasted robins, swift hummingbirds, and silent butterflies. Each one of them is a grandfather or grandmother, or even further back to Alois and Teresia, or someone else lost along the way and always remembered. The great bald eagle will always conjure my two grandfathers. Grandpa Albert Reisinger, calling me "Smart Eagle Bird" as a little boy, giving me faith to follow my dreams, believing somehow that I would make him proud someday wherever I flew. Grandpa Roman Ripp, always spotting the eagle perched in the tree when he took us fishing up north, later guiding me in those intervening years when I had walked away from farming with my dad but not yet found my path back to our way of life. Not far from the farm is a place called Sauk City—what Grandpa Albert called "going to town"—where the American bald eagle famously congregates, in a small flatland along the Mississippi River surrounded by the hills of the Driftless region spared by the glaciers centuries ago.

In the days since we sold the cows and Malia began to operate our farm with my dad on new terms, there has been joy, and sadness, and many moments we have looked to our ancestors. It was back in the woods at my cabin where my dad first got his sense of smell back from his bout with long COVID. Sitting there, in the fresh wood of the place I'd dedicated to Albert and Anna, with memories of both sides of our family hanging on the walls, he looked at me and told me he could smell the white pine. We talked a lot there, and out in the farmyard and in the living room of the farmhouse, about the path the farm would take. Through many informal chats and family meetings with all four of us, we shared hopes, discussed what was working and what wasn't, planned for the future, worked through legal and financial issues, and untangled the emotions around a family business we all felt we were failing at, one time or another. We ultimately had to have the local fire department burn down the old homestead where Alois and Teresia settled and Albert and his siblings grew up. It was simply too old and run-down to be habitable, a barrier to something new and useful being done with the land. It was a bittersweet day as we watched the flames begin, flashing and dancing—as they had when Albert and Sophie escaped the enflamed house as children—before this time consuming the old rough-sawn farmhouse in full.

I began a new journey in 2023, in California of all places, when Rachael got a new job near where she grew up. It was a chance to advance her career and be near her family—just as I had done when I moved back home to Wisconsin from my travels in Tennessee and Washington, DC. Wanting that for her, and not wanting to leave my home behind, we decided I'd split my time between the small town we moved to in northern California and the family farm where I grew up. Keeping my job in Wisconsin and continuing my writing, I began to work remotely when I was in California and live on the farm when I was in Wisconsin, for the first time since I was eighteen. I've come to love life in both places. Rachael gave birth to our daughter, Ana

Elizabeth Reisinger—named for my Grandma Anna and Rachael's Abuelita Ana—as I was completing the draft of this book. My little baby girl waited a few extra days to come as I rushed to finish and prepared for my most important job of fatherhood. She has saved her daddy from himself in so many ways.

And so I return, over and over, to my roots, winding the way of life I grew up with into my own. Through it all the place I most love to breathe the clean country air is the small cabin I'd formally named St. Albert's Retreat—that place my dad and I created together, on that sacred ground our family walked through the generations, and where he and I hunted, and where we mourned the loss of his cows, and where we both regained so much. I sit there on the porch as the summer sun warms the forest floor and the wind moves through the trees; as fall turns the leaves to their boldest oranges, reds, and yellows before falling to the ground; and as the snow falls. Sometimes the snow is light and swirling from the cold sky of deep winter like stars turning in space. Sometimes it is soft and wet to gather on the branches of the trees before slipping in graceful tufts to the ground. Later it melts, and the air fills with the life of spring, greening in the intermittent rhythm of gentle sun and falling rain. I'm surrounded in all seasons by the tracks of animals: squirrel and rabbit and turkey and deer and coyote and bobcat. It's in the spring that the spirits of our loved ones begin again to show themselves—those oddly timed robins, hummingbirds, butterflies. The eagles in the trees beyond.

I step off the porch sometimes, especially in the light rain falling from the heavens above, and walk back toward the rock shelf where I missed my first deer with my dad so many years ago. I think of the tracks and other traces of the animals moving across the land and wonder if perhaps I'll even find those of our family's cows from yesteryear, though I know they've long since washed away. I think also of those things more permanent, like the bond between the members of a family and a piece of land, so long as they can hold onto it. Taking my hat off, I look skyward and watch and feel and smell the rain falling on me and on our land, as though we are one.

We've each found such fragile peace in the face of a struggle that is ongoing. Our faith is constantly challenged and renewed, not only through our own struggles or the family arguments that crop up but also through those mishaps that can befall a farm anytime. Dry years killing crops. Animals falling sick. One fall morning, my sister bravely fought a fire to protect our animals, as Alois and Teresia had a century before to protect their home. Those are the kinds of moments—tragedies often the fault of no one—when farms already ground so far into the ground can finally go under. And yet, we continue onward.

It is the tragic cost of the beauty our way of life offers, to face those perils as our ancestors did. Maybe that is why we look to them. As we did not that long after we sold the cows, when the money was especially tight and my dad and sister struggled with where best to sell their corn from that fall's harvest. It was no longer feed for the cows, but rather a main revenue source with which we had to make top dollar, at a time when income from our new lines of business had not yet come in and expenses were still high from our dairying days. And then, in the middle of these and so many other worries, a great American bald eagle flew through the farmyard—his wings broad and powerful as he soared down from above and glided among the tractors and the cattle and the family fretting that day. It was on that same day that the eagle flew that we found a buyer in extra need of corn, if we could spare it.

We decided the eagle must have been Grandpa Albert. Flying down from his place of rest, no longer weighted with guilt or sadness or drink, to give us the kind of faith born only in hardship.

FINAL NOTE ON MENTAL HEALTH

One of my home state's great writers, Michael Perry, wrote a novella about a farmer struggling with mental health as his farm faltered. That book, *40 Acres Deep*, came out as I was writing this book, and it reminded me of how important it is to bring mental health out into the light.

If you are struggling, you are not alone. Please talk to someone. And don't hesitate to get professional help—it is a sign of strength, not shame.

Contact the National Suicide Prevention Lifeline for urgent help at 1-800-273-8255, or text HELLO to 741741. There are also support groups, like the Farmer Angel Network, which began in my home county and has a growing presence in Wisconsin: https://www. farmerangelnetwork.com/.

ACKNOWLEDGMENTS

This book would not have been possible without the support of so many people, to a degree that I never could have imagined. Thank you first, foremost, and always, to my wife Rachael for your love, and patience. I am always amazed by the charity you have for others, least deservingly so me. You are not only my soulmate and best friend but also an incredible mother, friend, editor, and more, truly the center of my universe around which all other things—including an overwhelming project like this—orbit.

Thank you to my dad for being more honest about your life than I could have imagined anyone being. I want to also thank my mom for the hours of stories, many years of encouragement, and the stacks of photos, facts, and feelings you have carefully preserved in our family's scrapbooks—they are a treasure for all who see them, and a crucial record in a book project like this. Thank you, Malia, for the fearless heart you show each day in your work and life, and also in the memories you shared for this book. Thank you to my wife's family, for being so welcoming to someone from such a different place.

I appreciate the many other members of my family across multiple generations and members of the local community where I grew up, whom I interviewed about multiple eras of family and community history—some of whom were willing to appear in the book, some of whom wished to remain in the background but were still willing to offer their knowledge, all of whom were invaluable. Thank you especially to Great-Aunt Helene Dederich for your patient and joyful sharing of stories that combined with the interviews, stories, and memories from so many others in our family going back to my grandfather's generation, including those still living and those now passed on. A special thank you to Helene's son, Stan Dederich, for your generous help and the invaluable family genealogical archives you maintain and have shared with so many. The facts of family history that are woven into this book—alongside the interviews, family recollections, and my own observations—are drawn from the research you have carried on from your dad.

Thank you also to the many subject-matter experts, keepers of historical records and data and more, whom I interviewed or bothered so often for information, with special thanks to Mary Jayne Liegel at the Old Franklin Township Historical Society, the talented data specialists at the US Department of Agriculture, and others.

I want to thank the many people who have helped me in my writing career through the journalism, public policy, and consulting worlds, including my first newspaper editor Art Drake—the first person willing to pay me for the written word and open an entire world to me—and all the many editors and other colleagues I've had since. Thank you also to my mentors in other professional walks (and on both sides of the aisle), including Tom Ingram, for special advice; Dave Cooley, for commonsense wisdom; David Cleary, for always being in my corner; Tony Blando and Betsy Ankney, for bringing me home; and so many more. I'd also like to thank Senator Lamar Alexander, for the special interest you've always shown in my writing and the wisdom you've shared about public policy and life. Thank you to Keith Gilkes, for not only mentoring me upon my return to Wisconsin but also giving me a shot at helping to build a small business with you, and to the many members of the Platform team who help us keep it thriving, including Kathryn Kotowski, Anthony Birch, Rusty Schultz, and others—sometimes, a business

ACKNOWLEDGMENTS

feels like a family, even when it isn't passed down through the generations.

I want to thank my agent, Nena Madonia, for giving me honest advice, heartfelt support in times of need, and above all else encouragement to be myself. Thank you to my editor Jesse McHugh and the entire team at Skyhorse, for seeing what this story could be and for your thoughtful consideration and encouragement all along the way. Thank you to Sara Rath and Tim Mahoney, the first authors who took the time and care to read my writing, in addition to the many other writers who've offered advice and encouragement. Special thanks to Lisa Scofield and Mick Showen, teachers who saw something in a talkative farm boy. Thank you to the many others who gave crucial feedback on the pages of this book, including Collin Roth, Luke Woodard, Mark Schaaf, and Nick Halter.

All of you helped me improve not only this book but also my understanding of what this all means.

ENDNOTES

1   Analysis of shifts in number of farms and per capita data based upon US Census of Agriculture and US Census, 1920. Throughout this book, I use data from the US Census of Agriculture from 1850 through 2022. Given the long period that it covers, the data has changed over the years as the US Department of Agriculture has adjusted its approach to collecting or presenting the data to better reflect realities on the ground. Some researchers have done work to compensate for changing realities in other ways, and the data has both its champions and critics, which I will note as relevant. I use the raw data from the Census of Agriculture because it allows us to look at important farm statistics in any given point in history, without getting bogged down by more technical studies. In all cases I used the most recent data, as numbers were revised over the years, and I have noted in other endnotes where changes in the USDA's approach amounted to a relevant difference from one year to another.

2   Thomas Jefferson, "Jefferson Quotes and Family Letters," Thomas Jefferson Foundation, https://tjrs.monticello.org/letter/2355.

3   Public opinion surveys throughout the past two decades, including "Consumer Attitudes About Farmers and Sustainability," American Farm Bureau Federation; "National Survey of Registered Voters Regarding Crop Insurance," National Crop Insurance Services; "Roper Poll Shows Consumers Trust Family Farms," Institute for Agriculture and Trade Policy.

4   Analysis of numbers based upon US Census of Agriculture and US Census, 1920, 2017, 2020. The two million farms statistic is from 2017, the most recent year available from the US Department of Agriculture when the 2020 US Census was completed.

5   Wisconsin Department of Agriculture, Trade, and Consumer Protection, "2019 Wisconsin Agricultural Statistics," 2019, 41.

6   John Oncken, "The 'Other' Story Behind the Decline in Farm Numbers in Wisconsin," *Wisconsin State Farmer*, January 19, 2022, https://www.wisfarmer.com/story/opinion/columnists/2022/01/19/other-story-behind-decline-farm-numbers-wisconsin/9192910002/.

7   Economic Research Service, "Productivity Growth in U.S. Agriculture (1948–2021)," US Department of Agriculture, last modified January 12, 2024, https://www.ers.usda.gov/data-products/agricultural-productivity-in-the-u-s/productivity-growth-in-u-s-agriculture/

8   US Bureau of Labor Statistics, "Prices for Food at Home up 13.5 Percent for Year Ended August 2022," *The Economics Daily*, September 15, 2022, https://www.bls.gov/opub/ted/2022/prices-for-food-at-home-up-13-5-percent-for-year-ended-august-2022.htm

9   James M. MacDonald, "Tracking the Consolidation of U.S. Agriculture," *Applied Economic Perspectives and Policy* 42, no. 3 (September 2020): 361–379, https://doi.org/10.1002/aepp.13056.

10   Cary Funk, Brian Kennedy, and Meg Hefferon, "Public Perspectives on Food Risks," Pew Research Center, November 19, 2018, https://www.pewresearch.org/internet/2018/11/19/public-perspectives-on-food-risks/.

11   Clay Newcomb, "From the Earth—Civilization, Humans, and Whitetails," September 22, 2021, in *Bear Grease*, podcast, transcript and audio, 1:10:15, https://omny.fm/shows/bear-grease-1/ep-20-from-the-earth-civilization-humans-and-white.

12   Farm Service Agency, *Foreign Holdings of U.S. Agricultural Land Through December 31, 2022* (Washington, DC: US Department of Agriculture, 2023), abstract, https://www.fsa.usda.gov/Assets/USDA-FSA-Public/usdafiles/EPAS/PDF/2022_afida_annual_report_12_14_23.pdf.

13   Aaron Sussell et al., "Suicide Rates by Industry and Occupation—National Vital Statistics System, United States, 2021," Centers for Disease Control and Prevention, December 15, 2023, https://www.cdc.gov/mmwr/volumes/72/wr/mm7250a2.htm.

14   Wisconsin Department of Agriculture, Trade, and Consumer Protection, "2019 Wisconsin Agricultural Statistics," 41. The source tracks the number of milk herds per month from 2016 to 2019.

15   James M. MacDonald, Jonathan Law, and Roberto Mosheim, "Consolidation in U.S. Dairy Farming," US Department of Agriculture, July 2020, 9.

16   US Census of Agriculture, 1920–2022.

17   John Oncken, "The Milk Continues to Flow," *Wisconsin State Farmer*, last modified January 28, 2021, https://www.wisfarmer.com/story/opinion/columnists/2021/01/27/milk-continues-flow-california-and-wisconsin/6664991002/.

18   Administrative Office of the US Courts, "US Bankruptcy Courts—Business and Nonbusiness Cases Filed, by Chapter of the Bankruptcy Code, District, and County," https://www.uscourts.gov/statistics-reports/caseload-statistics-data-tables?tn=F-5A&pn=32&t=534&m%5Bvalue%5D%5Bmonth%5D=12&y%5Bvalue%5D%5Byear%5D=2020.

19   James M. MacDonald and Robert A. Hoppe, "Examining Consolidation in U.S. Agriculture," US Department of Agriculture, March 14, 2018,

20 Sarah K. Mock, *Farm (And Other F Words): The Rise and Fall of the Small Family Farm* (Washington, DC: New Degree Press, 2021), 44–46.

21 David Yaffe-Bellany and Michael Corkery, "Dumped Milk, Smashed Eggs, Plowed Vegetables: Food Waste of the Pandemic," *New York Times*, last modified March 6, 2022, https://www.nytimes.com/2020/04/11/business/coronavirus-destroying-food.html.

22 Maegan Vazquez, "Trump announces multi-billion dollar coronavirus food assistance program," CNN, April 17, 2020, https://www.cnn.com/world/live-news/coronavirus-pandemic-intl-04-17-20/h_2b614fb5164e8b5020591c49e2950ef2; and Joseph R. Biden, "President Biden Remarks on the Economy," speech, January 22, 2021, transcript and video, 19:29, https://www.c-span.org/video/?508234-1/president-biden-remarks-economy#.

23 US Bureau of Labor Statistics, "Consumer Price Index: 2022 in Review," *The Economics Daily*, January 17, 2023, https://www.bls.gov/opub/ted/2023/consumer-price-index-2022-in-review.htm

24 Corey Geiger, "Wisconsin Upends Texas in New Milk Growth," *Hoard's Dairyman*, February 28, 2022, https://hoards.com/article-31578-wisconsin-upends-texas-in-new-milk-growth.html.

25 US Census of Agriculture, 1850–1910.

26 Robert C. Nesbit, *Urbanization and Industrialization, 1873–1893*, vol. 3 of *The History of Wisconsin* (Madison: State Historical Society of Wisconsin, 1985), 12–13.

27 Nesbit, *Urbanization and Industrialization*, 10.

28 US Census of Agriculture, 1910.

29 US Census of Agriculture, 1910.

30 "The Little Things Around Home," *The Weekly Home News*, May 6, 1909.

31 National Centers for Environmental Information, "Statewide Time Series," n.d., https://www.ncei.noaa.gov/access/monitoring/climate-at-a-glance/statewide/time-series. Search was for the dates 1895–2022.

32 "The Great Blue Norther of November 11, 1911," National Weather Service, n.d., https://www.weather.gov/oun/events-19111111.

33 US government land patent documents, 1858, 1859.

34 Nesbit, *Urbanization and Industrialization*, 12–13.

35 Raghuram Rajan and Rodney Ramcharan, "Local Financial Capacity and Asset Values: Evidence from Bank Failures," *Journal of Financial Economics* 120, (January 2016): 230.

36 US Census of Agriculture, 1850–2022.

37 Federal Reserve Bank of St. Louis, "Exports from the United States Before and After the Outbreak of the War," *Federal Reserve Bulletin*, October 1919, 952.

38 Theodore Saloutos and John D. Hicks, *Agricultural Discontent in the*

Middle West, 1900–1939 (Madison: (University of Wisconsin Press, 1951), 100.

39   Rajan and Ramcharan, "Local Financial Capacity," 232.

40   US Census of Agriculture, 1920, 481–482.

41   Rajan and Ramcharan, "Local Financial Capacity," 232.

42   Stanley W. Trimble, *Historical Agriculture and Soil Erosion in the Upper Mississippi Valley Hill Country* (Boca Raton, FL: CRC Press, 2013), 55.

43   Joshua K. Hausman, Paul W. Rhode, and Johannes F. Wieland, "Recovery from the Great Depression: The Farm Channel in Spring 1933," *American Economic Review*, February 2019, 432.

44   Jerome M. Stam and Bruce L. Dixon, "Farmer Bankruptcies and Farm Exits in the United States, 1899–2002," US Department of Agriculture, March 2004, 11–12.

45   Paul W. Glad, *War, a New Era, and Depression, 1914–1940*, vol. 5 of *The History of Wisconsin* (Madison: State Historical Society of Wisconsin, 1990), 410.

46   Glad, *War, a New Era, and Depression*, 419.

47   Suyin Haynes, "'The Saddest, Bitterest Thing of All.' From the Great Depression to Today, a Long History of Food Destruction in the Face of Hunger," *Time*, May 28, 2020, https://time.com/5843136/covid-19-food-destruction/.

48   William F. Thompson, *Continuity and Change, 1940–1960*, vol. 6 of *The History of Wisconsin* (Madison: (State Historical Society of Wisconsin, 1988), 152–155.

49   Harold F. Breimyer, *Individual Freedom and the Economic Organization of Agriculture* (Urbana: University of Illinois Press, 1965), 71.

50   US Census of Agriculture, 1940.

51   Tim Sablik, "Electrifying Rural America," *Econ Focus*, Federal Reserve Bank of Richmond, First Quarter 2020, 24, https://www.richmondfed.org/publications/research/econ_focus/2020/q1/economic_history.

52   Natural Resources Conservation Service, "A Brief History of NRCS," US Department of Agriculture, accessed August 15, 2023, https://www.nrcs.usda.gov/about/history/brief-history-nrcs.

53   Thompson, *Continuity and Change*, 130–131, 134–135.

54   US Census of Agriculture, 1920–1935.

55   Jerry Apps, *Wisconsin Agriculture: A History* (Madison: Wisconsin Historical Society Press, 2015), 198.

56   US Census of Agriculture, 1850–1940.

57   Kenneth Johnson and Daniel Lichter, "Is Rural America Failing or Succeeding? Maybe Both," University of New Hampshire, Carsey School of Public Policy, September 8, 2020, https://carsey.unh.edu/publication/rural-america-failing-or-succeeding-maybe-both.

58   Charles J. Haulk, "Changes in Industry Shares of National Output," in *History of the US Economy Since World War II*, ed. Harold G. Vatter and John F. Walker (New York: M. E. Sharpe, 1996), 65.

59 Kenneth Johnson and Daniel Lichter, "Rural Depopulation in a Rapidly Urbanizing America," University of New Hampshire, Carsey School of Public Policy, February 6, 2019, https://carsey.unh.edu/publication/rural-depopulation-rapidly-urbanizing-america.

60 US Census Bureau, "Agriculture," in Historical Statistics of the United States, Colonial Times to 1970 (Washington, DC: US Department of Commerce, September 1975), 488–89, table Series K 344–353, https://www2.census.gov/library/publications/1975/compendia/hist_stats_colonial-1970/hist_stats_colonial-1970p1-chK.pdf.

61 "Research Starters: U.S. Military by the Numbers," National World War II Museum, accessed August 2023, https://www.nationalww2museum.org/students-teachers/student-resources/research-starters/research-starters-us-military-numbers.

62 "Deferment of Farm Workers," CQ Almanac 1945, 1st ed., (Washington DC: Congressional Quarterly, 1946), http://library.cqpress.com/cqalmanac/cqal45-1402876.

63 John D. Buekner, *The Progressive Era, 1893–1914*, vol. 4 of *The History of Wisconsin* (Madison: State Historical Society of Wisconsin, 1998), 37.

64 "Timeline: Oscar Mayer History in Madison Dates Back to 1919," *Wisconsin State Journal*, November 4, 2015, https://madison.com/news/local/timeline-oscar-mayer-history-in-madison-dates-back-to-1919/article_41702049-9971-5530-87c3-392fafb2dce7.html.

65 Michael Ratcliffe, "A Century of Delineating a Changing Landscape: The Census Bureau's Urban and Rural Classification, 1910 to 2010," US Census Bureau. The Census Bureau uses definitions of *urban* and *rural* that are different than US Office of Management and Budget definitions that inform the other population research featured in this chapter and are sometimes preferred by rural demographers. Census data is used here because of its reach back to 1910.

66 County-specific data comes from Net Migration Patterns for US Counties project, David Egan-Robertson et al., "Age-Specific Net Migration Estimates for US Counties, 1950–2020," Applied Population Laboratory, University of Wisconsin-Madison, 2023.

67 Hannah Hartig et al., "Republican Gains in 2022 Midterms Driven Mostly by Turnout Advantage," Pew Research Center, July 2023.

68 Stephen K. McNees, "A Brief Overview of Post–World War II Expansions," in *History of the U.S. Economy Since World War II* ed. Harold G. Vatter and John F. Walker (New York: M.E. Sharpe, 1996), 48.

69 US Census of Agriculture, 1850–1950.

70 Thompson, *Continuity* and *Change*, 106–107.

71 Economic Research Service, "Productivity Growth in U.S. Agriculture."

72 Eric Schlosser, *Fast Food Nation: The Dark Side of the All-American Meal* (Boston: Houghton Mifflin, 2002), 19–20.

73 Schlosser, *Fast Food Nation*, 21–25.

ENDNOTES

74 Harold G. Vatter, "The Inheritance of the Preceding Decades," *in History of the US Economy Since World War II* (New York: M. E. Sharpe, 1996), 11–12.

75 Breimyer, *Individual Freedom*, 61, 95–97.

76 Haulk, "Changes in Industry Shares," 65–67.

77 US Census Bureau, "Agriculture," 488–489, table Series K 344–353, https://www2.census.gov/library/publications/1975/compendia/hist_stats _colonial-1970/hist_stats_colonial-1970p1-chK.pdf.

78 US Census of Agriculture, 1950–2002. The only year where the amount of farmland would increase was 1997, when the US Department of Agriculture adjusted the way it counted farms, after which it would continue to fall. The decrease in farmland was slower than other indicators, but still a notable shift compared to growing or steady farm acreage in prior decades.

79 US Census of Agriculture, 1850–1959.

80 Thompson, *Continuity* and *Change*, 122–123.

81 Council of Economic Advisors, "Strengthening the Rural Economy— Improving America's Support of Agriculture," President Barack Obama White House Archives, accessed September 2023, https://obamawhitehouse .archives.gov/administration/eop/cea/factsheets-reports/strengthening -the-rural-economy/improving-americas-support-of-agriculture.

82 Anton Bekkerman, Eric J. Belasco, and Vincent H. Smith, "Where the Money Goes: The Distribution of Crop Insurance and Other Farm Subsidy Payments," American Enterprise Institute, January 2018.

83 Emily Featherston et al., "Secret Subsidies: Payments to Farms Allowed to Stretch Far Beyond Rural America, Sowing Concern About Who Gets What," KCRG-TV, May 17, 2021, article and video, 9:54, https://www .kcrg.com/2021/05/17/secret-subsidies-payments-to-farms-allowed-to -stretch-far-beyond-rural-america-sowing-concern-about-who-gets -what/.

84 Michael Barbaro, "Who Do You Want Controlling Your Food?," January 28, 2022, in *The Daily*, produced by Diana Nguyen, Lynsea Garrison, and Robert Jimison, podcast, 55:59, https://www.nytimes.com/2022/01 /28/podcasts/the-daily/beef-prices-cattle-ranchers.html.

85 Diane Bartz, "Biden Administration Continues Trump Antitrust Focus on Tech Giants," Reuters, January 24, 2023, https://www.reuters.com /technology/biden-administration-continues-trump-antitrust-focus -tech-giants-2023-01-24/.

86 Eleanor Mueller, "The New Power Couple Taking on Wall Street: J. D. Vance and Elizabeth Warren," Politico, July 6, 2023, https://www.politico .com/news/2023/07/05/j-d-vance-senate-banks-00104432.

87 Federal Trade Commission and states of California, Colorado, Illinois, Indiana, Iowa, Minnesota, Nebraska, Oregon, Texas, and Wisconsin v. Sygenta Crop Protection AG, Syngenta Corporation, Syngenta Crop

Protection, LLC, and Corteva, Inc., 22-cv-828 (United States District Court, Middle District of North Carolina).

88 Mike Scarcella, "Pesticide Antitrust Cases Consolidated in North Carolina Federal Court," Reuters, February 7, 2023, https://www.reuters.com/legal/pesticide-antitrust-cases-consolidated-north-carolina-federal-court-2023-02-07/.

89 May Peters, Suchada Langley, and Paul Westcott, "Agricultural Commodity Price Spikes in the 1970s and 1990s: Valuable Lessons for Today," US Department of Agriculture, March 1, 2009, https://www.ers.usda.gov/amber-waves/2009/march/agricultural-commodity-price-spikes-in-the-1970s-and-1990s-valuable-lessons-for-today/.

90 Hedrick Smith, "Big US Grain Deal with Soviet Gains," New York Times, April 1972.

91 The Farm Crisis, produced and written by Laurel Bower Burgmaier, narrated by Harry Smith, aired on Iowa PBS, July 1, 2013, transcript and audio, 1:29:50, https://www.iowapbs.org/shows/farmcrisis/documentary/5311/farm-crisis.

92 US Census of Agriculture, 1969 and 1974.

93 Thompson, Continuity and Change, 112–113.

94 Wendell Berry, The Unsettling of America: Culture & Agriculture, (San Francisco: Sierra Club Books, 1977), 8.

95 James M. MacDonald, Robert A. Hoppe, and Doris Newton, Three Decades of Consolidation in U.S. Agriculture (Washington, DC: US Department of Agriculture, March 2018), 35–36, https://www.ers.usda.gov/webdocs/publications/88057/eib-189.pdf?v=6112.4.

96 US Census of Agriculture, 1950–1992.

97 Board of Governors of the Federal Reserve System, Federal Funds Effective Rate, Federal Reserve Bank of St. Louis, graph, last modified May 1, 2024, https://fred.stlouisfed.org/series/FEDFUNDS.

98 Jimmy Carter, "Address to the Nation on the Soviet Invasion of Afghanistan," The American Presidency Project, January 4, 1980, transcript, https://www.presidency.ucsb.edu/documents/address-the-nation-the-soviet-invasion-afghanistan.

99 Lindsay H. Metcalf, Farmers Unite! Planting a Protest for Fair Prices, (Honesdale, PA: Calkins Creek, 2020), 6, 11, 23–25.

100 Marguerite Roby, "Tractorcade," Smithsonian Institution Archives, February 21, 2012, https://siarchives.si.edu/blog/tractorcade.

101 Metcalf, Farmers Unite!, 42–43.

102 Board of Governors of the Federal Reserve System, Federal Funds Effective Rate, https://fred.stlouisfed.org/series/FEDFUNDS.

103 David A. Stockman and Jack F. Kemp, "Memo to Reagan: 'Avoiding an Economic Dunkirk,'" New York Times, December 14, 1980, https://www.nytimes.com/1980/12/14/archives/economics-memo-to-reagan-avoiding-an-economic-dunkirk-gathering.html.

ENDNOTES

104 Nebraska Public Media, "Bankers: Villains or Victims?," Nebraskastudies. org, accessed September 2023, article and video, 0:20, https://nebraskas tudies.org/en/1975-1999/foreclosures-lead-to-violence/bankers-villains -or-victims/.

105 "Farm Aid: Nearly 40 Years of Action for Family Farmers and the Good Food Movement," FarmAid.org, accessed October 2023, https://www .farmaid.org/issues/roots-and-vision/farm-aid-nearly-40-years-of-action -for-family-farmers/.

106 Ronald Reagan, "Remarks on Signing the Agricultural Credit Act of 1987," Ronald Reagan Presidential Library and Museum, January 6, 1988, https://www.reaganlibrary.gov/archives/speech/remarks-signing -agricultural-credit-act-1987.

107 Sarah Vogel, "The Legacy of *Coleman v. Block*," Sarahmvogel.com, accessed September 2023, https://sarahmvogel.com/learnmore/the-legacy-of -coleman-v-block/.

108 US Census of Agriculture, 1982–1992.

109 George M. Gregorash and James Morrison, "Lean Years in Agricultural Banking," *Economic Perspectives* 9 (November/December 1985), 17–21, https://www.chicagofed.org/publications/economic-perspectives/1985 /november-december-gregorash.

110 Kayode Ajewole et al., *Do Free Trade Agreements Benefit Developing Countries? An Examination of U.S. Agreements* (Washington, DC: US Department of Agriculture, September 2022), 14, https://www.ers.usda .gov/webdocs/publications/104855/eib-240.pdf.

111 Benjamin Lorr, *The Secret Life of Groceries: The Dark Miracle of the American Supermarket* (New York: Avery 2020), 5.

112 US Census of Agriculture, 1992, 1997–2022. Note: The USDA updated its methodology in 1997, resulting in a jump in the number of plots of land counted as "farms" in federal data from 1992 to 1997 under the new measure, even though earlier USDA methodology showed a decline from 1992 to 1997 as well.

113 MacDonald, Hoppe, and Newton, *Three Decades of Consolidation*, 27.

114 MacDonald, Hoppe, and Newton, *Three Degrees of Consolidation*, 28.

115 John G. Murphy, "We Can't Stand Still: How U.S. Farmers and Ranchers Depend on Trade," US Chamber of Commerce, November 4, 2022, https://www.uschamber.com/international/we-cant-stand-still-how-u-s -farmers-and-ranchers-depend-on-trade.

116 Kristina Johnson and Samuel Fromartz, "NAFTA's 'Broken Promises': These Farmers Say They Got the Raw End of Trade Deal," NPR, August 7, 2017, https://www.npr.org/sections/thesalt/2017/08/07/541671747/nafta -s-broken-promises-these-farmers-say-they-got-the-raw-end-of-trade -deal.

117 Mary K. Hendrickson, "Resilience in a Concentrated and Consolidated Food System," *Journal of Environmental Studies and Sciences* 5, no. 2 (July 2015), Introduction, Table 1, https://doi.org/10.1007/s13412-015-0292-2.

118 Mary K. Hendrickson et al., *The Food System: Concentration and Its Impacts* (Mexico, MO: Farm Action Alliance, May 2021), 3–4, 9, https://farmaction.us/wp-content/uploads/2021/05/Hendrickson-et-al.-2020.-Concentration-and-Its-Impacts_FINAL_Addended.pdf.

119 Economic Research Service, "Productivity Growth in U.S. Agriculture."

120 Oncken, "The Milk Continues to Flow."

121 "Wisconsin vs. California: Whose Cows Are 'Happier?'," May 10, 2007, https://www.wrn.com/wisconsin-vs-california-whose-cows-are-happier/.

122 MacDonald, Hoppe, and Newton, *Three Decades of Consolidation*, 24–28.

123 Analysis of changes in commodity prices based upon US Department of Agriculture "Quick Stats" database providing statistics on the prices received index, 2001–2002. Trends in prices for individual commodities, such as wheat or milk, can vary widely depending upon market conditions, but the data across all types of commodities remains a useful overall measure for the general direction of agricultural income.

124 Analysis of changes in commodity prices based upon U.S. Department of Agriculture "Quick Stats" database providing statistics on the prices received index, 2007-2011.

125 John Weinberg, "The Great Recession and Its Aftermath," Federal Reserve History (website), November 22, 2013, https://www.federalreservehistory.org/essays/great-recession-and-its-aftermath.

126 Robert Rich, "The Great Recession," Federal Reserve History (website), November 22, 2013, https://www.federalreservehistory.org/essays/great-recession-of-200709.

127 Mathew Shane et al., *The 2008/2009 World Economic Crisis: What It Means for U.S. Agriculture* (Washington, DC: US Department of Agriculture, March 2009), 21, https://www.ers.usda.gov/webdocs/outlooks/40467/9650_wrs0902.pdf?v=8466.6.

128 Paul Sundell and Mathew Shane, *The 2008-09 Recession and Recovery: Implications for Growth and Financial Health of U.S. Agriculture* (Washington, DC: US Department of Agriculture, May 2012), 12, https://downloads.usda.library.cornell.edu/usda-esmis/files/6t053f96k/dj52w807c/0k225f57b/WRS-05-22-2012.pdf.

129 Analysis of changes in commodity prices based upon U.S. Department of Agriculture "Quick Stats" database providing statistics on the prices received index, 2001–2011.

130 Ajewole et al., "Do Free Trade Agreements Benefit Developing Countries?," 16.

131 Ajewole et al., "Do Free Trade Agreements Benefit Developing Countries?," 14.

132 MacDonald, Hoppe, and Newton, *Three Decades of Consolidation*, 33, 36.

133 MacDonald, Hoppe, and Newton, *Three Decades of Consolidation*, 36.

134 MacDonald, Hoppe, and Newton, *Three Decades of Consolidation*, iii–15.

135 John Flesher, "Factory Farms Provide Abundant Food, but Environment Suffers," Associated Press, February 6, 2020, https://apnews.com/article

/mo-state-wire-in-state-wire-ia-state-wire-mi-state-wire-iowa-8546
6c302a7436070b913aeee071b16a.

136 2017 Census of Agriculture, *Farm Typology* (Washington, DC: US
     Department of Agriculture, January 2021), 1–14, table 1, https://www
     .nass.usda.gov/Publications/AgCensus/2017/Online_Resources
     /Typology/typology.pdf.

137 I heard debates about government data acknowledged by a wide range of
     experts who work with the US Department of Agriculture's data, includ-
     ing those who find it invaluable, in addition to critics. And, while the data
     does help identify a minority of farms that are corporate owned, it does
     not survey specific corporate structures in a comprehensive way or the
     motivations of various owners as it pertains to government assistance.
     Whatever the wisdom of its assumptions, the data is thorough, accessible,
     and meticulously handled by the researchers who compile it.

138 National Farmers Union, *121st Anniversary Convention Policy Book*
     (Washington DC: National Farmers Union, 2023), https://nfu.org/wp
     -content/uploads/2023/03/2023-NFU-Policy-Book.pdf.

139 American Farm Bureau Federation, "American Farm Bureau Establishes
     2023 Policies," news release, January 10, 2023, https://www.fb.org/news
     -release/american-farm-bureau-establishes-2023-policies.

140 Wisconsin Department of Agriculture, Trade, and Consumer Protection,
     "2019 Wisconsin Agricultural Statistics," 2019, 41, https://www.nass
     .usda.gov/Statistics_by_State/Wisconsin/Publications/Annual_Statistical
     _Bulletin/2019AgStats-WI.pdf.

141 Alana Semuels, "'They're Trying to Wipe Us Off the Map.' Small
     American Farmers Are Nearing Extinction," *Time*, November 27, 2019.

142 David J. Lynch and Damian Paletta, "Trump Announces Steel and
     Aluminum Tariffs Thursday over Objections from Advisers and
     Republicans," *Washington Post*, March 1, 2018, https://www.washington
     post.com/news/business/wp/2018/03/01/white-house-planning
     -major-announcement-thursday-on-steel-and-aluminum-imports/.

143 Mariam Khan, "US-China Trade War Spurs Unease on Capitol Hill,"
     ABC News, May 14, 2019, https://abcnews.go.com/Politics/trump-rare
     -support-democrats-us-china-trade-war/story?id=63027877.

144 Clark Packard, "Trump's Trade Wars Have Made Bad Agriculture
     Policies Worse," *Foreign Policy*, October 27, 2020, https://foreignpolicy
     .com/2020/10/27/trump-trade-wars-farmers/.

145 Shuyang Qu et al., "Midwest Crop Farmers' Perceptions of the U.S.-
     China Trade War," Center for Agricultural and Rural Development, Iowa
     State University, October 2019, https://www.card.iastate.edu/products
     /policy-briefs/display/?n=1294.

146 Menzie Chinn and Bill Plumley, "What Is the Toll of Trade Wars on U.S.
     Agriculture?," PBS NewsHour, January 16, 2020, https://www.pbs.org
     /newshour/economy/making-sense/what-is-the-toll-of-trade-wars
     -on-u-s-agriculture.

147 John Newton, "Farm Bankruptcies Rise Again," American Farm Bureau Federation, October 30, 2019, https://www.fb.org/market-intel/farm -bankruptcies-rise-again.

148 Niv Elis, Morgan Chalfant, and Sylvan Lane, "Trump Takes Victory Lap with USMCA Signing," The Hill, January 19, 2020, https://thehill.com /policy/finance/480493-trump-takes-victory-lap-with-usmca-signing/.

149 Murphy, "We Can't Stand Still."

150 Tobias Burns, "How Trump and Biden Killed the Free-Trade Consensus," The Hill, September 25, 2023, https://thehill.com/business/4222035-how -trump-and-biden-killed-the-free-trade-consensus/.

151 Rakesh Kochhar, "Unemployment Rose Higher in Three Months of COVID-19 Than It Did in Two Years of the Great Recession," Pew Research Center, June 11, 2020, https://www.pewresearch.org/short -reads/2020/06/11/unemployment-rose-higher-in-three-months-of -covid-19-than-it-did-in-two-years-of-the-great-recession/.

152 "Business Cycle Dating Committee Announcement," National Bureau of Economic Research, July 19, 2021, https://www.nber.org/news/business -cycle-dating-committee-announcement-july-19-2021.

153 Jonathan W. Dyal et al., "COVID-19 Among Workers in Meat and Poultry Processing Facilities—19 States, April 2020," Centers for Disease Control and Prevention, May 2020, https://www.cdc.gov/mmwr/vol- umes/69/wr/mm6918e3.htm?s_cid=mm6918e3_x.

154 Terry Nguyen, "You Can Buy Stuff Online, but Getting It Is Another Story," Vox (website), September 2, 2021, https://www.vox.com/the -goods/22650965/supply-chain-delays-2021-ongoing.

155 Robert Johansson, "America's Farmers: Resilient Throughout the COVID Pandemic," US Department of Agriculture, September 24, 2020, https: //www.usda.gov/media/blog/2020/09/24/americas-farmers-resilient -throughout-covid-pandemic.

156 Hendrickson et al., *Food System*, 13.

157 Quingbin Wang et al., "Impacts of the COVID-19 Pandemic on the Dairy Industry: Lessons from China and the United States and Policy Implications," *Journal of Integrative Agriculture* 19, no. 12 (December 2020), 2904, https:doi.org/10.1016/s2095-3119(20)63443-8.

158 Shelby Myers, "Too Many to Count: Factors Driving Fertilizer Prices Higher and Higher," American Farm Bureau Federation, December 13, 2021, https://www.fb.org/market-intel/too-many-to-count-factors-driving -fertilizer-prices-higher-and-higher.

159 US Census of Agriculture, 1920–2022.

160 Brenna Ellison and Maria Kalaitzandonakes, "Food Waste and COVID- 19: Impacts Along the Supply Chain," farmdoc daily, September 10, 2020, https://origin.farmdocdaily.illinois.edu/2020/09/food-waste-and -covid-19-impacts-along-the-supply-chain.html.

161 Yaffe-Bellany and Corkery, "Dumped Milk."

162 National Meat Institute, "COVID At One Year: Infections in Meat Sector 85% Lower Than General Population With Urgent Need to Accelerate Vaccination," press release, March 22, 2021, https://www .meatinstitute.org/press/covid-one-year-infections-meat-sector-85-lower -general-population-urgent-need-accelerate.

163 Hendrickson et al., *Food System*, 11–13.

164 Farm Service Agency, *Foreign Holdings of U.S. Agricultural Land Through December 31, 2022* (Washington, DC: US Department of Agriculture, 2023), abstract, https://www.fsa.usda.gov/Assets/USDA-FSA-Public /usdafiles/EPAS/PDF/2022_afida_annual_report_12_14_23.pdf; Farm Service Agency, *Foreign Holdings of U.S. Agricultural Land Through December 31, 2020* (Washington, DC: US Department of Agriculture, 2021), abstract, https://www.fsa.usda.gov/Assets/USDA-FSA-Public/usdafiles /EPAS/PDF/2020_afida_annual_report.pdf.

165 Patricia Zengerle, "U.S. Senate Backs Measure Requiring Reporting on China Tech Investments," Reuters, July 25, 2023, https://www.reuters .com/technology/us-senate-backs-measure-requiring-reporting-china -tech-investments-2023-07-25/.

166 National Institute on Drug Abuse, "Drug Overdose Death Rates," National Institutes of Health, May 14, 2024, https://nida.nih.gov /research-topics/trends-statistics/overdose-death-rates.

167 Sussell et al., "Suicide Rates by Industry and Occupation." My conclusions were based also on comparison to the previous 2021 report.

168 Hartig et al., "Republican Gains."

169 Hendrickson et al., *Food System*, 13.

170 Tom Polansek, "Bird Flu Infects Arkansas Poultry as US Cases Rise," Reuters, November 3, 2023, https://www.reuters.com/world/us/bird-flu -infects-arkansas-poultry-us-cases-rise-2023-11-03/.

171 Schlosser, *Fast Food Nation*, 195–96.

172 US Bureau of Labor Statistics, "Prices for Food at Home."

173 US Census of Agriculture, 1920–2022.

174 2017 Census of Agriculture, *Farm Typology*, 1–14, table 1.

175 2017 Census of Agriculture, *Farm Typology*, 1–14, table 1.

176 I heard these issues acknowledged by a wide range of experts who work with the US Department of Agriculture's data, including those who find it invaluable, in addition to critics. Whatever the wisdom of its assumptions, the data is thorough, accessible, and meticulously handled by the researchers who compile it.

177 Anne Grimmelt et al., "Hungry and Confused: The Winding Road to Conscious Eating," McKinsey & Company, October 5, 2022, https: //www.mckinsey.com/industries/consumer-packaged-goods/our -insights/hungry-and-confused-the-winding-road-to-conscious-eating.

178 Kenneth Johnson, "Population Redistribution Trends in Nonmetropolitan America, 2010 to 2021," *Rural Sociology* 88, no. 1 (March 2023): 193–219, https://doi.org/10.1111/ruso.12473.

179 Alicia Wallace, "Food Price Hikes Are No Longer Outpacing Overall Inflation," CNN, December 12, 2023, https://www.cnn.com/2023/12/12 /economy/food-inflation-november-cpi/index.html.

180 J. Agnew and S. Hendery, 2023 *Global Agricultural Productivity Report: Every Farmer, Every Tool*, ed. T. Thompson (Blacksburg, VA: Virginia Tech College of Agriculture and Life Sciences, 2023), 5–6, https: //globalagriculturalproductivity.org/wp-content/uploads/2024/01/2023 -GAP-Report.pdf.

181 Kelly P. Nelson and Keith Fuglie, "Investment in U.S. Public Agricultural Research and Development Has Fallen by a Third Over Past Two Decades, Lags Major Trade Competitors," US Department of Agriculture, June 6, 2022, https://www.ers.usda.gov/amber-waves/2022/june/investment -in-u-s-public-agricultural-research-and-development-has-fallen-by-a -third-over-past-two-decades-lags-major-trade-competitors/.

182 Joe Mariani, et al., "Revisiting the Government's Role in Catalyzing Modern Innovation," July 20, 2023, https://www2.deloitte.com/us/en /insights/industry/public-sector/role-of-government-in-innovation.html.

183 Asim Anand, "Sustainable Aviation Fuel: Agriculture's Ticket to Redemption?" S&P Global, September 21, 2023, https://www.spglobal .com/commodityinsights/en/market-insights/blogs/agriculture /092123-sustainable-aviation-fuel-agricultures-ticket-to-redemption.

184 Grace Connaster, "Wisconsin's Master Cheesemaker Program Shows Quality and Commitment," *Wisconsin State Farmer*, June 2, 2021, https: //www.wisfarmer.com/story/news/2021/06/02/wisconsins-master -cheesemaker-program-shows-quality-and-commitment/7499027002/.